ISNM 73:
International Series of Numerical Mathematics
Internationale Schriftenreihe zur Numerischen Mathematik
Série internationale d'Analyse numérique
Vol. 73

Edited by
Ch. Blanc, Lausanne; A. Ghizzetti, Roma;
R. Glowinski, Paris; G. Golub, Stanford;
P. Henrici, Zürich; H. O. Kreiss, Pasadena;
A. Ostrowski, Montagnola; J. Todd, Pasadena

Birkhäuser Verlag
Basel · Boston · Stuttgart

Constructive Methods for the Practical Treatment of Integral Equations

Proceedings of the Conference at the Mathematisches Forschungsinstitut Oberwolfach, June 24–30, 1984

Edited by

G. Hämmerlin and
K.-H. Hoffmann

1985

Birkhäuser Verlag
Basel · Boston · Stuttgart

Editors

Prof. Dr. G. Hämmerlin
Mathematisches Institut der
Ludwig-Maximilians-Universität
Theresienstraße 39
D–8000 München 2

Prof. Dr. K.-H. Hoffmann
Mathematisches Institut
der Universität Augsburg
Memminger Straße 6
D–8900 Augsburg

Library of Congress Cataloging in Publication Data
Main entry under title:

Constructive methods for the practical treatment of integral equations.
(International series of numerical mathematics ; vol. 73)
1. Integral equations -- Numerical solutions -- Congresses. I. Hämmerlin, G. (Günther), 1928– II. Hoffmann, K.-H. (Karl-Heinz) III. Series: International series of numerical mathematics ; v. 73.
QA431.C594 1985 515.4'5 85–1237
ISBN 3–7643–1685–3

CIP-Kurztitelaufnahme der Deutschen Bibliothek

Constructive methods for the practical treatment of integral equations : proceedings of the conference held at the Math. Forschungsinst. Oberwolfach, June 24–30, 1984 / ed. by G. Hämmerlin and K.-H. Hoffmann. – Basel ; Boston ; Stuttgart : Birkhäuser, 1985.
(International series of numerical mathematics ; Vol. 73)
ISBN 3–7643–1685–3
NE: Hämmerlin, Günther [Hrsg.]; Mathematisches Forschungsinstitut ⟨Oberwolfach⟩; GT

Printed in Germany
ISBN 3-7643-1685-3

P r e f a c e

Among the numerous problems arising in the field of constructive methods for the practical treatment of integral equations, several focal points can be made out. They are also reflected in this collection of 23 papers presented at the conference.

First of all, we mention the numerical treatment of integral equations of the Volterra type, weakly singular kernels and stability questions being in the foreground; weakly singular Fredholm equations are treated as well. Further, there is great interest in collocation and Galerkin methods, in particular in using splines to produce approximate solutions. Several papers are devoted to nonlinear integral equations and to their applications, for instance in scattering theory. Integral equations of the first kind and the investigation of regularization methods represent a connection with improperly posed problems, the latter being of particularly actual importance.

The editors' thanks go to all contributors and participants who made the conference a success; to the management of the Oberwolfach Institute with its unique atmosphere; to the Birkhäuser Verlag for the possibility to publish the volume in the well-known ISNM series and to the co-workers of the editors for their assistance in organisation and editorial work.

G. Hämmerlin
München

K.-H. Hoffmann
Augsburg

C O N T E N T S

List of participants

Dr. G. Akrivis
University of Crete
Department of Mathematics
P.O. Box 470
Iraklion Crete
Greece

Prof. Dr. J. Albrecht
Technische Universität Clausthal
Institut für Mathematik
Erzstraße 1
D 3392 Clausthal-Zellerfeld
Germany (FRG)

Priv.-Doz. Dr. H. Arndt
Institut für Angewandte
Mathematik der Universität Bonn
Wegelerstraße 6
D 5300 Bonn 1
Germany (FRG)

Prof. Dr. K. Atkinson
Department of Mathematics
University of Iowa
Iowa City, Iowa 52242
U.S.A.

Dr. C.T.H. Baker
Department of Mathematics
University of Manchester
Oxford Road
Manchester M13 9PL
U.K.

Dipl.-Math. L. Bamberger
Mathematisches Institut
der Universität München
Theresienstraße 39
D 8000 München 2
Germany (FRG)

Prof. Dr. M. Brannigan
University of Georgia
Department of Computer Science
Athens, Georgia 30602
U.S.A.

Prof. Dr. H. Braß
Naturwissenschaftliche Fakultät
Lehrstuhl E für Mathematik
Pockelsstraße 14
D 3300 Braunschweig
Germany (FRG)

Dr. M. Brokate
Mathematisches Institut
der Universität Augsburg
Memminger Straße 6
D 8900 Augsburg
Germany (FRG)

Prof. Dr. H. Brunner
Université de Fribourg Suisse
Institut de Mathématiques
CH-1700 Fribourg
Switzerland

Dr. S. Christiansen
Laboratory of Applied
Mathematical Physics
The Techn. Univ. of Denmark
DK-2800 Lyngby
Denmark

Prof. Dr. L. Collatz
Institut für Angewandte
Mathematik der Universität Hamburg
Bundesstraße 55
D 2000 Hamburg 13
Germany (FRG)

Prof. Dr. D.L. Colton
University of Delaware
Dep. of Mathematical Sciences
501 Ewing Hall
Newark, Delaware 19716
U.S.A.

Prof. Dr. P. Eggermont
University of Delaware
Dep. of Mathematical Sciences
501 Ewing Hall
Newark, Delaware 19716
U.S.A.

Prof. Dr. H. Engl
Johannes Kepler Univ. Linz
Institut für Mathematik
A-4040 Linz
Austria

Dr. David Eyre
National Research Institute
for Mathematical Sciences
of the CSIR
P.O. Box 395
Pretoria 0001
South Africa

Dr. Tharwat Fawzy
Head of Mathematics Department
Faculty of Science
Suez-Canal University
Ismailia
Egypt

Prof. Dr. R. Gorenflo
Freie Universität Berlin
Institut für Mathematik, WE3
Arnimallee 2-6
D 1000 Berlin 33
Germany (FRG)

Prof. Dr. G. Hämmerlin
Mathematisches Institut
der Universität München
Theresienstraße 39
D 8000 München 2
Germany (FRG)

Prof. Dr. K.-H. Hoffmann
Mathematisches Institut
der Universität Augsburg
Memminger Straße 6
D 8900 Augsburg
Germany (FRG)

Prof. Dr. P.J. van der Houwen
Dep. of Numerical Mathematics
Centre for Mathematics
Kruislaan 413
1098 SJ Amsterdam
The Netherlands

Dr. D. Kershaw
Department of Mathematics
University of Lancaster
Lancaster LA1 4YL
Lancashire, U.K.

Dr. A. Kirsch
Georg August Universität
Lotzestraße 16-18
D 3400 Göttingen
Germany (FRG)

Prof. Dr. R. Kress
Institut für Numerische
und Angewandte Mathematik
Universität Göttingen
Lotzestraße 16-18
D 3400 Göttingen
Germany (FRG)

Prof. Dr. F. Kuhnert
Technische Hochschule
Karl-Marx-Stadt
Sektion Mathematik
Postschließfach 964
DDR-9010 Karl-Marx-Stadt

Prof. Dr. A. Louis
Universität Kaiserslautern
Mathematik
Postfach 3049
D 6750 Kaiserslautern
Germany (FRG)

Prof. Dr. J. Marti
Seminar f. Angew. Mathematik
ETH-Zentrum, Hauptgebäude
CH-8092 Zürich
Switzerland

Prof. Dr. F. Natterer
Mathematisches Institut
Universität Münster
Einsteinstraße 64
D 4400 Münster
Germany (FRG)

Prof. Dr. G. Opfer
Inst. f. Angewandte Mathematik
Universität Hamburg
Bundesstraße 55
D 2000 Hamburg 13
Germany (FRG)

Dr. Vu Quoc Phong
Institute of Mathematics
P.O. Box 631, Bo Ho
Ha noi
Vietnam

Dr. H.J.J. te Riele
Centre for Mathematics
and Computer Science
Kruislaan 413
1098 SJ Amsterdam
The Netherlands

Priv.-Doz. Dr. E. Schäfer
Mathematisches Institut
der Universität München
Theresienstraße 39
D 8000 München 2
Germany (FRG)

Dr. Claus Schneider
Johannes Gutenberg-Universität
Mainz
Fachbereich 17 - Mathematik
Postfach 3980
D 6500 Mainz
Germany (FRG)

Prof. Dr. E. Schock
Universität Kaiserslautern
Fachbereich Mathematik
Postfach 3049
D 6750 Kaiserslautern
Germany (FRG)

Dr. Jennifer Scott
Oxford University Computing
Laboratory
8-11 Keble Road
Oxford OX1 3QD, U.K.

Dr. I.H. Sloan
Dep. of Applied Mathematics
University of New South Wales
Sydney, NSW 2033
Australia

Dr. A. Spence
School of Mathematics
University of Bath
Claverton Down
Bath, BA2 7AY, U.K.

Prof. Dr. J. Sprekels
Mathematisches Institut
Universität Augsburg
Memminger Straße 6
D 8900 Augsburg
Germany (FRG)

Dr. Sergio Vessella
c/o I.A.G.A. (C.N.R.)
via S. Marta 13/A
50139 Firenze
Italy

Prof. Dr. H. Voss
Fachbereich Mathematik
Gesamthochschule Essen
Universitätsstraße 2
D 4300 Essen
Germany (FRG)

Prof. Dr. W.L. Wendland
Fachbereich Mathematik
TH Darmstadt
Schloßgartenstraße 7
D 6100 Darmstadt
Germany (FRG)

International Series of
Numerical Mathematics, Vol. 73

DIE FEHLERNORM SPEZIELLER GAUSS-QUADRATURFORMELN

G. Akrivis

Mathematisches Institut, Universität München

Abstract. We consider Gaussian quadrature formulae Q_n, $n \in \mathbb{N}$, approximating the integral $I(f) := \int_{-1}^{1} w(x)f(x)dx$. Let $f(z) = \sum_{i=0}^{\infty} \alpha_i^f z^i$ be analytic in $K_r := \{z \in \mathbb{C} : |z| < r\}$, $r > 1$ and $|f|_r := \sup\{|\alpha_i^f| r^i : i \in \mathbb{N}_0, R_n(q_i) \neq 0\} < \infty$, where $R_n := I - Q_n$ is the error functional and $q_i(x) := x^i$. R_n is continuous with respect to $|\cdot|_r$ and $\|R_n\| = \sum_{i=0}^{\infty} [|R_n(q_i)|/r^i]$ holds. For

$$w(x) = \frac{1}{c-x^2} (1-x)^{\alpha}(1+x)^{\beta}, \quad \alpha,\beta = \pm\frac{1}{2}, \quad c > 1 ,$$

we explicitly calculate the norm of R_n .

1. Einleitung

Wir betrachten die Approximation des Integrals I,

$$I(f) = \int_{-1}^{1} w(x)f(x)dx, \quad w \geq 0, \quad \|w\|_1 > 0 ,$$

durch die Gauß-Quadraturformel Q_n ,

$$Q_n(f) = \sum_{i=1}^{n} w_i f(x_i) .$$

Sei $R_n := I - Q_n$ das Fehlerfunktional.

Für eine im Kreis K_r, $K_r := \{z \in \mathbb{C} : |z| < r\}$, $r > 1$, holomorphe Funktion f,

$$f(z) = \sum_{i=0}^{\infty} \alpha_i^f z^i, \quad z \in K_r ,$$

sei

(1.1) $$|f|_r := \sup\{|\alpha_i^f| r^i : i \in \mathbb{N}_0 \text{ und } R_n(q_i) \neq 0\}, \quad q_i(x) := x^i .$$

In

$$X_r := \{f : f \text{ holomorph in } K_r \text{ und } |f|_r < \infty\}$$

ist $|\cdot|_r$ eine Seminorm. Das Fehlerfunktional R_n ist in $(X_r, |\cdot|_r)$ stetig, und für $\|R_n\|$,

$$\|R_n\| := \sup\{|R_n(f)| : |f|_r = 1\} ,$$

gilt die Identität

(1.2) $$\|R_n\| = \sum_{i=0}^{\infty} \frac{|R_n(q_i)|}{r^i} .$$

Dieser Zugang zu ableitungsfreien Abschätzungen des Fehlerterms $R_n(f)$,

(1.3) $$|R_n(f)| \leq \|R_n\| \, |f|_r$$

geht auf Hämmerlin [4] zurück.

Erfüllt die Gewichtsfunktion w eine der Bedingungen

(1.4.a) $$\frac{w(t_1)}{w(-t_1)} \leq \frac{w(t_2)}{w(-t_2)} \quad \text{für} \quad t_1 < t_2$$

beziehungsweise

(1.4.b) $$\frac{w(t_1)}{w(-t_1)} \geq \frac{w(t_2)}{w(-t_2)} \quad \text{für} \quad t_1 < t_2 ,$$

so gilt mit $p_n(x) = (x-x_1)\ldots(x-x_n)$ für die Fehlernorm

(1.5.a) $$\|R_n\| = \frac{r}{p_n(r)} \int_{-1}^{1} w(x) \frac{p_n(x)}{r-x} dx$$

beziehungsweise

(1.5.b) $$\|R_n\| = \frac{r}{p_n(-r)} \int_{-1}^{1} w(x) \frac{p_n(x)}{r+x} dx .$$

Die Darstellung (1.5) wurde in [1] mit Hilfe eines Ergebnisses von Gautschi [2] über das Vorzeichen von $R_n(q_i)$ hergeleitet und war dort der Ausgangspunkt zur Berechnung der Norm des Fehlerfunktionals für die Gewichtsfunktionen

$$w(x) = \frac{1}{c \pm x} W(x) , \quad c > 1 ,$$

$$w(x) = \frac{1}{c + x^2} W(x) , \quad c > 0 ,$$

mit $W(x) = (1-x)^{\alpha}(1+x)^{\beta}$, $\alpha,\beta = \pm\frac{1}{2}$. Hier gehen wir analog vor und berechnen $\|R_n\|$ für

$$w(x) = \frac{1}{c - x^2} (1-x)^{\alpha}(1+x)^{\beta}, \quad c > 1, \quad \alpha,\beta = \pm\frac{1}{2} .$$

2. Die Norm des Fehlerfunktionals

Der einfacheren Schreibweise wegen schreiben wir die hier betrachteten Gewichtsfunktionen in der Form

$$(2.1) \qquad w(x) = \frac{1}{a^2-(2a-1)x^2}(1-x)^{\alpha}(1+x)^{\beta}, \quad a>1, \quad \alpha,\beta = \pm\frac{1}{2},$$

vgl. Kumar [5]. Sind R_n und R_n^* die Fehlerfunktionale zur obigen Gewichtsfunktion mit $\alpha = -\beta = 1/2$ bzw. $\alpha = -\beta = -1/2$, so gilt offensichtlich $R_n(q_i) = (-1)^i \; R_n^*(q_i)$ und damit nach (1.2) $\|R_n\| = \|R_n^*\|$. Es genügt also, im folgenden die Fälle $\alpha = \beta = \pm 1/2$ und $\alpha = -\beta = 1/2$ zu betrachten. Dann ist die Bedingung (1.4.b) erfüllt, und $\|R_n\|$ läßt sich aus (1.5.b) berechnen.

<u>Satz.</u> Sei $w(x) = \frac{1}{a^2-(2a-1)x^2}(1-x)^{\alpha}(1+x)^{\beta}$, $a>1$ und $\tau := r-\sqrt{r^2-1}$.

Dann gilt für die Norm des Fehlerfunktionals R_n

$$(2.2) \qquad \|R_n\| = \frac{4\pi r\tau^{2n}}{(a-r\tau)[(2a-1)(1+\tau^{2n})-\tau^2(1+\tau^{2n-4})]\sqrt{r^2-1}}$$

für $\alpha = \beta = -1/2$, $n>1$,

$$(2.3) \qquad \|R_n\| = \frac{4\pi r\tau^{2n+2}\sqrt{r^2-1}}{(a-r\tau)[(2a-1)(1-\tau^{2n+2})-\tau^2(1-\tau^{2n-2})]}$$

für $\alpha = \beta = 1/2$, $n>1$, und

$$(2.4) \qquad \|R_n\| = \frac{4\pi r\tau^{2n+1}}{(a-r\tau)[(2a-1)(1+\tau^{2n+1})-\tau^2(1+\tau^{2n-1})]}\left(\frac{r+1}{r-1}\right)^{1/2}$$

für $\alpha = -\beta = 1/2$, $n>2$.

Beweis. Sei zunächst $\alpha = \beta = -1/2$. Die Knoten $x_1,\dots,x_n$ der Gauß-

Quadraturformel Q_n zu dieser Gewichtsfunktion sind die Nullstellen von $(2a-1)T_n-T_{n-2}$. Hierbei ist T_i das Tschebyscheff-Polynom erster Art vom Grad i. Zu dieser Charakterisierung der Stützstellen vergleiche man das Vorgehen von Kumar [6], [5] und dessen Verallgemeinerung von Price [7]. Nach (1.5.b) gilt also

$$(2.5)\qquad \|R_n\| = \frac{(-1)^n\, r}{(2a-1)T_n(r)-T_{n-2}(r)} \int_{-1}^{1} \frac{(2a-1)T_n(x)-T_{n-2}(x)}{(r+x)[a^2-(2a-1)x^2]\sqrt{1-x^2}}\, dx .$$

Sei $I_n(a,r)$ das Integral in (2.5). Die Transformation $x = \cos y$ liefert

$$I_n(a,r) = \int_0^{\pi} \frac{(2a-1)\cos(ny)-\cos[(n-2)y]}{(r+\cos y)[a^2-(2a-1)\cos^2 y]}\, dy .$$

Dieses Integral läßt sich in der Form

$$I_n(a,r) = \frac{1}{a^2-(2a-1)r^2}\left\{\int_0^{\pi} \frac{(2a-1)\cos(ny)-\cos[(n-2)y]}{r+\cos y}\, dy + C_n(a,r)\right\}$$

mit $\quad C_n(a,r) = (2a-1)\displaystyle\int_0^{\pi} \frac{\cos y - r}{a^2-(2a-1)\cos^2 y}\, dy \quad$ schreiben .

Wegen (1.2) gilt $\|R_n\| = O(r^{-2n})$ für $r \to \infty$, und damit nach (2.5) $I_n(a,r) = O(r^{-n-1})$ für $r \to \infty$. Folglich verschwindet $C_n(a,r)$, und es gilt

$$I_n(a,r) = \frac{1}{a^2-(2a-1)r^2} \int_0^{\pi} \frac{(2a-1)\cos(ny)-\cos[(n-2)y]}{r+\cos y}\, dy .$$

Mit $\quad \displaystyle\int_0^{\pi} \frac{\cos(my)}{r+\cos y}\, dy = \frac{(-1)^m \pi \tau^m}{\sqrt{r^2-1}} \quad$ (siehe etwa [3; S. 112]),

erhält man

$$I_n(a,r) = (-1)^n \frac{(2a-1)\tau^2-1}{a^2-(2a-1)r^2} \frac{\pi\, \tau^{n-2}}{\sqrt{r^2-1}} , \quad \text{d.h.}$$

$$(2.6) \qquad I_n(a,r) = (-1)^n \frac{2\pi\tau^n}{(a-r\tau)\sqrt{r^2-1}} .$$

Mit $T_m(r) = [(r-\sqrt{r^2-1})^m + (r+\sqrt{r^2-1})^m]/2$ (siehe z.B. [8; S. 5]) folgt aus (2.5) und (2.6) die Behauptung.

(2.3) und (2.4) lassen sich analog zeigen. Die Knoten $x_1,\ldots,x_n$ der entsprechenden Quadraturformeln sind die Knoten von

$(2a-1)U_n-U_{n-2}$ für $\alpha = \beta = 1/2$ und $n > 1$ bzw. von

$(2a-1)(U_n+U_{n-1})-U_{n-2}-U_{n-3}$ für $\alpha = -\beta = 1/2$ und $n > 2$. U_i sind dabei die Tschebyscheff-Polynome zweiter Art.

Bemerkung. Im allgemeineren Fall der Gewichtsfunktionen

$$w(x) = \frac{1}{(a-x)(b-x)} W(x), \quad a,b > 1 \quad \text{oder} \quad a,b < -1 ,$$

$$w(x) = \frac{1}{(a-x)(x-b)} W(x), \quad a > 1 , \quad b < -1 ,$$

mit $W(x) = (1-x)^\alpha(1+x)^\beta$, $\alpha,\beta = \pm 1/2$, läßt sich $\|R_n\|$ analog berechnen.

3. Beispiel

Sei $f(z) = \frac{z^4}{4-z^2}$, $f \in X_r$, $r \in (1,2]$. Bei der Approximation des Integrals $\int_{-1}^{1} \frac{1}{(4-3x^2)\sqrt{1-x^2}} f(x)dx$ mit der Gauß-Formel Q_2 zur Gewichtsfunktion $w(x) = \frac{1}{(4-3x^2)\sqrt{1-x^2}}$ beträgt der exakte Fehler $7.11 \cdot 10^{-2}$.

Für dieses f gilt in

$$(3.1) \qquad |R_2(f)| \leq \inf_{1<r\leq 2} (\|R_2\| \, |f|_r)$$

(siehe (1.3)) Gleichheit. Das Infimum wird für r=2 angenommen. $\|R_2\|$ erhält man aus (2.2) mit a=2, n=2. Schätzt man in (3.1) $|f|_r$ durch

$$\|f\|_{2,r} := \frac{1}{\sqrt{2\pi r}} \left(\int_{|z|=r} |f(z)|^2 |dz| \right)^{1/2}$$

bzw. durch $\max_{|z|=r} |f(z)|$ (siehe [4]) ab, so erhält man für $|R_2(f)|$ die Schranken $1.28 \cdot 10^{-1}$ (für r=1.65) beziehungsweise $2.62 \cdot 10^{-1}$ (für r=1.50) .

Literatur

1. Akrivis, G.: The error norm of certain Gaussian quadrature formulae. Eingereicht zur Veröffentlichung.
2. Gautschi, W. (1983) On Padé approximants associated with Hamburger series, Calcolo 20, 111-127.
3. Gröbner, W., N. Hofreiter (Hrsg.)(1961) Integraltafel, II. Teil, 3., verb. Aufl. (Springer Verlag, Wien).
4. Hämmerlin, G. (1972) Fehlerabschätzungen bei numerischer Integration nach Gauß. In: Methoden und Verfahren der mathematischen Physik, Bd. 6 (B. Brosowski, E. Martensen, Hrsg.) 153-163 (Bibliographisches Institut, Mannheim, Wien, Zürich).
5. Kumar, R. (1974) Certain Gaussian quadratures, J. Inst. Maths Applics 14, 175-182.
6. Kumar, R. (1974) A class of quadrature formulas, Math. Comp. 28, 769-778.
7. Price, Jr., T.E. (1979) Orthogonal polynomials for nonclassical weight functions, SIAM J. Numer. Anal. 16, 999-1006.
8. Rivlin, T.J. (1974) The Chebyshev polynomials (John Wiley and Sons, New York, London, Sydney, Toronto).

Dr. Georgios Akrivis, Mathematisches Institut der Universität München, Theresienstraße 39, D-8000 München 2, Germany (FRG).

Now at University of Crete, Department of Mathematics, Iraklion Crete, P.O. Box 470, Greece.

International Series of
Numerical Mathematics, Vol. 73

SOLVING INTEGRAL EQUATIONS ON SURFACES IN SPACE

Kendall E. Atkinson*, The University of Iowa

1. Introduction

Consider solving the integral equation

$$\lambda f(P) - \int_S K(P,Q)f(Q)dS = g(P), \quad P \in S, \tag{1.1}$$

where S denotes a surface in space. Such equations occur in a number of situations, and very often the integral operator is compact from $C(S)$ into itself. We will consider a collocation method for numerically solving (1.1), with the approximating solution a function that is piecewise quadratic in a parameterization of the surface. The numerical method is of independent interest, but we have chosen the method as a means to focus on the problems of solving integral equations on piecewise smooth surfaces in space. Unlike the case for functions of one variable with domain an interval, the use of surfaces S leads to the problem of approximating the domain. This makes the solution of (1.1) more than a simple generalization of the theory for integral equations of one variable.

The following paper is an extension of ATKINSON (1984),

---

* This research was supported in part by NSF Grant MCS-8002422.

in which the quadratic collocation method for (1.1) was introduced. Along with some review of that earlier paper, we will discuss additional aspects of the problem, particularly practical questions of implementation of the method. Section 2 discusses the triangulation of S, including the implementation of this on a computer. Section 3 reviews results on the interpolation of functions on the triangulation of S, including the approximation of S by interpolation. Section 4 defines the collocation method for solving (1.1), along with its practical implementation where $K(P,Q)$ is well-behaved. Section 5 gives an iterative method for the resulting finite linear systems. The final section 6 discusses the solution of the integral equation (1.1) arising from solving Laplace's equation using a double layer representation.

2. The Surface and its Triangulation

The surface S is assumed to be piecewise smooth. More precisely,

$$S = S_1 \cup \cdots \cup S_J \tag{2.1}$$

with each $S_i \subset \mathbb{R}^3$ and satisfying the following. For each i, there is a mapping

$$F_i : R_i \xrightarrow[\text{onto}]{1-1} S_i \tag{2.2}$$

with R_i a closed polygon in the plane $\mathbb{R}^2$. We further assume that F_i can be extended to an open set $\Omega_i \supset R_i$, with

$$F_i : \Omega_i \xrightarrow{1-1} \mathbb{R}^3$$

and

$$F_i \in C^3(\Omega_i). \tag{2.3}$$

Convergence of the numerical scheme of this paper can be proven under a condition weaker than (2.3), but the order of convergence will not be optimal.

For each surface S_i, let

$$\{\hat{\Delta}_{1,i},\cdots,\hat{\Delta}_{r(i),i}\}$$

denote a triangulation of the polygon R_i. Define a triangulation of S_i by

$$\Delta_{k,i} = F_i(\hat{\Delta}_{k,i}) , \quad k=1,\cdots,r(i). \tag{2.4}$$

Collect together the triangulations of $S_1,\cdots,S_J$ and denote them by

$$\{\Delta_1,\cdots,\Delta_N\}.$$

This gives a triangulation of S.

To aid in interpolating and integrating functions defined on a triangular face (or element) Δ_k, we introduce a parametric representation of Δ_k in terms of the unit simplex σ in $\mathbb{R}^2$,

$$\sigma = \{(s,t) \mid s,t \geq 0,\ s+t \leq 1\},$$

shown in Figure 1. For $\hat{\Delta}_k \subset S_i$, let $\hat{v}_1,\hat{v}_2,\hat{v}_3$ be the three

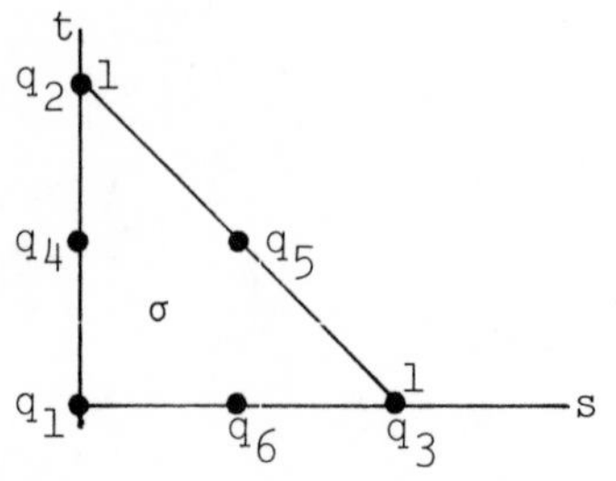

Fig. 1. Unit simplex σ.

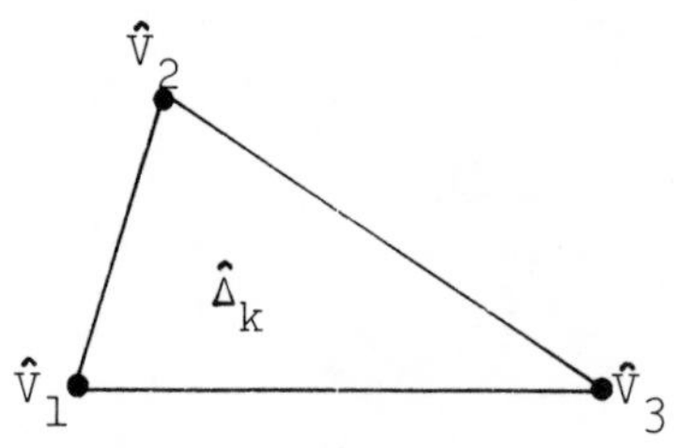

Fig. 2. Schematic of $\hat{\Delta}_k$.

vertices of $\hat{\Delta}_k$, as shown in Figure 2. Define

$$m_k : \sigma \xrightarrow[\text{onto}]{1-1} \Delta_k$$

by

$$m_k(s,t) = F_i(u\hat{v}_1 + t\hat{v}_2 + s\hat{v}_3) \ , \quad (s,t) \in \sigma \tag{2.5}$$

with $u = 1-s-t$. This is the composition of F_i with an affine mapping of σ onto $\hat{\Delta}_k$.

As additional notation, let $q_1,\cdots,q_6$ be the vertices and midpoints of the boundary of σ, as shown in Figure 1. Also define

$$v_{j,k} = m_k(q_j) \ , \quad j = 1,\cdots,6. \tag{2.6}$$

These six points of Δ_k are shown in Figure 3. They will be used as interpolation points on Δ_k. These three vertices and three 'midpoints' will be collectively referred to as node points or, more simply, nodes. The three vertices also give an orientation to Δ_k, by their order. This is needed when constructing a normal to Δ_k, which is needed with some applications.

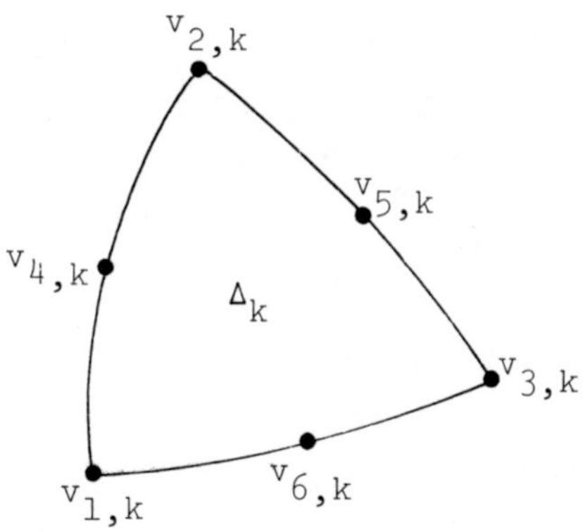

Fig. 3. Schematic of Δ_k.

When collectively referring to the nodes in the triangulation $\{\Delta_1,\cdots,\Delta_N\}$ of S, we will denote them by $\{v_1,\cdots,v_{N_v}\}$. The index N_v is the total number of distinct node points.

Computer Implementation

We are writing a package of subroutines to define and manipulate triangulations of S, to perform interpolation and integration over a triangulation, and to solve common types of integral equations. These programs are written in Fortran 77, in a portable form, and the total package will be referred to as TRIPACK.

To store the node points, we use an array VERTEX(3,*). Column #I contains the node v_I, with the rectangular coordinates (x,y,z) in rows 1, 2, and 3, respectively. To allow storage of additional information about each node, if needed, a one-dimensional array INDEXV is permitted. The element INDEXV(I) is associated with node v_I, and it can be a pointer to additional information or it can be used directly. For example, we have often used the definition

$$\text{INDEXV(I)} = \begin{cases} 2, & v_I \text{ is a vertex of the surface } S \\ 1, & v_I \text{ is on an edge of } S, \text{ but is not a vertex} \\ 0, & \text{otherwise.} \end{cases} \qquad (2.7)$$

This is used in defining variable or adaptive mesh refinements of the triangulation $\{\Delta_k\}$. Often the solution of the integral equation can have bad behaviour near edges or vertices of S, and this can be taken into account in the refinement of $\{\Delta_k\}$, based on using (2.7).

The faces in $\{\Delta_1,\cdots,\Delta_N\}$ are stored in an integer array IFACE(7,*). Face #K is stored in column K of IFACE. The entries IFACE(J,K) contain the indices (relative to VERTEX) of the six nodes $v_{J,K}$ for $J=1,\cdots,6$. The final entry IFACE(7,K) allows for additional information to be stored about Δ_K, and this information will be carried along to all subsequent subdivisions of Δ_K. For example, if $\Delta_K \subset S_\ell$ for some ℓ, then one can let IFACE(7,K) = ℓ. This may be useful in defining the user supplied subroutine MIDPT, described below.

To define the surface S and its triangulation, the user must supply two subroutines.

(1) INIT. This sets an initial triangulation of S by initializing VERTEX, INDEXV, and IFACE. For many standard surfaces, such routines INIT are available in TRIPACK.

(2) MIDPT. This defines the surface S implicitly in an operational manner. The routine MIDPT accepts as input (a) the index K of a face Δ_K, and (b) the indices of two adjoint nodes in Δ_K. The user is to then supply a 'midpoint' on S, located approximately midway between the given nodes. Again, such routines for many standard surfaces are given in TRIPACK.

Refinement of a Triangulation

Given a triangular element Δ, it is refined by connecting the midpoints of its sides, forming four new triangular faces. This is shown in Figure 4. The midpoints of the sides of the four new faces are obtained using the subroutine MIDPT, supplied by the user.

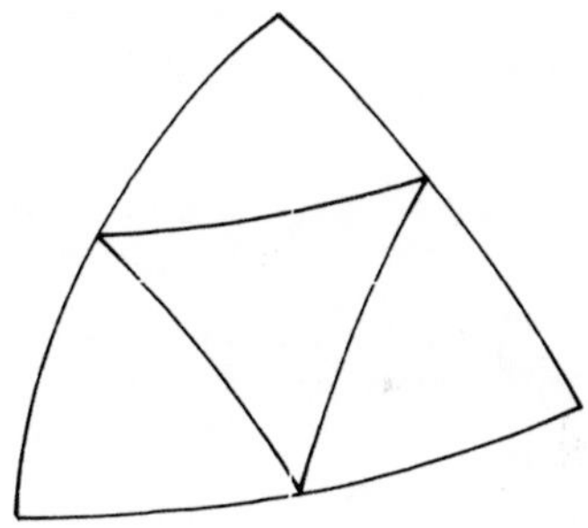

Fig. 4. Refining Δ.

To carry out the refinement or subdivision process on all triangular faces in a given triangulation $\{\Delta_k \mid 1 \le k \le N\}$, use subroutine REFINE. It will update VERTEX, INDEXV, and IFACE. The number of faces will increase by a factor of four. Alternatively, to carry out an adaptive subdivision based on INDEXV as defined in (2.7), subroutine ADAPT can be used. It will subdivide only those faces containing a node for which the corresponding index is nonzero. A discussion of uniform and nonuniform triangulations is considered in the earlier paper ATKINSON (1984), but we consider only uniform triangulations in the present paper.

3. Piecewise Quadratic Interpolation

Let $f \in C(S)$. On each face of a triangulation $\{\Delta_k\}$

of S, we define an isoparametric quadratic interpolant to f as follows. Begin by defining the interpolation basis functions $\ell_1,\cdots,\ell_6$ on σ by

$$\begin{aligned} \ell_1(s,t) &= u(2u-1) & \ell_2(s,t) &= t(2t-1) \\ \ell_3(s,t) &= s(2s-1) & \ell_4(s,t) &= 4tu \\ \ell_5(s,t) &= 4st & \ell_6(s,t) &= 4su \end{aligned} \tag{3.1}$$

with $u = 1-s-t$ and $(s,t) \in \sigma$. For the points q_j of σ (see Figure 1),

$$\ell_i(q_j) = \delta_{ij};$$

and degree $(\ell_i) = 2$, $1 \le i \le 6$. It is also convenient to define corresponding functions on a face Δ_k; let

$$\ell_{j,k}(m_k(s,t)) = \ell_j(s,t)\ , \quad (s,t) \in \sigma \tag{3.2}$$

for $1 \le j \le 6$, $1 \le k \le N$.

For the continuous function f on S, define its interpolant over $\{\Delta_k\}$ and $\{v_i\}$ as follows. On Δ_k, let

$$(\mathcal{P}_N f)(m_k(s,t)) = \sum_{j=1}^{6} f(v_{j,k})\ell_j(s,t)\ , \quad (s,t) \in \sigma, \tag{3.3}$$

or equivalently,

$$(\mathcal{P}_N f)(Q) = \sum_{j=1}^{6} f(v_{j,k})\ell_{j,k}(Q)\ , \quad Q \in \Delta_k. \tag{3.4}$$

For uniform triangulations, $\mathcal{P}_N : C(S) \longrightarrow C(S)$ and $\|\mathcal{P}_N\| = 5/3$.

Let

$$\delta_N = \underset{1 \le k \le N}{\operatorname{Max}} \ \operatorname{diameter}(\Delta_k).$$

Then easily

$$\underset{1 \le k \le N}{\text{Max}} \ \text{Area}(\Delta_k) = O(\delta_N^2) = O(\tfrac{1}{N}). \tag{3.5}$$

For $f \in C(S)$, one can show

$$\|f - \mathcal{P}_N f\|_\infty \le \frac{5}{3}\, \omega(f;\delta_N) \tag{3.6}$$

with ω the modulus of continuity of f. For $f \in C(S)$, we will say f <u>is smooth on</u> S if $f \in C^3(S_j)$, $j = 1,\cdots,J$, for the surfaces S_j making up S. In such a case, we can show

$$\|f - \mathcal{P}_N f\|_\infty = O(\delta_N^3). \tag{3.7}$$

These and other results given below, for both uniform and adaptive triangulations, are discussed in ATKINSON (1984).

<u>Surface Interpolation</u>

Each triangular face Δ_k is known explicitly at only its nodes $\{v_{j,k}\}$. This is often not sufficient, and for that reason we define an approximant to Δ_k. For the mapping $m_k(s,t)$, define an interpolant to it,

$$\begin{aligned} \tilde{m}_k(s,t) &= \sum_{j=1}^{6} m_k(q_j)\ell_j(s,t) \\ &= \sum_{j=1}^{6} v_{j,k}\ell_j(s,t)\,, \qquad (s,t) \in \sigma. \end{aligned} \tag{3.8}$$

Let $\tilde{\Delta}_k = \tilde{m}_k(\sigma)$. The approximate face $\tilde{\Delta}_k$ coincides with Δ_k at the six nodes $v_{j,k}$. Using the assumption (2.3), it can be shown that

$$\underset{1 \le k \le N}{\text{Max}} \ \underset{(s,t)\in\sigma}{\text{Max}} |m_k(s,t) - m_k(s,t)| = O(\delta_N^3). \tag{3.9}$$

Define $D_s m_k(s,t)$ and $D_t m_k(s,t)$ to be the derivatives of $m_k(s,t)$ with respect to s and t, and define $D_s\tilde{m}_k$ and $D_t\tilde{m}_k$ analogously. Then

$$D_s m_k, D_t m_k, D_s\tilde{m}_k, D_t\tilde{m}_k = O(\delta_N) \tag{3.10}$$

and

$$D_s m_k \times D_t m_k - D_s \tilde{m}_k \times D_t \tilde{m}_k = O(\delta_N^4). \tag{3.11}$$

The normal to Δ_k $[\tilde{\Delta}_k]$ at $m_k(s,t)$ $[\tilde{m}_k(s,t)]$ is

$$\nu_k = \frac{D_s m_k \times D_t m_k}{|D_s m_k \times D_t m_k|} , \quad \left[\tilde{\nu}_k = \frac{D_s \tilde{m}_k \times D_t \tilde{m}_k}{|D_s \tilde{m}_k \times D_t \tilde{m}_k|} \right]. \tag{3.12}$$

From (3.10) and (3.11),

$$\nu_k - \tilde{\nu}_k = O(\delta_N^2). \tag{3.13}$$

4. The Projection Method

Let $\mathcal{K}$ denote a bounded linear operator on $C(S)$ to $C(S)$. Usually this will be an integral operator

$$(\mathcal{K}f)(P) = \int_S K(P,Q)f(Q)dS , \quad P \in S. \tag{4.1}$$

We will give a numerical method for solving the equation of the second kind

$$(\lambda-\mathcal{K})f = g , \quad g \in C(S); \tag{4.2}$$

and it will be assumed that $(\lambda-\mathcal{K})^{-1}$ is defined and bounded on $C(S)$ to $C(S)$.

The collocation method for solving (4.2), using the interpolation scheme of section 3, is defined by

$$(\lambda-\mathcal{P}_N\mathcal{K})f_N = \mathcal{P}_N g. \tag{4.3}$$

If

$$\|\mathcal{K}-\mathcal{P}_N\mathcal{K}\| \longrightarrow 0 \quad \text{as} \quad N \longrightarrow \infty \tag{4.4}$$

then the convergence and stability theory for (4.3) is straightforward; see ATKINSON (1976, p. 228). The cited results say that for sufficiently large N, say $N \geq N_0$, $(\lambda-\mathcal{P}_N\mathcal{K})^{-1}$ exists and is uniformly bounded on $C(S)$,

$$\|(\lambda-\mathcal{P}_N\mathcal{K})^{-1}\| \leq c , \quad N \geq N_0. \tag{4.5}$$

Moreover,

$$\|f-f_N\|_\infty \leq c\|f-\mathcal{P}_N f\|_\infty. \tag{4.6}$$

And if f is smooth on S, then (3.7) and (4.6) imply $f-f_N = O(\delta_N^3)$. (Note: We will use c to denote a generic constant.) The condition (4.4) will be satisfied automatically if $\mathcal{K}$ is compact (see ATKINSON (1976, p. 53, Lemma 2)). Otherwise (4.5) must be shown directly.

The Collocation Linear System

Using the formula

$$f_N(Q) = \sum_{j=1}^{6} f_N(v_{j,k})\ell_{j,k}(Q) , \quad Q \in \Delta_k, \tag{4.7}$$

the collocation equation (4.3) leads to the equivalent linear system

$$\lambda f_N(v_i) - \sum_{k=1}^{N} \sum_{j=1}^{6} f_N(v_{j,k})\int_{\Delta_k} K(v_i,Q)\ell_{j,k}(Q)dS = g(v_i), \tag{4.8}$$

for $i = 1,\cdots,N_v$. Denote this linear system by

$$(\lambda-A_N)\tilde{f}_N = \tilde{g} , \quad \tilde{f}_N,\tilde{g} \in \mathbb{R}^{N_v}$$

with $\tilde{g}$ the restriction of g to the nodes of the triangulation. From ATKINSON (1976, p. 78), it follows that

$$\|(\lambda-A_N)^{-1}\| \leq \tfrac{5}{3}\|(\lambda-\mathcal{P}_N\mathcal{K})^{-1}\| , \quad N \geq N_0, \tag{4.9}$$

where the matrix norm is the row norm induced by the maximum norm on $\mathbb{R}^{N_v}$.

The integrals in (4.8) can be rewritten as

$$\int_\sigma K(v_i, m_k(s,t))\ell_j(s,t)|D_s m_k \times D_t m_k| ds\ dt. \tag{4.10}$$

These must almost always be further approximated before the system (4.8) can be obtained explicitly. This will lead to a further approximating linear system,

$$(\lambda - B_N)\tilde{h}_N = g\ , \quad \tilde{h}_N \in \mathbb{R}^{N_v}. \tag{4.11}$$

Assume

$$\|A_N - B_N\| \longrightarrow 0 \quad \text{as} \quad N \longrightarrow \infty. \tag{4.12}$$

Then using (4.9) and (4.5), $(\lambda - B_N)^{-1}$ exists and is uniformly bounded for all sufficiently large N, say $N \geq N_1$. Moreover,

$$\|\tilde{f}_N - \tilde{h}_N\|_\infty \leq c[\|A_N - B_N\|\|\tilde{f} - \tilde{f}_N\|_\infty + \|(A_N - B_N)\tilde{f}\|_\infty]. \tag{4.13}$$

The first term on the right will go to zero faster than $\|f - \mathcal{P}_N f\|_\infty$, using (4.6) and (4.13). To have $\|\tilde{f}_N - \tilde{h}_N\|_\infty$ be $O(\delta_N^3)$ for smooth functions f, we must have

$$\|(A_N - B_N)\tilde{f}\|_\infty \leq O(\delta_N^3). \tag{4.14}$$

From (4.8), component #i of $A_N \underset{\sim}{f}$ is

$$(A_N\tilde{f})_i = (\mathcal{K}\mathcal{P}_N f)(v_i). \tag{4.15}$$

Using this, $\|f - \mathcal{P}_N f\|_\infty = O(\delta_N^3)$, and the boundedness of $\mathcal{K}$, (4.14) is equivalent to

$$\underset{1 \leq i \leq N_v}{\text{Max}} |\mathcal{K}f(v_i) - (B_N\tilde{f})_i| = O(\delta_N^3). \tag{4.16}$$

Showing this condition when $K(P,Q)$ is smooth is discussed below, and showing it when K is singular is discussed in both section 6 and in ATKINSON (1984).

Before proceeding with the construction of B_N, we note that the mapping $m_k(s,t)$ in (4.10) is known at only the six nodes of Δ_k. Because of this we replace m_k by $\tilde{m}_k$. This changes $\mathcal{K}f(v_i)$ to

$$\int_\sigma K(v_i,\tilde{m}_k(s,t))f(\tilde{m}_k(s,t))|D_s\tilde{m}_k \times D_t\tilde{m}_k|ds\ dt. \qquad (4.17)$$

To carry this out, we must assume that on each piece S_j of S, f and $K(v_i,\cdot)$ can be extended smoothly to a nearby open neighboring region. This is not a problem in theory; and in practice, we know such a K exactly or we will need $K(v_i,\cdot)$ and f at only the nodes of Δ_k. The resulting use of (4.17) over the entire surface S, together with (3.9) and (3.11), would seem to imply an error of $O(\delta_N^2)$ in approximating (4.16). But using an argument in NEDELEC (1976), it can be shown that the actual error is $O(\delta_N^3)$.

<u>Smooth Kernel Functions</u>

Let $K(P,Q)$ belong to $C^3(S_i \times S_j)$ for $i,j = 1,\cdots,J$; we will simply say that K <u>is smooth on</u> S. To approximate the integral in (4.17), we use the formula

$$\int_\sigma G(s,t)ds\ dt \doteq \frac{1}{6}[G(q_4) + G(q_5) + G(q_6)]. \qquad (4.18)$$

For polynomials in (s,t), this has degree of precision 2. Applying this to (4.17), we obtain a final formula for approximating $\mathcal{K}f(v_i)$,

$$\begin{aligned}\mathcal{K}f(v_i) &\doteq \sum_{k=1}^{N}\sum_{j=4}^{6} K(v_i,v_{j,k})f(v_{j,k})\frac{1}{6}|D_s\tilde{m}_k \times D_t\tilde{m}_k(q_j)| \\ &= \sum_{\ell=1}^{N_V} w_\ell K(v_i,v_\ell)f(v_\ell) \equiv (B_N\tilde{f})_i. \end{aligned} \qquad (4.19)$$

The weight w_ℓ equals the sum of all weights $|D_s\tilde{m}_k \times D_t\tilde{m}_k(q_j)|/6$

where $v_{j,k} = v_\ell$. This definition of B_N can be shown to satisfy the requirements (4.12) and (4.16). Thus the use of (4.19) in (4.11) will lead to a collocation solution $\tilde{h}_N$ that is in error by $O(\delta_N^3)$.

Using (4.19), introduce the numerical integration operator

$$(\mathcal{K}_N f)(P) = \sum_{\ell=1}^{N_v} w_\ell K(P,v_\ell)f(v_\ell) , \quad P \in S. \tag{4.20}$$

Then the system $(\lambda-B_N)\tilde{h}_N = \tilde{g}$ is the linear system associated with the Nystrom method

$$(\lambda-\mathcal{K}_N)h_N = g \tag{4.21}$$

for approximating (4.2). It would have been difficult to prove directly that $f-h_N = O(\delta_N^3)$, although it follows from the results shown above.

Example. (1) Consider the error in $\mathcal{K}_N f$ in (4.20) when $K,f \equiv 1$ and the surface S is the ellipsoid

$$x^2 + (y/1.5)^2 + (z/2)^2 = 1. \tag{4.22}$$

The calculation of $\mathcal{K}f$ in this case is just the calculation of the surface area of S using

$$\int_S dS \doteq \sum_{\ell=1}^{N_v} w_\ell . \tag{4.23}$$

The errors in this numerical integration are shown in Table I. The true integral (the surface area) is 27.886442, to eight digits. The column labeled "Ratio" refers to the ratio of successive errors. Using it and (3.5), the errors are approximated $O(\delta_N^4)$, better than was expected.

(2) Using the same ellipsoidal surface, solve $(\lambda-\mathcal{K})f = g$ with

$$K(P,Q) = \frac{\partial}{\partial \nu_Q}(|P-Q|^2), \quad f(x,y,z) = e^z, \quad \lambda = 80. \qquad (4.24)$$

Table I. Errors in numerical integration (4.23)

N	N_v	Rel.Error	Ratio	N	N_v	Rel.Error	Ratio
8	18	1.07E-1		20	42	3.05E-2	
			6.8				11.0
32	66	1.57E-2		80	162	2.78E-3	
			12.0				14.5
128	258	1.31E-3		320	642	1.92E-4	
			14.9				
512	1026	8.78E-5					

We calculated the kernel exactly, not by using the approximation $\tilde{\nu}_k$ in (3.12). Also, $\|\mathcal{K}\| = 24\pi \doteq 75$, and λ is only slightly outside the spectral radius, in a relative sense. The numerical results are shown in Table II. The rate of convergence appears to be $O(\delta_N^3)$ or faster.

Table II. Errors in solving $(\lambda-\mathcal{K})f = g$ with (4.24)

N	N_v	$\|\tilde{f}-\tilde{h}_N\|_\infty$	Ratio	N	N_v	$\|\tilde{f}-\tilde{h}_N\|_\infty$	Ratio
8	18	1.25		20	42	.603	7.8
			5.1				
32	66	.247		80	162	.0774	
			8.0				12.2
128	258	.0307		320	642	.00633	

5. Iterative Solution: Smooth Kernels

Regard the linear system (4.11) as coming from the Nyström method associated with the numerical integral operator $\mathcal{K}_N$ of (4.20). Then there are iterative variants of the Nyström method which can be used to iteratively solve the linear system; see ATKINSON (1976, Chapter 4, Part II).

Assume that the linear system $(\lambda-B_N)\tilde{h}_N = \tilde{g}$ can be solved directly for some N, for any right-hand side $\tilde{g}$.

Usually this will mean that its LU factorization has been computed previously and saved, and the linear system can be solved rapidly for new right-hand sides $\tilde{g}$. We will use this information to construct an iterative method for solving

$$(\lambda - B_M)\tilde{h}_M = \tilde{g} \tag{5.1}$$

for values $M > N$.

Using the numerical integral operator (4.20), define the iteration as follows. Let $h_M^{(0)}$ be an initial guess for the solution of $(\lambda - \mathcal{K}_M)h_M = g$, the continuous approximating equation. For $\nu \geq 0$, define

$$\begin{aligned} r^{(\nu)} &= g - (\lambda I - \mathcal{K}_M)h_M^{(\nu)} \\ h_M^{(\nu+1)} &= h_M^{(\nu)} + \frac{1}{\lambda}[r^{(\nu)} + (\lambda I - \mathcal{K}_N)^{-1}\mathcal{K}_M r^{(\nu)}]. \end{aligned} \tag{5.2}$$

This method is analyzed in ATKINSON (1976, pp. 142-147), and it is shown to converge for sufficiently large values of N. In particular,

$$\|h_M - h_M^{(\nu+1)}\|_\infty \leq c\|(\mathcal{K}_M - \mathcal{K}_N)\mathcal{K}_M\|\|h_M - h_M^{(\nu)}\|_\infty, \quad \nu \geq 0. \tag{5.3}$$

The multiplier $\|(\mathcal{K}_M - \mathcal{K}_N)\mathcal{K}_M\|$ can be shown to converge to zero as $N \to \infty$, uniformly for $M \geq N$.

The iteration (5.2) can be restricted to the values of $h_M^{(\nu)}$ at only the node points, thus iteratively solving (5.1). This is discussed in ATKINSON (1976, p. 146), and we omit it here. For the initial guess, use the Nyström interpolation formula

$$h_M^{(0)} := h_L = \frac{1}{\lambda}[g + \mathcal{K}_L h_L] \tag{5.4}$$

where L is the index of the previous triangulation used in approximating $(\lambda - \mathcal{K})f = g$. Evaluate (5.4) at the nodes of the triangulation of index M. Usually $L = M/4$; and we usually solve for a succession of values $M = 4N$, $16N$, etc.

The iteration (5.2) has an operations cost of

$$2M(N+M) + N^2 + 3M$$

multiplications per iterate; and more importantly, there are about $2M^2$ evaluations of $K(P,Q)$ per iteration, if these are not stored between iterations.

Example. Use the ellipsoidal surface (4.22) and the equation defined by (4.24). Table III contains the rates of convergence of the iteration method for various values of N and M,

Table III. Nyström iteration for $(\lambda - B_M)\tilde{h}_M = \tilde{g}$

N	N_v	M	M_v	Rate
8	18	32	66	2.0
32	66	128	258	6.2
20	42	80	162	3.5
20	42	320	642	3.2

with the rate defined as an empirical approximation of

$$\text{Rate} := \operatorname*{Limit}_{\nu \to \infty} \frac{\|\tilde{h}_M^{(\nu-1)} - \tilde{h}_M^{(\nu)}\|_\infty}{\|h_M^{(\nu)} - h_M^{(\nu+1)}\|_\infty} .$$

6. The Double Layer Potential Integral Equation

Consider solving the Dirichlet problem for Laplace's equation,

$$\begin{aligned} \Delta u(A) &= 0 , \quad && A \in D \\ u(P) &= g(P) , \quad && P \in S = \partial D \end{aligned} \tag{6.1}$$

where D is a simply-connected region in $\mathbb{R}^3$ and S is a piecewise smooth surface, as defined earlier in section 2. Represent u as a double layer potential,

$$u(A) = \int_S f(Q) \frac{\partial}{\partial \nu_Q}\left(\frac{1}{|A-Q|}\right) dS , \quad A \in D. \tag{6.2}$$

Letting $A \longrightarrow P \in S$, f will satisfy

$$2\pi f(p) + \int_S f(Q) \frac{\partial}{\partial \nu_Q}\left(\frac{1}{|P-Q|}\right) dS + [2\pi - \Omega(P)] f(P)$$
$$= g(P) , \quad P \in S. \tag{6.3}$$

Symbolically,

$$(2\pi + \mathcal{K}) f = g.$$

In this equation ν_Q is the inner normal to S at Q, and $\Omega(P)$ is the solid angle of S at P. We will assume

$$0 < \Omega(P) < 4\pi. \tag{6.4}$$

Under this and other assumptions on the edges and vertices of S, it can be shown that

$$\mathcal{K} : \mathcal{X} \longrightarrow \mathcal{X},$$

with $\mathcal{X} = C(S)$ or $L^\infty(S)$ and with $\mathcal{K}$ bounded. If S is smooth, then $\mathcal{K}$ is also compact. For smooth surfaces S, see GUNTER (1967); and for piecewise smooth surfaces, see WENDLAND (1968).

<u>Numerical Solution</u>

Applying the collocation method of section 4, we can carry out a convergence analysis using the ideas in WENDLAND (1968). In particular, if

$$\frac{5}{3} \sup_{P \in S} |2\pi - \Omega(P)| < 2\pi , \tag{6.5}$$

then we can show convergence, as in (4.6). If $f(P)$ is smooth on S (i.e., on each section of S), then the rate of convergence of f_N will be $O(\delta_N^3)$, as before. [However, if S is only piecewise smooth, then it is unlikely that $f(P)$ will be smooth for P near to an edge or vertex of S.] These are straightforward arguments and we omit them here. Instead we look at the problem of approximating the linear system $(2\pi - A_N)\tilde{f}_N = \tilde{g}$.

We begin by replacing integration over S, via the triangulation $\{\Delta_k\}$, by integration over $\{\tilde{\Delta}_k\}$, the piecewise quadratic isoparametric approximation of S. Define

$$K(P,Q) = \frac{\partial}{\partial \nu_Q}\left(\frac{1}{|P-Q|}\right) = \nu_Q \cdot \nabla_Q\left(\frac{1}{|P-Q|}\right). \qquad (6.6)$$

As stated earlier in section 4, following (4.17), if K is known exactly and is extended smoothly to a neighborhood of S, then the approximation of S will result in a further error of $O(\delta_N^3)$ in solving for f. Unfortunately, we cannot know ν_Q exactly in many cases and we must use the approximate inner normal $\tilde{\nu}_Q$ given earlier in (3.12),

$$\tilde{\nu}_Q = \frac{D_s\tilde{m}_k \times D_t\tilde{m}_k}{|D_s\tilde{m}_k \times D_t\tilde{m}_k|}, \qquad Q = \tilde{m}_k(s,t). \qquad (6.7)$$

Doing this causes an additional error of $O(\delta_N^2)$ in solving for f, at least based on our error analysis using (3.13).

<u>Evaluation of $\Omega(P)$</u>

The linear system for the collocation method applied to (6.3) is now given by

$$2\pi f_N(v_i) - \sum_{k=1}^{N} \sum_{j=1}^{6} f_N(v_{j,k}) \int_{\tilde{\Delta}_k} \tilde{K}(v_i,Q)\ell_{j,k}(Q)dS$$
$$+ [2\pi - \Omega(v_i)]f(v_i) = g(v_i), \quad 1 \le i \le N_v, \qquad (6.8)$$

with $\tilde{K}$ the result of using (6.7) in (6.6).

To approximate $\Omega(v_i)$, note that substituting

$f(P) \equiv 1$ into (6.3) will give an identity if $g(P) = 4\pi$. Thus the integral term yields

$$\int_S K(P,Q)dS = \Omega(P) , \quad P \in S. \tag{6.9}$$

We use the approximation to the integral term in (6.8) to approximate $\Omega(v_i)$, using (6.9). For our final linear system $(2\pi+B_N)\tilde{h}_N = \tilde{g}$, this results in the forced identity

$$(2\pi-B_N)\tilde{f}^* = 4\pi\tilde{f}^* \tag{6.10}$$

for the vector $\tilde{f}^* = [1,1,\cdots,1]^T$.

Examples. (i) Consider the ellipsoid given in (4.22). Table IV gives the values of $\Omega(v_i)$ obtained by the above schema. In all cases, the values are approaching 2π, the exact value for a smooth surface.

Table IV. Values of $\Omega(v_i)$ for the ellipsoid (4.22)

v_i	N=20	N=80	N=320
(0,0,2)	5.9107	6.2767	6.2902
(.9,0,.9)	6.0583	6.2701	6.2851
(.5,0,1.7)	5.8307	6.2508	6.2827

(ii) Let S be the surface of the unit cube $D = [0,1] \times [0,1] \times [0,1]$. Table V gives values for $\Omega(P)$ at three node points: (0,0,0) is a vertex of S, (.5,0,0) is a

Table V. Values of $\Omega(v_i)$ on a cube

v_i	N=12	N=48
(0,0,0)	1.5562	1.5706
(.5,0,0)	2.9286	3.1329
(.5,0,.5)	6.6276	6.2481

midpoint of an edge of S, and $(.5,0,.5)$ is a centroid of a face of S. In all cases, the correct values of $\Omega(v_i)$ are being obtained.

Numerical Integration of Collocation Integrals

We must evaluate the integrals

$$\int_\sigma K(v_i,\tilde{m}_k(s,t))\ell_j(s,t)|D_s\tilde{m}_k \times D_t\tilde{m}_k|\,ds\,dt \tag{6.11}$$

for $k=1,\cdots,N$, $i=1,\cdots,N_v$, and $j=1,\cdots,6$. There are three cases, depending on the distance of v_i from Δ_k.

Case (i). Let v_i be "far from Δ_k." This generally means that the distance d from v_i to Δ_k satisfies $d > \epsilon$, where ϵ is a given nonnegative constant. Then $K(P,Q)$ is non-singular, and we use the simple 3-point scheme (4.18) to perform the integration in (6.8) over $\tilde{\Delta}_k$. For best theoretical results, ϵ should be a positive constant, chosen independent of N.

Case (ii). Let v_i be "near to Δ_k," but not inside of it. The distance d between v_i and A_k satisfies $0 < d \le \epsilon$, and this means that $K(v_i,Q)$ can be very peaked when Q is near to v_i. In this case, we use an automatic integration scheme to calculate the integrals in (6.11) for $1 \le j \le 6$. The program uses the 7-point method T2:5-1, of degree of precision 5, from STROUD (1971). Continued uniform subdivisions of σ are carried out until sufficient accuracy is obtained.

Case (iii). Let v_i belong to Δ_k. Then $K(v_i,Q)$ is singular over $\tilde{\Delta}_i$. To treat (6.11) in this case, we use an idea of DUFFY (1982). To explain the general idea, consider first the integral

$$I = \int_\sigma G(s,t)\,ds\,dt \tag{6.12}$$

with $G(s,t)$ singular at the single point $(0,0)$. Introduce the change of variable

$$s = (1-u)x\ , \quad t = ux\ , \quad 0 \le u,x \le 1.$$

Then

$$I = \int_0^1 \int_0^1 x\, G((1-u)x, ux)\, du\, dx. \qquad (6.13)$$

For our case of a double layer kernel K, with $v_i = \tilde{m}_k(0,0)$, the new integrand in (6.13) will no longer have a singularity and it will be almost as smooth as the original element Δ_k. These results are also true for the single layer kernel $K(P,Q) = 1/|P-Q|$.

If a simple product Gaussian quadrature is applied to (6.13), very satisfactory results are obtained. We used an m-point Gaussian quadrature for each integral in (6.13), and very satisfactory results are obtained. We used an m-point Gaussian quadrature for each integral in (6.13), and very accurate results were obtained with $m = 2$, 3, or 4.

For cases where v_i is a node of Δ_k other than $m_k(0,0)$, we transform those integrals to the case (6.12) with the singularity at $(0,0)$ and then apply (6.13). If v_i is $m_k(0,1)$ or $m_k(1,0)$, then simply use an affine mapping of σ onto σ, to map the singular point of (6.11) onto $(0,0)$. For the cases where v_i corresponds to a midpoint of a side of σ, break the triangle into two pieces σ_1 and σ_2, with v_i corresponding to a vertex in each of the new triangles. For example, see Figure 5 for $v_i = m_k(0,\frac{1}{2})$. Write (6.11) as the sum of integrals over σ_1 and σ_2. For each such integral, map the domain onto σ, with the singular point mapped to $(0,0)$. Then apply (6.13) to that new integral, for both σ_1 and σ_2.

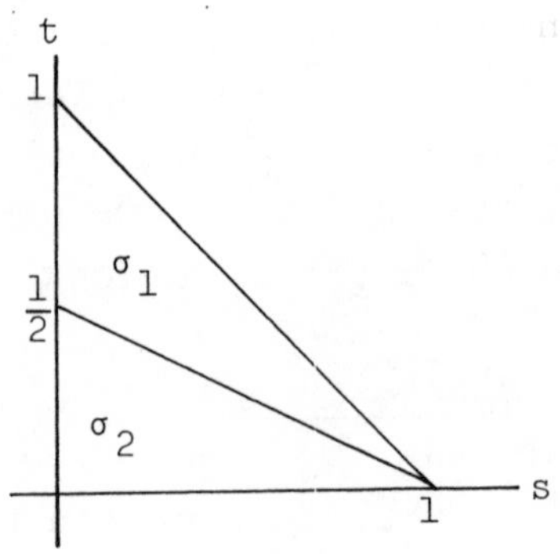

Fig. 5. Decomposition of σ.

Subroutines are given in TRIPACK to carry out all of the above forms for integrating (6.11), with the user allowed to set error tolerances.

Examples. (i) Let S be the ellipsoid in (4.22). We generate the Dirichlet boundary data from the harmonic function

$$u(x,y,z) = e^z \cos(y) + e^x \sin(z). \tag{6.14}$$

The integral equation (6.3) is solved for an approximate density function $f_N(P)$. This is then used to generate an approximate harmonic function from (6.2), which will be denoted by $u_N(x,y,z)$. There are various parameters needed in determining the numerical integration of (6.11), as derived in cases (i)-(iii) above. In the examples given here, we took $\epsilon = 0$, thus not considering case (ii). The results are shown in Table VI, for various points A inside the region D.

Empirically, the rate of convergence is consistent with $O(\delta_N^r)$, with $3.4 \le r \le 5.4$. This is better then the rate $O(\delta_N^2)$ that was expected on the basis of the approximation $\nu_Q \doteq \tilde{\nu}_Q$ in (3.13).

Table VI. Errors in solving $\Delta u = 0$: ellipsoid case

A	Error in $u_N(A)$ N=20	N=80	N=320
(.1,.1,.1)	1.4E-2	-7.2E-4	-4.8E-5
(.25,.25,.25)	7.2E-2	-9.4E-6	3.9E-5
(.5,.5,.5)	1.4E-1	6.2E-4	3.2E-4
(0,0,1.75)	1.9E-1	2.7E-2	1.8E-3

(ii) Let S be the elliptic paraboloid defined by

$$\begin{aligned} &S = S_1 \cup S_2 \\ &S_1 : \; z = x^2 + (y/2)^2 , \quad 0 \le z \le 1 \\ &S_2 : \; z = 1 , \quad 0 \le x^2 + (y/2)^2 \le 1. \end{aligned} \tag{6.15}$$

Initially both S_1 and S_2 are divided into four triangular elements. Again, the Dirichlet problem (6.1) was solved with the solution given by (6.14). The results at selected points inside S are given in Table VII. Empirically, the rate of convergence is consistent with $O(\delta_N^r)$ with $3.2 \leq r \leq 3.8$.

Table VII. Errors in solving $\Delta u = 0$: paraboloid case

A	Error in $u_N(A)$ N=8	N=32	N=128
(0,0,.2)	1.2E-1	4.4E-3	6.3E-4
(0,0,.5)	2.0E-1	6.9E-3	1.8E-3
(0,0,.8)	2.6E-1	5.6E-3	2.8E-3
(.3,.3,.5)	2.0E-1	8.9E-3	2.5E-3

Iterative Solution of Linear System

Denote the linear system arising from the numerical integration of the integrals in (6.8) by $(2\pi - B_N)\tilde{f}_N = \tilde{g}$. This system was solved iteratively by adapting the multigrid technique in HACKBUSCH (1981); we used his "simple method." For smooth boundaries S, the results were quite satisfactory, and the method has the same convergence properties as the method given earlier in section 5 for equations with a smooth kernel function.

For the case where S was only piecewise smooth, the numerical results were much less satisfactory. The iterative method converged in most cases, but quite slowly. The convergence behaviour seen earlier in (5.3) was no longer true. Increasing the order of the coarser approximation did not increase the rate of convergence of the iteration. The effect of S having edges or vertices is qutie pronounced, and it would appear that a scheme such as that in SCHIPPERS (1984) will be needed to take account of this effect.

7. REFERENCES

Atkinson, K. (1976) A survey of numerical methods for the solution of Fredholm integral equations of the second kind (SIAM Pub., Philadelphia).

Atkinson, K. (1984) Piecewise polynomial collocation for integral equations on surfaces in three dimensions. J. Int. Eqns., to appear.

Duffy, M. (1982) Quadrature over a pyramid or cube of integrands with a singularity at the vertex. SIAM J. Num. Anal. 19, 1260-1262.

Gunter, N. (1967) Potential theory (F. Ungar Pub., New York).

Hackbusch, W. (1981) Die schnelle Auflösung der Fredholmschen Integralgleichungen zweiter Art. Beitrage zur Numer. Math. 9, 47-62.

Nedelec, J. (1976) Curved finite element methods for the solution of singular integral equations on surfaces in $\mathbb{R}^3$. Computer Methods in Appl. Mech. and Eng. 8, 61-80.

Schippers, H. (1984) Multigrid methods for boundary integral equations. Submitted for publication.

Stroud, A. (1971) Approximate calculation of multiple integrals (Prentice-Hall, New Jersey).

Wendland, W. (1968) Die Behandlung von Randwertaufgaben im $\mathbb{R}^3$ mit Hilfe von Einfach- und Doppelschichtpotentialen. Numerische Math. 11, 380-404.

Kendall E. Atkinson, Department of Mathematics, The University of Iowa, Iowa City, Iowa, 52242, U.S.A.

International Series of
Numerical Mathematics, Vol. 73

An Adaptive Step Size Control for Volterra Integral Equations

H. ARNDT, BONN

1. INTRODUCTION

Consider the Volterra integral equation of the second kind

$$y(x) = f(x) + \int_a^x K(x,t,y(t))dt, \quad x \in [a,b]$$

with continuous f and continuous kernel K.

For simplicity we assume that K is defined on

$$G := \{(x,t,y) \in \mathbb{R} \times \mathbb{R} \times \mathbb{R}^n \mid a \le t \le x \le b, \quad y \in \mathbb{R}^n\} \quad ,$$

We suppose K to be Lipschitz continuous with respect to the last argument,

$$|K(x,t,y) - K(x,t,z)| \le L|y-z| \quad \text{for all} \quad (x,t,y),\ (x,t,z) \in G;$$

here $| \bullet |$ denotes a norm on $\mathbb{R}^n$.

Under these assumptions there exists a unique solution y on some interval $[a, \overline{x}]$; we assume $\overline{x} = b$.

This work has been partially supported by the Department of Mathematics and Computer Science of the University of Miami, Florida

Typeset by $\mathcal{A}_{\mathcal{M}}\mathcal{S}$-TEX

The purpose of this paper which is a sequel of [1] is to prove (at least for Extended Volterra Runge Kutta methods) that for the sake of reliable step size control we cannot proceed in the same way as in the case of ordinary differential equations. In the numerical solution of Volterra integral equations we have to test at earlier stages whether integrals that have to be computed later will be approximated according to the prescribed tolerance.

Before treating the case of Volterra integral equations let's take a short look on the special case of ordinary differential equations.

2. Ordinary Differential Equations

We consider the numerical solution of the initial value problem

$$y' = f(x, y)$$

$$y(x_0) = \eta$$

with f continuous and Lipschitz continuous with respect to the second argument

$$|f(x,v) - f(x,w)| \leq L|v - w| \quad \text{for all} \quad v, w.$$

Let $a = x_0 < x_1 < x_2 < ... < x_N = b$ denote a grid with step sizes $h_j := x_{j+1} - x_j$ and let u be the numerical solution on the grid. Furthermore let y_j be the (local) solution of the initial value problem

$$y_j' = f(x, y_j)$$

$$y_j(x_j) = u(x_j) \quad j = 0, 1, ..., N-1.$$

If y and z are two solutions of the differential equation, i.e.

$$y' = f(x, y) \quad \text{and} \quad z' = f(x, z)$$

then in a common interval I of existence with $x_j \in I$ we have

$$|y(x) - z(x)| \leq |y(x_j) - z(x_j)|e^{L|x - x_j|} \quad \text{for all} \quad x \in I. \tag{1}$$

Let

$$\begin{aligned} r\,[f,h]\,(x_j, u(x_j)) &:= \frac{1}{h}(y_j(x_j + h) - u(x_j + h)) \\ &= \frac{y_j(x_j + h) - y_j(x_j)}{h} - \varphi\,[f,h]\,(x_j, u(x_j)) \end{aligned}$$

be the local discretization error where φ is the increment function of a one step method. Assume that during the computation of u we get the following errors

$$\delta_j := |r[f, h_j](x_j, u(x_j))| \quad , \quad j = 0, 1, ..., N-1.$$

Then because of $u(x_i) = y_i(x_i)$ and $y = y_0$ we obtain for the global error

$$\begin{aligned} |y(x_i) - u(x_i)| &\leq \sum_{j=1}^{i} |y_j(x_i) - y_{j-1}(x_i)| \\ &\leq \sum_{j=1}^{i} |y_j(x_j) - y_{j-1}(x_j)| e^{L|x_i - x_j|} \end{aligned}$$

In view of

$$\begin{aligned} |y_j(x_j) - y_{j-1}(x_j)| &= |u(x_j) - y_{j-1}(x_j)| \\ &= |u(x_{j-1}) + h_{j-1}\varphi[f, h_{j-1}](x_{j-1}, u(x_{j-1})) - y_{j-1}(x_j)| \\ &= h_{j-1} \left| \frac{y_{j-1}(x_j) - y_{j-1}(x_{j-1})}{h_{j-1}} - \varphi[f, h_{j-1}](x_{j-1}, u(x_{j-1})) \right| \\ &= h_{j-1} |r[f, h_{j-1}](x_{j-1}, u(x_{j-1}))| \\ &= h_{j-1}\delta_{j-1} \end{aligned}$$

this leads to

(2)
$$|y(x_i) - u(x_i)| \leq \sum_{j=1}^{i} h_{j-1}\delta_{j-1} e^{L|x_i - x_j|}.$$

If $\delta_j \leq \delta$ for all $j = 0, 1, ..., N-1$, then we obtain the estimate

$$|y(x_i) - u(x_i)| \leq \delta \int_a^{x_i} e^{L(x_i - t)} dt \quad , \quad i = 0, 1, 2, ..., N.$$

This proof justifies the step size policy: Compute the step size h_j in such a way that

$$|r[f, h_j](x_j, u(x_j))| = \delta.$$

If a method of local order p is used then $\delta = \mathcal{O}(h^p)$ that is we have global order p. This known statement is normally proven in a different way:

If the local discretization error (along the exact solution) of the method is p and the *method is stable* (that is Lipschitz continuous) than the method has global order p. We have proven above: If the local discretization error (along all neighboring solutions) of the method is p and the *differential equation is stable* (i.e. Lipschitz continuous, cf.(1)) then the global order is p as well. The main difference between both proofs is that our proof follows the way the computation proceeds whereas the common proof uses local errors along the exact solution that almost never occur in practice.

The above proof has the disadvantage in that it uses (global) Lipschitz constants (the proof can easily be adapted to local Lipschitz constants). But note that the above estimate (2) of the global error may be sharp, e.g. when Euler's method is applied to the problem $y' = \lambda y$, $y(0) = 1$. A more sophisticated analysis would have to make use of the variational equations, which can be treated similar to the above arguments.

3. Extended Volterra Runge Kutta methods

We consider the integral equation

$$y(x) = f(x) + \int_{x_0}^{x} K(x, t, y(t))dt \quad . \tag{3}$$

We define (see Hairer, Lubich, Nørsett [4])

$$F_k(x) := f(x) + \int_{x_0}^{x_k} K(x, t, y(t))dt \quad \text{for} \quad x \in [x_k, b]$$

with the solution y of (3). We want to solve the integral equation by a one-step method

$$u_{k+1} = \tilde{F}_k(x_{k+1}) + h_k \Phi_k(x_{k+1}, \tilde{F}_k, h_k) \tag{4}$$

with numerical solution (u_j). This corresponds to an approximation of

$$y(x_{k+1}) = F_k(x_{k+1}) + \int_{x_k}^{x_{k+1}} K(x_{k+1}, t, y(t))dt \quad .$$

We restrict ourselves to Extended Volterra Runge Kutta methods. For these we have

$$\tilde{F}_0(x) := f(x)$$

$$\tilde{F}_k(x) := f(x) + \sum_{j=0}^{k-1} h_j \Phi_j(x, \tilde{F}_j, h_j) \quad , \quad x \in [x_k, b] \, .$$

For details see Baker [2].

For example a 2-stage method (of Pouzet type) is given by

$$u_{k+1} = \tilde{F}_k(x_{k+1}) + h_k \Phi_k(x_{k+1}, \tilde{F}_k, h_k).$$

Here the increment function is defined by

$$\Phi_j(x, \tilde{F}_j, h_j) := b_1 K(x, x_j + c_1 h_j, v_1) + b_2 K(x, x_j + c_2 h_j, v_2))$$

with

$$v_1 = \tilde{F}_j(x_j + c_1 h_j) + h_j(a_{11} K(x_j + c_1 h_j, x_j + c_1 h_j, v_1) + a_{12} K(x_j + c_1 h_j, x_j + c_2 h_j, v_2))$$

$$v_2 = \tilde{F}_j(x_j + c_2 h_j) + h_j(a_{21} K(x_j + c_2 h_j, x_j + c_1 h_j, v_1) + a_{22} K(x_j + c_2 h_j, x_j + c_2 h_j, v_2))$$

If the coefficients are chosen as the coefficients of the 2-stage Runge-Kutta method of order 4 known from ordinary differential equations then the above Extended Volterra Runge Kutta method has order 4 as well (see Brunner, Hairer, Nørsett [3]).

By $y(\bullet, \xi, g)$ we denote the (local) solution of

$$y(x) = g(x) + \int_{\xi}^{x} K(x, t, y(t))dt$$

LEMMA 1.

Let $a \leq \xi \leq \varsigma \leq b$ and $f, g \in C[a, b]$.

Let

$$y := y(\bullet, \xi, f) \quad , \quad z := y(\bullet, \varsigma, g)$$

Define

$$\alpha(x) := |f(x) - g(x) + \int_{\xi}^{\varsigma} K(x, t, y(t))dt| \quad \text{for} \quad x \geq \varsigma$$

and

$$\overline{\alpha}(x) := \max_{\varsigma \leq s \leq x} \alpha(s) \quad .$$

Then

$$|y(x) - z(x)| \leq \alpha(x) + L \int_{\varsigma}^{x} \alpha(t) e^{L(x-t)} dt$$

$$\leq \overline{\alpha}(x) e^{L(x-\varsigma)} \quad \text{for} \quad x \geq \varsigma \quad .$$

PROOF:

By definition of y and z we have

$$
\begin{aligned}
|y(x)-z(x)| &= |f(x)-g(x)+\int_{\xi}^{x} K(x,t,y(t))dt-\int_{\varsigma}^{x} K(x,t,z(t))dt| \\
&\leq |f(x)-g(x)+\int_{\xi}^{\varsigma} K(x,t,y(t))dt| + \left|\int_{\varsigma}^{x} [K(x,t,y(t))-K(x,t,z(t))]\,dt\right| \\
&\leq \alpha(x)+L\int_{\varsigma}^{x} |y(t)-z(t)|dt \quad x\geq\varsigma
\end{aligned}
$$

Application of Gronwall's lemma yields the desired result

$$
\begin{aligned}
|y(x)-z(x)| &\leq \alpha(x)+L\int_{\varsigma}^{x} \alpha(t)e^{L(x-t)}dt \\
&\leq \overline{\alpha}(x)e^{L(x-\varsigma)}
\end{aligned}
$$

Here we have used Gronwall's lemma in the following form:

If α, β and η are real-valued continuous functions on $[a,b]$ and $\beta\geq 0$ is integrable on $[a,b]$ with

$$\eta(x)\leq\alpha(x)+\int_{a}^{x}\eta(t)\beta(t)dt \quad , \quad a\leq x\leq b,$$

then

$$\eta(x)\leq\alpha(x)+\int_{a}^{x}\beta(t)\alpha(t)e^{\int_{t}^{x}\beta(\tau)d\tau}dt \quad , \quad a\leq x\leq b.$$

If, in addition, α is nondecreasing, we have

$$\eta(x)\leq\alpha(x)e^{\int_{a}^{x}\beta(\tau)d\tau} \quad , \quad a\leq x\leq b. \quad \blacksquare$$

DEFINITION. *(Hairer, Lubich, Nørsett [4])*

The one step method (4) has local order p if for any integral equation (3) (with sufficiently differentiable f and K)

$$|y(x_k)-\overline{y}_k|\leq c\, h^{p+1}$$

where $\overline{y}_k$ is the local error

$$\overline{y}_{k+1} = F_k(x_{k+1}) + h\Phi_k(x_{k+1}, F_k, h) \quad , \quad x_{k+1} = x_k + h$$

caused by the increment function Φ_k only. Here the coefficient c is independent of x_k and h. ∎

An Extended Volterra Runge Kutta method of local order p fulfills

$$|F_{k+1}(x) - F_k(x) - h\Phi_k(x, F_k, h)| \leq C\ h^{p+1} \quad \text{for all} \quad x \in [x_{k+1}, b]$$

with C independent of h, x_k and x (see [4]).

A consequence is the following

THEOREM 1.

Let

$$y_j := y(\bullet, x_j, \tilde{F}_j)$$

Assume that there are real numbers δ_j *such that*

$$\left| \int\limits_{x_j}^{x_{j+1}} K(x, t, y_j(t))dt - h_j\Phi_j(x, \tilde{F}_j, h_j) \right| \leq \delta_j\ h_j \tag{5}$$

for all $x \in [x_{j+1}, b]$ *and all* $j = 0, 1, 2, ..., N-1$. *If* $\delta := \max_j \delta_j$ *then*

$$|y(x_i) - u_i| \leq \delta \int\limits_a^{x_i} e^{L(x_i - t)}dt \quad \text{for} \quad i = 0, 1, ..., N \quad .$$

PROOF:

Because of $y = y_0$ and $u_i = y_i(x_i)$ we have

$$\begin{aligned} |y(x_i) - u_i| &\leq |y_0(x_i) - y_1(x_i)| + |y_1(x_i) - y_2(x_i)| + ... \\ &\quad + |y_{i-2}(x_i) - y_{i-1}(x_i)| + |y_{i-1}(x_i) - u_i| \\ &= \sum_{j=1}^{i} |y_j(x_i) - y_{j-1}(x_i)|. \end{aligned}$$

By definition of the local solutions we obtain

$$|y_j(x_i) - y_{j-1}(x_i)| = |\tilde{F}_j(x_i) + \int\limits_{x_j}^{x_i} K(x_i, t, y_j(t))dt - \tilde{F}_{j-1}(x_i) - \int\limits_{x_{j-1}}^{x_i} K(x_i, t, y_{j-1}(t))dt|$$

$$\leq \alpha_j(x_i) + |\int\limits_{x_j}^{x_i} [K(x_i, t, y_j(t)) - K(x_i, t, y_{j-1}(t))]\, dt|$$

$$\leq \alpha_j(x_i) + L \int\limits_{x_j}^{x_i} |y_j(t) - y_{j-1}(t)|dt$$

with

$$\alpha_j(x) := |\tilde{F}_j(x) - \tilde{F}_{j-1}(x) - \int\limits_{x_{j-1}}^{x_j} K(x, t, y_{j-1}(t))dt|$$

Application of Lemma 1 yields

$$|y_j(x_i) - y_{j-1}(x_i)| \leq \overline{\alpha}_j(x_i)e^{L(x_i - x_j)}$$

with

$$\overline{\alpha}_j(x) := \max_{x_j \leq s \leq x} \alpha(s)$$

Because of $\tilde{F}_j(s) = \tilde{F}_{j-1}(s) + h_{j-1}\Phi_{j-1}(s, \tilde{F}_{j-1}, h_{j-1})$ we get

$$\alpha_j(s) = |h_{j-1}\Phi_{j-1}(s, \tilde{F}_{j-1}, h_{j-1}) - \int\limits_{x_{j-1}}^{x_j} K(s, t, y_{j-1}(t))dt|$$

and therefore because of our assumption (5)

$$\overline{\alpha}_j(x_i) = \max_{x_j \leq s \leq x_i} \alpha_j(s)$$
$$\leq \delta_{j-1}h_{j-1}$$

Altogether this leads to

$$|y(x_i) - u_i| \leq \sum_{j=1}^{i} \delta_{j-1}h_{j-1}e^{L(x_i - x_j)}$$

$$\leq \delta \sum_{j=1}^{i} h_{j-1}e^{L(x_i - x_j)}$$

$$\leq \delta \int\limits_{a}^{x_i} e^{L(x_i - t)}dt \qquad \blacksquare$$

Condition (5) of the preceding theorem means that during the computation of u_{i+1} we have to control whether future integrations will be carried out according to the prescibed tolerances.

In practice (5) cannot be tested for all $x \in [x_{j+1}, b]$, but for instance on a (coarser) grid with grid points $\tilde{x}_1, \tilde{x}_2, ..., \tilde{x}_m$. If for instance extrapolation is used to determine the step size similar to the case of ordinary differential equations then by using the same formulas the step size can additionally be adjusted (that is perhaps reduced furthermore) such that (5) is fulfilled. This means that all integrations that occur on the triangle

$$\{(x,t) \mid a \leq t \leq x \leq b\}$$

are integrated according to the local tolerance δ.

This in turn allows it to integrate the lag term by different methods instead of the extended version and use a coarser grid in the lag term (cf. Kunkel [5]).

A numerical example which demonstrates the behavior of such a step size control is given in [1]. There the necessity of controlling (5) is pointed out, especially if the kernel behaves well near the diagonal $x = t$ and badly off the diagonal.

As in the case of ordinary differential equations we could define the local discretization error along such solutions that occur in the numerical process. This would lead to a similar statement as in the second section. But doing this would be a little bit tedious and would require an additional compactness argument. Therefore we omit it.

References

1. Arndt,H., *On Step Size Control for Volterra Integral Equations*, in: Collatz,L., Meinardus,G., Werner,H., Numerical Methods of Approximation Theory, ISNM **67**, Birkhäuser-Verlag, Basel (1983), 9–17.
2. Baker, C.T.H., *The Numerical Treatment of Integral Equations*, Clarendon Press, Oxford (1977).
3. Brunner,H., Hairer,E., Nørsett,S.P., *Runge-Kutta Theory for Volterra Integral Equations of the Second Kind*, Mathematics of Computation **39** (1982), 147–163.
4. Hairer,E., Lubich,Ch., Nørsett,S.P., *Order of One-Step Methods for Volterra Integral Equations of the Second Kind*, SIAM J. Numer. Anal. **20** (1983), 569–579.
5. Kunkel,P., *Ein adaptives Verfahren zur Lösung von Volterraschen Integralgleichungen zweiter Art*, Diplomarbeit, Heidelberg (1982).

Address:
Herbert Arndt, Institut für Angewandte Mathematik der Universität Bonn, Wegelerstr. 6, D-5300 Bonn

International Series of
Numerical Mathematics, Vol. 73
© 1985 Birkhäuser Verlag Basel

CONCERNING $A(\alpha)$-STABLE MIXED VOLTERRA RUNGE-KUTTA METHODS

Christopher T.H. Baker
University of Manchester, U.K.

Abstract. We establish the existence of $A(\alpha)$-stable mixed quadrature R-K methods and examine some of their aspects.

1. Some numerical methods.

1.1. We shall define some methods for integral equations in terms of those for differential equations. We recall that a choice of parameters $(\theta_r, b_r \equiv A_{pr}, A_{rs}$ $(r,s=0,1,\ldots,p-1))$ with $\theta_p=1$, defines a conventional Runge-Kutta *(R-K) tableau*

$$\left[\begin{array}{c|c} \theta & A^{\#} \\ \hline & b^T \end{array}\right] \tag{1.1}$$

where θ, b are vectors with components θ_r, b_r, and $A^{\#}$ has elements A_{rs}; this (see [8,10]) defines a R-K method for the initial-value problem

$$y'(t) = f(t,y(t)) \qquad (t \geq 0,\ y(0) \text{ given}). \tag{1.2}$$

We shall use (1.1) and we require, in addition, a choice of coefficients in the *quadrature formulae*

$$\int_0^{nh} \phi(s)\, ds \simeq h \sum_{j=0}^{n} \omega_{nj}\, \phi(jh) \qquad (n \geq n_0). \tag{1.3}$$

POUZET [13] used the coefficients in (1.1), (1.3) to devize R-K methods for the *Volterra integral equation of the second kind*

$$y(t) - \int_0^t K(t,s,y(s))\, ds = g(t) \quad (t \geq 0), \tag{1.4}$$

where $K(t,s,u)$ and $g(t)$ are prescribed smooth functions. Given a step $h > 0$, these R-K methods yield approximations $y_{n,r}$ to $y(nh+\theta_r h)$ $(n=0,1,2\ldots,$

This paper is in final form and no version of it will be submitted for publication elsewhere.

$r=0,1,\ldots,p;\ \theta_p = 1)$ wherein the values $\{y_{n+1} \equiv y_{n,p} \simeq y((n+1)h) \mid (n=0,1,2,\ldots\}$ are the "full-step" approximations of particular interest.

The formulae defining the *mixed quadrature-R-K method* for (1.4) are

$$(1.5)\qquad y_{n,r} - h\sum_{j=0}^{n} \omega_{nj}\, K(t_{nr}, jh, y_{j-1,p}) - h\sum_{s=0}^{p-1} A_{rs}\, K(t_{nr}, t_{ns}, y_{ns}) = g(t_{nr})$$

$(n \geqslant n_0;\ r=0,1,\ldots,p)$, where $A_{ps}=b_s$ and $t_{n,r} = nh + \theta_r h$. Starting values $y_{n,p}$ $(n < n_0)$ can be obtained by applying (for example) the self-starting *extended R-K methods* defined by the formulae

$$(1.6)\qquad y_{n,r} - h\sum_{j=0}^{n-1}\sum_{s=0}^{p-1} b_s K(t_{nr}, t_{js}, y_{js}) - h\sum_{s=0}^{p-1} A_{rs}\, K(t_{nr}, t_{ns}, y_{ns}) = g(t_{nr}),$$

$n \geqslant 0$. Related to the rules (1.3) are the *quadrature methods* yielding approximations y_n to $y(nh)$ satisfying for $n \geqslant n_0'$

$$(1.7)\qquad y_n - h\sum_{j=0}^{n} \omega_{nj}\, K(nh, jh, y_j) = g(nh).$$

1.2. A study of the mixed methods (1.5) (and of the method (1.7)) is [14] greatly facilitated by the assumption that the rules (1.3) are $\{\rho,\sigma\}$*-reducible* where $\rho(\mu)$, $\sigma(\mu)$ denote the first and second characteristic polynomials of a zero-stable consistent linear multistep method [8] for (1.2), viz.:

$$(1.8)\qquad \rho(\mu) = \alpha_0\mu^k + \alpha_1\mu^{k-1} + \ldots + \alpha_k;\quad \sigma(\mu) = \beta_0\mu^k + \beta_1\mu^{k-1} + \ldots + \beta_k.$$

Definition. The rules (1.3) are $\{\rho,\sigma\}$-reducible if $\sum_{\ell=0}^{k} \alpha_\ell \omega_{n-\ell,j} = \beta_{n-j}$, where $\beta_\ell = 0$ if $\ell \notin \{0,1,\ldots,k\}$ and $\omega_{n,j} = 0$ if $j < 0$ or $j > n$.

Example. The Gregory quadrature rules [1] are $\{\rho,\sigma\}$-reducible, where ρ,σ correspond to the Adams-Moulton formula of appropriate order.

1.3. The issues to be considered when choosing a type of formula as the basis of a numerical method are accuracy, preservation of the qualitative behaviour of the solution and stability, and implementational details such as work per step. We do not have space to consider all aspects here. Because of the amount of work involved per step with the R-K methods as a whole, support for them has been variable over the years. However, it is possible to find moderately high-order extended R-K methods which have good stability properties. At present, the mixed quadrature-R-K methods do no appear to be in vogue, but they are cheaper per step than their extended counterparts. One of our aims is to suggest (by drawing attention to the existence of mixed methods of moderately high order with large stability regions) that the mixed methods should not be discarded too readily. This is a limited objective;

we are not yet in a position to advocate mixed methods as sufficiently robust for adoption as the basis of an algorithm.

2. A stability analysis.

2.1. Much analysis of the *accuracy* of methods is based upon the situation as h tends to zero. In order to effect a *stability* analysis, one must select a concept of stability and a class of paradigms. NOBLE [12] and KOBAYASI [9] chose to consider stability properties, for quite general equations, by studying asymptotic properties as h tends to zero. More recently, the emphasis has been on the stability for arbitrary h; this has necessitated the choice of a class of test equations. The simplest test equation is the *basic equation*

$$(2.1) \qquad y(t) - \lambda \int_0^t y(s)ds = g(t) \qquad (t \geq 0),$$

(which has also been used in a discussion of accuracy by HAIRER [6]). Other equations considered in discussions of numerical stability are of the form

$$(2.2) \qquad y(t) - \lambda \int_0^t k(t-s)y(s)ds = g(t),$$

(the *convolution* or *renewal equation* [7,11]) and those of the form

$$(2.3) \qquad y(t) - \lambda \int_0^t \sum_{r=0}^{R} X_r(t)Y_r(s)ds = g(t),$$

(the *separable case*). It is commonly, if not universally, agreed that (2.1) is useful in order to obtain insight before considering the more difficult test equations; this is a view which will be adopted here, with the *caveat* indicated below. We also need a concept of stability, applicable to (2.1), for which we here adopt the following.

Definitions. A method applied with $h>0$ is said to be *strictly stable when applied to (2.1)* if the numerical solution decays when $g(t)$ is a constant. The *region of strict stability*, S, of the method is the region of the complex λh-plane for which the method applied to (2.1) is strictly stable. The method is called $A(\alpha)$-*stable* if S contains $\{\lambda h \in C \mid Re(\lambda h) < 0, \arg(\lambda h) \in (\pi-\alpha, \pi+\alpha)\}$, and A_0-*stable* if S contains the negative real line. $A(\pi/2)$-stability is called A-*stability*.

Caveat. A related property for (2.2) is called C-*stability* [7] (C= Convolution). A-stability does not imply C-stability; consequently it is not necessarily sufficient to use an A-stable method for more general types of equation. However, a certain relevance to the study of (2.2) of the concepts defined here is seen in [7,11], and a number of numerical tests also suggest the relevance, to more general equations than the basic model, of definitions in terms of (2.1).

2.2. Having placed the role of (2.1) in perspective, we proceed. If (2.1) is differentiated, we obtain a differential equation. If the numerical methods are applied to (2.1), then (in the cases to be considered) we can difference the discretized equations to produce a *finite-term recurrence with constant coefficients*. Recurrence relations of this form can be re-written invariably as a *two-term vector recurrence* [4] between vectors ϕ_n whose components are the computed approximations:

$$\phi_{n+1} = M\,\phi_n + \gamma_{n+1}, \qquad M = M(\lambda h).$$

This is strictly stable ($\phi_n \to 0$ as $n \to \infty$ when $g(\cdot)$ is constant) if and only if $\rho(M) < 1$ where $\rho(M)$ is the spectral radius of M. Equivalently, $\det(M - \mu I)$ should be a Schur polynomial. (A polynomial is called *Schur* if and only if all its zeros have absolute value less than unity.) It may be remarked that for such a strictly stable method, if $g(\cdot)$ is bounded it follows that $\{\|\phi_n\|\}$ is a bounded sequence.

Using the above concepts, it is not difficult to establish the following results in which the reader will recognise expressions from the theory of methods for (1.2):

Theorem [4]. (a) Let (1.3) be $\{\rho, \sigma\}$-reducible. Then the formulae (1.7) applied to (2.1) are strictly stable if and only if $\rho(\mu) - \lambda h\sigma(\mu)$ is Schur. (b) The formulae (1.6) applied to (2.1) are strictly stable if and only if $\mu - \hat{\mu}(\lambda h)$ is Schur (viz., $|\hat{\mu}(\lambda h)| < 1$) where

$$\hat{\mu}(\lambda h) := 1 + \lambda h\, b^T (I - \lambda h A^{\#})^{-1} \mathbb{1} \tag{2.4}$$

and where $A^{\#}$ denotes the matrix $\{A_{rs}\}$ of order p, $b^T = [b_0, b_1, \ldots b_{p-1}]$ and $\mathbb{1} = [1, 1, \ldots, 1]^T$.

The preceding theorem relates our theory to the existing theory [8] for (a) linear multistep methods and (b) Runge-Kutta methods for (1.2) and as a consequence we know not to look for high-order A-stable reducible quadrature methods, but we know that we can find A-stable extended R-K methods of moderately high order. More intriguing than the above results, however, are those for mixed quadrature-R-K methods.

3. Basic Stability of Mixed Quadrature-R-K Methods.

3.1. The following is a particular case of a theorem appearing in Section 4.

Lemma. Let the mixed formula (1.5) be applied to (2.1). Denote by y_{n+1} the resulting $y_{n,p}$. Then for $n \geqslant n_0$,

$$y_{n+1} - \lambda h \hat{\mu}(\lambda h) \sum_{j=0}^{n} \omega_{nj}\, y_j = \gamma'_{n+1,\lambda h} \tag{3.1}$$

where $\gamma'_{n+1,\lambda h}$ depends upon $g(\cdot)$ and upon λh, and $\hat{\mu}(\lambda h)$ is the value (2.4) associated with (1.1).

We also require the following consequence of $\{\rho,\sigma\}$-reducibility.

Lemma. Suppose that the quadrature method with weights (1.3) is $\{\rho,\sigma\}$-reducible. Then the quadrature method with weights $\Omega_{n,j} = \omega_{n-1,j}$ is $\{\mu\rho(\mu),\sigma(\mu)\}$-reducible.

To utilize these results we note that (3.1) represents an application of the quadrature method, with the weights $\Omega_{n,j}$ shown, to the basic equation (2.1) in which λh is replaced by $\lambda h\hat{\mu}(\lambda h)$. This indicates a new proof of the result [4]:

Theorem. The mixed quadrature-R-K method using $\{\rho,\sigma\}$-reducible rules is strictly stable when applied to (2.1) if and only if $\mu\rho(\mu)-\lambda h\hat{\mu}(\lambda h)\sigma(\mu)$ is Schur.

It is plain from the above that to investigate the stability of mixed methods with $\{\rho,\sigma\}$-reducible rules (1.3), one should examine the region S' of the complex plane for which $\mu\rho(\mu) - \Lambda\sigma(\mu)$ is Schur:

$$S' = \{\Lambda \mid |\mu| < 1 \text{ if } \mu\rho(\mu) - \Lambda\sigma(\mu) = 0\}. \tag{3.2a}$$

The stability region S of the mixed method is then the region

$$S = \{\lambda h \in C \mid \lambda h\hat{\mu}(\lambda h) \in S'\}. \tag{3.2b}$$

The stability polynomial $\mu^m\rho(\mu)-\Lambda\sigma(\mu)$ occurs in the treatment by linear multistep methods of *delay-differential equations* where the delay is a fixed multiple m of the stepsize h. Our interest is with $m = 1$.

3.2. If the multistep method $\{\rho,\sigma\}$ is consistent and (zero-)stable then the method $\{\mu\rho(\mu), \sigma(\mu)\}$ is clearly consistent and zero-stable; see [8] for the definitions of such terms. If $\rho(\mu)$ satisfies the strong root condition (i.e. $\rho(1) = 0$, and $\rho(\mu)/(\mu-1)$ is Schur) then so does $\mu\rho(\mu)$. Under these conditions, the region S' is bounded and includes a region of the left half-plane with zero on its boundary. The latter follows simply because the dominant zero of (3.2) is $1 + \Lambda + O(|\Lambda|^2)$. The boundary locus method [8] provides a well-known technique for the investigation of S': we determine the curve

$$\gamma(\theta) := e^{i\theta} \rho(e^{i\theta})/\sigma(e^{i\theta}) \tag{3.3}$$

parametrized by $\theta \in [0,2\pi]$, say, and the boundary $\partial S'$ is (part of) this locus.

Examples. (a) Let the quadrature rules (1.3) be repeated rectangle (backward Euler) rules. Then $\rho = \mu-1$, $\sigma = \mu$; then $\partial S'$ is the unit circle centred upon -1. (b) If (1.3) are the trapezoidal rules, then $\rho=\mu-1$, $\sigma = (\mu+1)/2$, $\partial S'$ asymptotes to the imaginary axis, and intercepts the real axis at -2.

The preceding examples are not wholly typical, being primitive cases. The sketch in Fig. 1 indicates a boundary locus typical of $\{\rho,\sigma\}$ of some Adams method: part of the boundary locus determines $\partial S'$, and S' is shaded.

3.3. To proceed, it is necessary (as above examples suggest) to specialize the choice of $\{\rho,\sigma\}$, and it is convenient to consider the *Adams methods* which correspond to $\rho(\mu) = \mu^k-\mu^{k-1}$ and the choice of $\sigma(\mu)$ which maximizes the order of the formula given $\beta_0 = 0$ for the Adams-Bashforth methods, $\beta_0 \neq 0$ for the Adams-Moulton methods. Recall that the latter methods correspond to the Gregory rules (1.3) with an appropriate order and choice of n_0. A feeling for the extent of the stability region can be obtained by considering the intercept of $\partial S'$ with the negative real axis.

Lemma. Let the locus $\gamma(\theta)$ be defined by (3.3) for an Adams method. $\gamma(\theta)$ assumes a real negative value when $\theta = \phi$, $\sum_0^k \beta_r \cos(\{r+1/2\}\phi) = 0$, $\phi\varepsilon(0,\pi)$. Thus, the boundary locus $\partial S'$ is the locus

$$\{\exp(i\{k+1\}\theta)-\exp(ik\theta)\}/\{\Sigma\beta_{k-r}\exp(ir\theta)\}, \qquad \theta\varepsilon[-\phi,\phi]. \tag{3.4}$$

Further, $\partial S'$ intersects the negative real axis at

$$\frac{-2\,\Sigma\beta_r\sin(\{r+1/2\}\phi)\times\sin(\phi/2)}{[\Sigma\,\beta_{k-r}\cos r\phi]^2 + [\Sigma\,\beta_{k-r}\sin r\phi]^2}. \tag{3.5}$$

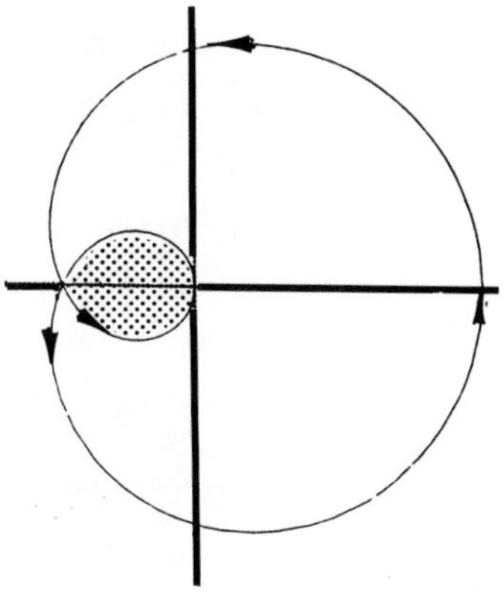

Fig. 1. S' and the boundary locus curve where $\{\rho,\sigma\}$ is an Adams method (k=3), $\beta_0 \neq 0$.

It can be verified computationally that in the case of the Adams-Moulton $\{\rho,\sigma\}$ (corresponding to Gregory quadrature), $S' \supset (-1.37,0)$ for $k \leq 4$, and for the Adams-Bashforth formulae $S' \supset (-0.415,0)$ for $k \leq 4$. Thus, we have the result:

<u>Lemma</u>. Let (1.3) be $\{\rho,\sigma\}$-reducible. For the Adams $\{\rho,\sigma\}$ with $k \leq 4$, $S' \supset [-(\sqrt{2}-1)-e, 0)$ for a suitably small positive quantity e.

3.4 We next require an appropriate R-K tableau (1.1). Our interest is in the corresponding 'amplification factor' $\hat{\mu}(\lambda h)$, in our quest for mixed methods with large S. Since S' is bounded, we think of a choice of $\hat{\mu}(\lambda h)$ for which $\lambda h \hat{\mu}(\lambda h)$ is bounded, for all negative $\mathrm{Re}(\lambda h)$, and the most primitive case is $\hat{\mu}(\lambda h) := 1/(1-\lambda h)$. With this choice, when $\mathrm{Re}(\lambda h)$ is negative, $\lambda h \hat{\mu}(\lambda h)$ has negative real part and absolute value bounded by unity; in fact, choosing $\rho(\mu)=\mu-1$, $\sigma(\mu)=\mu$, gives us $S' = \{\Lambda \mid |\Lambda+1|<1\}$ and yields a very simple A-stable mixed method. Choosing $\rho(\mu) = \mu - 1$, $\sigma(\mu) = (\mu + 1)/2$ also provides an A-stable method (see Fig.2 for an indication of S).

Building upon our experience, we examine the choice

$$\hat{\mu}(\lambda h) = 1/t_n(-\lambda h) \tag{3.6}$$

where $t_n(x)$ is the Maclaurin sum for $\exp(x)$ of degree n. With this choice, we can establish the existence of A_0-*stable mixed methods of modest order.* For this purpose, note (see [2]) that if $n \geq 2$ then $-(\sqrt{2}-1) \leq \lambda h t_n(-\lambda h) < 0$

when $-\infty < \lambda h < 0$, and $S' \supset (-(\sqrt{2}-1),0)$ in the case of the $\{\rho,\sigma\}$ for Adams methods with $k \lesssim 4$; this statement can be strengthened, but it establishes the existence of A_0-stable methods. The question then arises whether certain of the mixed methods based on $\{\rho,\sigma\}$ defined by the Adams methods, and with (1.1) yielding (3.6) as the amplification factor, are $A(\alpha)$-stable. We display in Fig. 3 (appearing in the Appendix 1) an indication of the stability region S for such a method. Although plotting the portion of the boundary ∂S lying in a finite region of the negative half-plane necessarily does not allow us to establish $A(\alpha)$-stability, our results prompt us to seek a proof of the following theorem.

Theorem. Let the rules (1.3) be $\{\rho,\sigma\}$-reducible, where $\{\rho,\sigma\}$ defines an Adams method with $k \lesssim 4$, and let the amplification factor $\hat{\mu}(\lambda h)$ be as in (3.6) for some $n \gtrsim 2$. Then the corresponding mixed method is $A(\alpha)$-stable for some sufficiently small α which depends, inter alia, upon n.

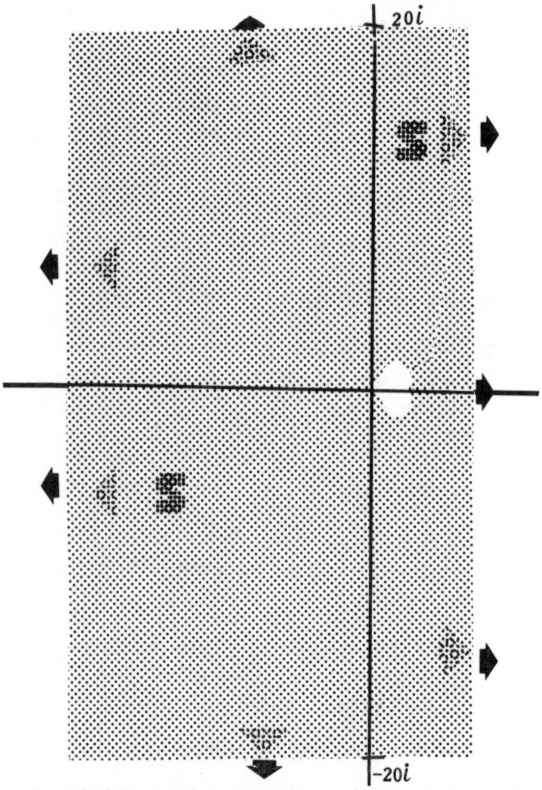

Fig. 2 Stability region for the mixed method where (1.3) is the repeated trapezium rule and $\hat{\mu}(\lambda h) = 1/(1-\lambda h)$,

(Outline Proof: Suppose that $\Lambda=\lambda h$, $\arg(\Lambda)\in(\pi-\alpha,\pi+\alpha)$ where $n\alpha$ is sufficiently small. For $\hat{\mu}(\Lambda)={}^1/t_n(-\Lambda)$, $\arg(\hat{\mu}(\Lambda))$ can be ascertained as $|\Lambda|\to\infty$ or $\to 0$. Then simple arguments show that $\gamma:=\Lambda\mu(\Lambda)$ lies in a sector in the left half-plane ($|\gamma|\leqslant(\sqrt{2}-1)+e$, $\arg(\gamma)\in(\pi-\psi,\pi+\psi)$ where $e=e(n,\alpha)$ and $\psi=\psi(n,\alpha)$), which lies in the region S' for sufficiently small α. Indeed, since $(-\sqrt{2}+1-e,0)$ lies in the stability region S', the latter result is a consequence of Rouche's theorem. The result follows.)

The technique used in the proof of the last theorem does not appeal to us as a practical method for estimating the value α of our theorem. For this purpose, we prefer to determine the trajectories of $\Lambda\hat{\mu}(\Lambda)$ with $\Lambda=re^{i\theta}$, as r varies in $(0,\infty)$, with $\theta=\pi,\pi-\delta,\pi-2\delta,\ldots\pi-\upsilon\delta,\upsilon\in\mathbb{Z}_+$. (Computation of the trajectories is reduced to a finite one since r, θ, are made to vary discretely and the limiting behaviour as $r\to\infty$ is known analytically.) From the trajectories, noting that $\bar{\Lambda}\hat{\mu}(\bar{\Lambda})=\overline{\Lambda\hat{\mu}(\lambda)}$, we are able to determine, for various θ, the regions

$$S_{-\theta,\theta}=\{\Lambda\hat{\mu}(\Lambda)\mid\arg(\Lambda)\in(\pi-\theta,\pi+\theta)\}$$

and to compare $S_{-\theta,\theta}$ with the region S'; we refer to Fig. 4, appearing in the Appendix 1. If $S_{-\alpha,\alpha}\subset S'$, the mixed method is $A(\alpha)$-stable.

Example. Let (1.3) be chosen as the Gregory rules, corresponding to the polynomials (1.8) of the Adams-Moulton methods. For $k=3$, and $n=3$ in (3.6), we can set $\alpha=\pi/4$; for $k=5$ and $n=5$ we can set $\alpha=\pi/9$. Analytical and computational experience suggests that increasing n decreases α.

3.5. We have to complete the discussion of methods by revealing the form of the tableau (1.1) which gives the amplification factor (3.6). It suffices to derive the required tableau from another in which the amplification factor is instead $t_n(\lambda h)$; for various n, many such "*ancestor*" tableaux are found in the literature **[10]**, whilst others are quite readily derived. The construction of the required tableau (1.1) is then immediate, as the following example indicates, involving only elementary operations on the rows of the ancestor tableau.

Example. The three-stage third order explicit method with tableau indicated.

$$\begin{array}{c|ccc} 0 & 0 & 0 & 0 \\ 1/2 & 1/2 & 0 & 0 \\ 1 & -1 & 2 & 0 \\ \hline 1 & 1/6 & 2/3 & 1/6 \end{array} \qquad \text{and } \hat{\mu}(\lambda h)=t_3(\lambda h)$$

yields

$$\begin{array}{c|ccc} 1 & 1/6 & 2/3 & 1/6 \\ 1/2 & -1/3 & 2/3 & 1/6 \\ 0 & 7/6 & -4/3 & 1/6 \\ \hline 1 & 1/6 & 2/3 & 1/6 \end{array} \qquad \text{with } \hat{\mu}(\lambda h)=1/t_3(-\lambda h).$$

Of course, the first is explicit and the second implicit. The algorithm for deriving a tableau (1.1) from its ancestor involves subtraction of the last row of the ancestor from its earlier rows and changing the sign, to produce new rows. The abscissae θ_r can be reordered by permuting rows and columns if this is desired.

4. Convolution kernels.

The study of stability of quadrature methods using $\{\rho,\sigma\}$-reducible quadrature rules (1.2) is greatly facilitated in the convolution case (2.2) by the fact that the weights $h\omega_{n,j}$ in (1.2) are, under the given assumption, of the form hw_{n-j}, if $j \geq j_0, j_0$ a fixed integer. In consequence, the equations (1.7) assume the form of discrete convolution equations, say

$$(4.1) \qquad y_n - h\sum_{j=j_0}^{n} w_{n-j}\, k(nh-jh)y_j = g_n^{\#} \quad (n \geq j_0),$$

The basis of a stability result is provided by an inversion theorem of Wiener which has been exploited in the specific context of quadrature methods in the work of LUBICH [11], and for extended R-K methods in [7]. For general discrete convolution equations, the essentials required for a stability analysis appear to be already imbedded in the results of GOHBERG and FELDMAN, who make an early appeal to the theorem of Wiener referred to above [5, p.4].

The above discussion is significant because, when one applies a reducible quadrature-R-K method to a convolution equation, the approximate values satisfy (as we shall show) a set of discrete convolution equations. By itself, this result does not lead to a simple and clear-cut criterion for stability (because λh enters non-linearly), but the following "almost-theorem" gives some practical insight, particularly in the case that λh is small.

Almost-Theorem. Suppose the rules (1.3) are $\{\rho,\sigma\}$-reducible, and the mixed method (1.5) is applied to the convolution equation (2.2). The full-step values y_n are bounded when $g(t)$ is bounded (in brief, the equations are *stable*) almost if the discrete convolution equations

$$y_{n+1} - \lambda h\hat{\mu}(\lambda h k(0)) \sum_{j=j_0}^{n} w_{n-j}\, k(nh-jh)y_j = g^{o}_{n,\lambda h} \qquad (n \geq j_0), \tag{4.2}$$

have bounded solutions, where $g^{o}_{n,\lambda h}$ is bounded if $g(t)$ is bounded.

We shall present the rigorous analysis which we summarized in these terms. We shall require some additional notation.

4.1. First, we denote by A the matrix

$$A = \left[\begin{array}{c|c} A^{\#} & \\ \hline b^T & 0 \end{array}\right] \tag{4.3}$$

and we denote by K_n the matrix with (r,s)-th elements $k(nh+(\theta_r-\theta_s)h)$; these matrices are of order $(p+1)$: we generally require $k(x)$ for $x < 0$. We denote by $\{e_r\}$ the successive columns of the identity of order $p+1$, and e denotes their sum. We set $\kappa_n = K_n e_p$. We write $\tilde{y}_n$ for the vector $[y_{n,0}, y_{n,1}, \ldots y_{n,p}]^T$, whilst g_n is the vector with components $g(nh+\theta_r h)$, $r=0,1,\ldots,p$. (For $n=-1$, only the last components $y_{-1,p}=y(0)=g(0)$ of these vectors have either meaning or relevance.) For use in (4.6) below, we note that

$$\hat{\mu}(\lambda h) = e_p^T(I - \lambda hA)^{-1}\, e. \tag{4.4}$$

If the Schur (or pointwise) product of two matrices is denoted by the symbol $*$, then the scalar equations which define the values $\{y_{n,r}\}$ obtained by application of the mixed method to (2.2) can be re-written as

$$(I - \lambda hA{*}K_0)\tilde{y}_n = g_n + \lambda h \sum_{j=0}^{n} \omega_{nj}(\kappa_{n-j}\, e_p^T)\tilde{y}_{j-1}. \tag{4.5}$$

The method is feasible if $(I - \lambda hA{*}K_0)$ is invertible; on this assumption, with $g^{*}_{n,\lambda h} = (I - \lambda hA{*}K_0)^{-1}g_n$, we deduce:

Theorem. For a mixed quadrature-RK method applied to (2.2), the values $y_{n+1} = y_{n,p}$ satisfy the equations

$$y_{n,p} - \lambda h \sum_{j=0}^{n} \omega_{nj}\, e_p^T(I - \lambda hA{*}K_0)^{-1}\, \kappa_{n-j}\, y_{j-1,p} = e_p^T g^{*}_{n,\lambda h}. \tag{4.6}$$

For a smooth kernel $k(\cdot)$, or when h is small, K_n is approximately the multiple $k(nh)$ of the matrix all of whose elements are unity, so that

$\kappa_n \simeq k(nh)e$. In consequence, using (4.4),

(4.7) $$e_p^T(I - \lambda hA^*K_0)^{-1}\ \kappa_{n-j} \simeq \widehat{\mu}(\lambda hk(0))\ \ k((n-j)h).$$

Making this approximation in (4.6) whilst recognising that $y_{j,p} = y_{j+1} \simeq y((j+1)h)$ gives (4.2) as an approximate relation under $\{\rho,\sigma\}$-reducibility conditions which ensure $\omega_{nj} = w_{n-j}$ for $j \geq j_0$. Observe that (4.6) and (4.7) are exact if $k(x)$ is constant, which establishes (3.1).

4.2. The relation (4.6) provides the basis for a fast and efficient numerical method for the approximate solution of (2.2) when the quadrature rules are $\{\rho,\sigma\}$-reducible.

4.3. The preceding analysis permits an abstract criterion for stability (which we give for completeness) in the case of $\{\rho,\sigma\}$-reducible quadrature. We assume $\{\rho,\sigma\}$ to be zero-stable, so that $\sup |w_n|$ is finite. First, we note that, with

(4.8) $$a_{n-j} = e_p^T(I - \lambda hA^*K_0)^{-1}\ \kappa_{n-j},$$

(4.9) $$\zeta_{n+1} = e_p^T g^*_{n,\lambda h} + \lambda h \sum_{j=0}^{j_0-1} w_{n-j}\ a_{n-j}\ y_{j-1,p}$$

then

(4.10) $$y_{n,p} - \lambda h \sum_{j=j_0}^{n} w_{n-j}\ a_{n-j}\ y_{j-1,p} = \zeta_{n+1}$$

If $g(\cdot)$ and $k(\cdot)$ are bounded, $\{\zeta_n\}$ is a bounded sequence. For stability, in the terms defined above, we seek conditions that ensure that $\{y_n = y_{n-1,p}\ |n \geq 0\}$ is bounded. The equations (4.10) are explicit for $y_{n,p}$ in terms of $y_{0,p},\ldots, y_{n-1,p}$ and can be solved formally in terms of $\{\zeta_n\}$: $y_{n,p} = \sum_{j=j_0}^{n} b_{n-j}\ \zeta_{j+1}$ where

(4.11) $$\{b_0 + b_1z + b_2z^2 + b_3z^3 + \ldots\}\ \{1 - \lambda h(w_0a_0z + w_1a_1z^2+w_2a_2z^3+\ldots)\} = 1.$$

In consequence, we require $\Sigma|b_j| < \infty$, for stability, where $b_j = b_j(\lambda h)$.

Now $\Sigma|a_j|$ converges if $\Sigma\,|k(t+jh)|$ converges for $t\varepsilon\{\theta_r\}$, in particular if $|k(x)|$ is monotonic decreasing and $\int_0^\infty |k(x)|\,dx$ converges. Then, since the weights w_j are uniformly bounded, the second term in (4.11) has radius of convergence at least 1. By appealing to Wiener's inversion theorem we establish:

Theorem. With the foregoing assumptions, the mixed method is stable if $(1 - \lambda h(w_0a_0z + w_1a_1z^2 + w_2a_2z^3 + \ldots)\} \neq 0$ when $|z| \leq 1$.

This result provides a criterion which is in general difficult to test (this is not surprising in view of the difficulty of establishing $A(\alpha)$-stability for the simpler basic equation). Thus, the almost-theorem may have some appeal despite its lack of rigour.

5. Acknowledgements: I am grateful to the Sonderforschungsbereich 72 and Prof. H. Werner and Dr. H. Arndt of the University of Bonn for support and hospitality during the preparation of part of this work. I also acknowledge computational assistance in running programmes from Messrs. Derakhshan, Gilvary and Riddell and related support under SERC grant GR/A/6458.7.

References.

[1] Baker, C.T.H. (1978) The numerical treatment of integral equations, 2nd printing.(Clarendon, Oxford).

[2] Baker, C.T.H. (1983) Approximations to the exponential function arising in the numerical analysis of Volterra equations. Numer. Anal. Tech. Tep. 87, Manchester University.

[3] Baker, C.T.H. and Miller, G.F. (1982) (editors). Treatment of integral equations by numerical methods.(Academic, London).

[4] Baker, C.T.H. and Wilkinson, J.C. (1981) Stability analysis of Runge-Kutta methods applied to a basic Volterra integral equation. J. Austral. Math. Soc. (B) 22, 515-538.

[5] Gohberg, I.C. and Feldman, I.A. (1971) Convolution equations and projection methods for their solution. (Amer. Math. Soc., Providence).

[6] Hairer, E. (1982) Extended Volterra-Runge-Kutta methods in [3], pp.221-232.

[7] Hairer, E., and Lubich, C. (1984) On the stability of Volterra Runge-Kutta methods. SIAM J. numer. Anal. 21,123-135.

[8] Hall, G. and Watt, J.M. (1976) Modern numerical methods for ordinary differential equations. (Clarendon, Oxford).

[9] Kobayasi, M. (1966) On numerical solution of the Volterra integral equations of the second kind by linear multistep methods. Rep. Statistic. Applic. Res. Tokyo 13, 1-21.

[10] Lapidus, L. and Seinfeld, J.H. (1971) Numerical solution or ordinary differential equations. (Academic, New York).

[11] Lubich, C. (1983) On the stability of linear multistep methods for Volterra convolution equations. IMA J. numer. Anal. 3, 439-466.

[12] Noble, B. (1969) Instability when solving Volterra integral equations of the second kind by multistep methods. Lect. notes in Math. 109, 23-39.

[13] Pouzet, P. (1962) Etude, en vue de leur traitement numérique, d'équations intégrales et intégro-différentielles de type Volterra pour des problèmes de conditions initiales. Thesis, University of Strasbourg

[14] Wolkenfelt, P.H.M. (1981) The numerical analysis of reducible quadrature methods for Volterra integral and integro-differential equations. Academisch proefschrift, MC. Amsterdam.

Appendix 1

C.T.H. Baker and B. Gilvary

In this appendix we provide a sample of graphical output connected with our investigations. Fig. 3 gives an indication of the infinite stability region associated with a mixed method based on the Gregory rule (1.3)

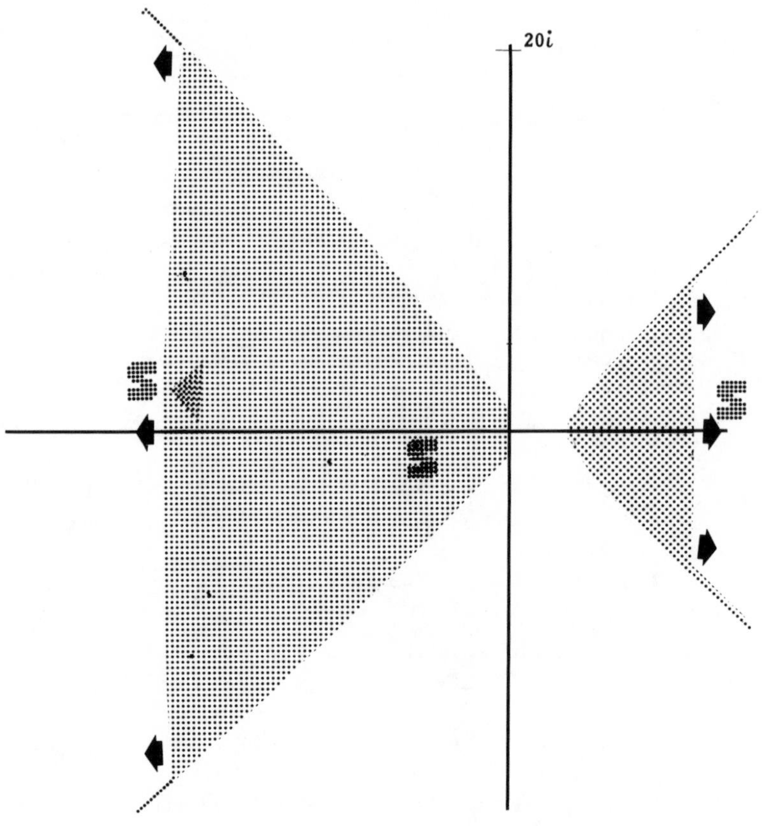

Fig. 3. Graphical indication of a stability region.

(corresponding to $k = 3$ in (1.8) of the Adams parameters), combined with the implicit three-stage RK tableau in the example in §3.5. The corresponding region S', and $S_{-\theta,\theta}$ for $\theta = \pi/2$ and (heavily shaded) $\theta = \pi/4$ appear in Fig. 4. in the case $n = 3$ in (3.6).

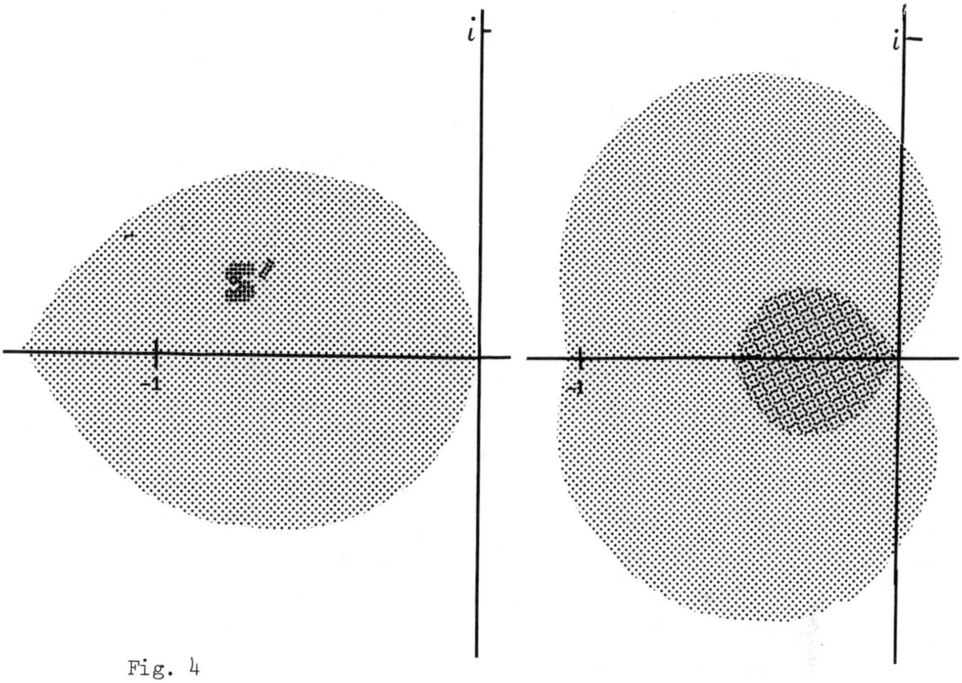

Fig. 4

Appendix 2.

C.T.H. Baker and M.S. Derakhshan.

The method discussed in Appendix 1 has been applied to a number of examples and the results will be presented in a forthcoming report. We have room here to give results for the case (2.2) with $k(x)= \frac{1}{2}x^2\exp(-x), g(x) = k(x)$. With $h=0.1$ the absolute errors for $x = 1.0\ (1.0)5.0$ are 4.4×10^{-6}, 4.9×10^{-6}, 5.2×10^{-6}, 5.7×10^{-6} and 6.3×10^{-6}.

Christopher T. H. Baker, Reader in Mathematics, The Victoria University of Manchester, Oxford Road, Manchester M13 9PL, United Kingdom.

International Series of
Numerical Mathematics, Vol. 73

CONSTRAINED APPROXIMATION TECHNIQUES FOR SOLVING INTEGRAL EQUATIONS

M. Brannigan
Computer Science Department
University of Georgia
Athens, GA 30602, U.S.A.

Introduction

The two standard techniques for numerically solving integral equations are collocation and Galerkin. Both these methods find an approximation via interpolation in that an approximating subspace of dimension n is provided, and the n parameters are found by solving n equations. These methods work well in practice for many equations as is seen for example in [1,2]. However, circumstances may arise when due to numerical error the number of basis functions n needs to be increased to an excessively large value. Also many real problems prescribe conditions on the underlying function, thus constraints on the approximation are introduced. Both these problems can be overcome if instead of interpolating we consider the approximation problem.

The method we suggest relies on the theory of best constrained Chebyshev approximation, and algorithms for solving semi-infinite linear programming problems. The approach we suggest uses stable numerical techniques, and hence integral equations of the first and second kind can be solved in this manner. Also as is shown in the example extension to multivariate equations is simple.

Theory

For the sake of brevity we shall consider integral equations of the second kind, and leave the development of the theory for first kind equations

This work was partially funded by a National Science Foundation grant number DMS8319727.

to the reader.

Consider, therefore,

$$f(s) + \int_a^b K(s,t)f(k)dt = \phi(s).$$

The problem that is posed is:- find a good approximation to the unknown function f(s). To solve this problem we take a linear space $V = \text{span}(g_1, g_2, \ldots, g_n)$ continuous on [a,b]. We then let f be defined as

$$f = \sum_{i=1}^{n} \alpha_i g_i ,$$

and our problem becomes :- find $\alpha = (\alpha_1, \alpha_2, \ldots, \alpha_n)$ so that the integral equation is approximated. As all known values are functions, namely K and ϕ then the Chebyshev norm has to be used, that is

$$||f|| = \max\{|f(x)|: x \varepsilon [a,b]\}.$$

Hence we need to determine α_i, i = 1, ..., n such that

$$||\phi - \sum_{i=1}^{n} \alpha_i g_i - \int_a^b \sum_{i=1}^{n} \alpha_i g_i(t)K(\cdot,t)dt||$$

is minimized. For convenience we define functions h_i, i = 1, ..., n by

$$h_i = g_i + \int_a^b g_i(t)K(\cdot,t)dt$$

As our method will be of a general nature then constraints are easily incorporated. We note here that if the known function ϕ has given properties, such as positivity or monotonicity then our choice of α should reflect this on the left hand side of the equation. We can now consider our original problem as follows:-

problem P:

$$\min_{\alpha} ||\phi - \sum_{i=1}^{n} \alpha_i h_i||$$

subject to

$$a(s) \leq \sum_{i=1}^{n} \alpha_i h_i(s) \leq b(s) ,$$

$$c(s) \leq \sum_{i=1}^{n} \alpha_i \psi_i(s) \leq d(s), \; s \varepsilon [a,b].$$

This problem can be written as a semi-infinite linear program in the following manner:-

Determine $\rho = \min \alpha_{n+1}$: over$(\alpha_1, \alpha_2, \ldots, \alpha_{n+1})$
subject to

$$\sum_{i=1}^{n} \alpha_i h_i(s) + \alpha_{n+1} - \phi(s) \geq 0,$$

$$-\sum_{i=1}^{n} \alpha_i h_i(s) + \alpha_{n+1} + \phi(s) \geq 0,$$

$$\sum_{i=1}^{n} \alpha_i h_i(s) - a(s) \geq 0,$$

$$-\sum_{i=1}^{n} \alpha_i h_i(s) + b(s) \geq 0,$$

$$\sum_{i=1}^{n} \alpha_i \psi_i(s) - c(s) \geq 0,$$

$$-\sum_{i=1}^{n} \alpha_i \psi_i(s) + d(s) \geq 0, \; s \in [a,b]$$

For computational, and theoretical purposes a useful concept is that of H-sets, first defined in [4]. In our setting we have:-

Definition $[\{x_i\}, \{y_j\}, \{\lambda_i\}, \{\mu_j\}, p, q]$ is an H-set for problem P if and only if

$$\lambda_i > 0, \; x_i \in [a,b], \qquad i = 1, \ldots, p;$$

$$\mu_j > 0, \; y_j \in [a,b], \qquad j = 1, \ldots, q;$$

and there are signs $\sigma_i = \pm 1$, $i = 1, \ldots, p$; $\tau_j = \pm 1$, $j = 1, \ldots, q$ such that

$$\sum_{i=1}^{p} \lambda_i \sigma_i h(x_i) + \sum_{j=1}^{q} \mu_j \tau_j \psi(y_j) = 0$$

$$\sum_{i=1}^{p} \lambda_i = 1,$$

where $h = (h_1, h_2, \ldots, h_n)^T$, $\psi = (\psi_1, \psi_2, \ldots, \psi_n)^T$.

An H-set is said to be minimal if no subset of the set of points $\{x_i\} \cup \{y_j\}$ forms an H-set.

Consider now the following sets defined for a trial solution α to problem P

$$M_\alpha = \{x \in [a,b] : | \phi(x) - \sum_{i=1}^{n} \alpha_i h_i(x)| = ||\phi - \sum_{i=1}^{n} \alpha_i h_i||\}$$

$$\bar{M}_\alpha = \{x \in [a,b] : \sum_{i=1}^{n} \alpha_i h_i(x) = a(x) \text{ or } b(x)\}$$

$$N_\alpha = \{y \in [a,b] : \sum_{i=1}^{n} \alpha_i \psi_i(j) = c(x) \text{ or } d(x)\}$$

We then obtain the characterization,

<u>Theorem 1</u> [3] A necessary and sufficient condition that α solves P is that there exist point $x_i \in M_\alpha$, $i = 1, \ldots, p_1$; $x_i \in \bar{M}_\alpha$, $i = p_1 + 1, \ldots, p$; $y_j \in N_\alpha$, $j = 1, \ldots, q$; appropriate multipliers λ_i, $i = 1, \ldots, p$; μ_j, $j = 1, \ldots, q$; and signs σ_i, $i = 1, \ldots, p$; τ_j; $j = 1, \ldots, q$ such that $[\{x_i\}, \{y_j\}, \{\lambda_i\}, \{\mu_j\}, p, q]$ forms an H-set for P and

$$\sigma_i = \operatorname{sgn}[\phi(x_i) - \sum_{k=1}^{n} \alpha_k h_k(x_i)], \quad i = 1, \ldots, p_1$$

$$\sigma_i = \begin{cases} +1, & \sum_{k=1}^{n} \alpha_k h_k(x_i) = a(x_i), \\ -1, & \sum_{k=1}^{n} \alpha_k h_k(x_i) = b(x_i), \end{cases} \quad i = p_1 + 1, \ldots, p$$

$$\tau_j = \begin{cases} +1, & \sum_{k=1}^{n} \alpha_k \psi_k(y_j) = c(y_j), \\ -1, & \sum_{k=1}^{n} \alpha_k \psi_k(y_j) = d(y_j), \end{cases} \quad j = 1, \ldots, q.$$

For approximating sets V, such as cubic splines, or multivariate problems, uniqueness of approximation is not guaranteed. However, we can state the following theorem

<u>Theorem 2</u> [3] Let S_α be the union of all minimal H-sets for P from a solution α to P in $M_\alpha \cup \bar{M}_\alpha \cup N_\alpha$; similarly define S_β for a further solution β to P, then

$$S_\alpha = S_\beta ,$$

and the signs $\{\sigma_i\}$, $\{\tau_j\}$ are the same.

<u>Corollary</u> If S_α contains an H-set of size $n + 1$ which is minimal for P then α is a unique solution to P.

<u>Computation</u>

Most algorithms for solving such problems P solve the dual of P. The dual function for P is given by the function θ where for an H-set of P $[\{x_i\}, \{y_j\}, \{\lambda_i\}, \{\mu_j\}, p, q]$ we have

$$\theta(\rho) = \sum_I [\lambda_i \sigma_i \phi(x_i) - \lambda_i \rho] + \sum_J \lambda_i \sigma_i \delta(x_i) + \sum_{j=1}^{q} \mu, \tau_j \, \varepsilon \, (y_j),$$

where

$$\delta(x_i) = \begin{cases} a(x_i), & \sigma_i = 1, \\ b(x_i), & \sigma_i = -1, \end{cases}$$

$$\delta(y_j) = \begin{cases} c(y_j), & \tau_j = 1, \\ d(y_j), & \tau_j = -1, \end{cases}$$

the index sets I, J are such that

$$I \cup J = \{1, \ldots, p\}$$

$$i \in I \text{ if } \rho \leq \begin{cases} \phi(x_i) - a(x_i), & \sigma_i = 1, \\ b(x_i) - \phi(x_i), & \sigma_i = -1. \end{cases}$$

$i \in J$ otherwise.

The dual problem is to maximize the root of $\theta(\rho)$ over all H-sets of P.

The following two theorems are computationally useful.

Theorem 3 [3] Let $[\{x_i\}, \{y_j\}, \{\lambda_i\}, \{\mu_j\}, p, q]$ be a minimal H-set for P, if ρ_0 is the root of $\theta(\rho)$ then

$$\rho_0 \leq \rho \leq ||\phi - \sum_{i=1}^{n} \beta_i h_i||,$$

where β is the solution to P on $\{x_i\} \cup \{y_j\}$.

Theorem 4 [3] If P is inconsistent then a minimal H-set for P exists for which the associated function $\theta(\rho)$ has no root.

For a good algorithm which uses stable matrix decompositions see [5,6]. Using this algorithm effectively gives you a solution on a very large discreet set.

Example Find f(x,y) which satisfies

$$f(x,y) + \int_0^1 \int_1^{2.5} f(s,t)(xt + ys)dtds = \ln(x + y) \sin x.$$

Using polynomials as basis functions approximate f by

$$f = \sum_{i=0}^{6} \sum_{j=0}^{i} \alpha_{ij} x^{i-j} y^j.$$

The program successfully finds the solution with an accuracy of 3.97×10^{-5}.

REFERENCES

1. Brannigan, M., Eyre, D. Splines and the collocation method for solving integral equations in scattering theory. J. Math. Phys., 24 (1983), 177-183.

2. Brannigan, M., Eyre, D. Splines and the Galerkin method for solving integral equations in scattering theory. J. Math. Phys. 24 (1983), 1548-1554.

3. Brannigan, M., Gustafson, S-A. H-sets, convex programming and constrained approximation. IMA J. Numer. Anal. to appear.

4. Collatz, L. Approximation von Funktionen bei einer und bei mehreren unabhangigen Veranderlichen. ZAMM 36 (1956), 198-211.

5. Hettich, R., Zencke, P. Numerische Methoden der Approximation und Semi-infiniten Optimierung. Teubner, Stuttgart. 1982.

6. Hettich, R. An implementation of a discretization method for semi-infinite programming. Technical Note, University of Trier, 1984.

Prof. Michael Brannigan, Department of Computer Science, University of Georgia, Athens, Georgia 30602 U.S.A.

International Series of
Numerical Mathematics, Vol. 73

ON THE NUMERICAL SOLUTION BY COLLOCATION OF VOLTERRA INTEGRODIFFERENTIAL EQUATIONS WITH NONSMOOTH SOLUTIONS

Hermann Brunner
University of Fribourg (Switzerland)

We study the attainable order of (global) convergence of collocation approximations in certain polynomial spline spaces to nonsmooth solutions of Volterra integro-differential equations; here, equations characterized by weakly singular kernels form, in view of practical applications, a particularly interesting subclass of such integro-differential equations. It is shown that even though the use of suitably graded meshes yields optimal convergence rates, such meshes have their limitations and drawbacks.

1980 *Mathematics Subject Classification*. Primary 65R20, 45J05. Secondary 41A25.

1. Introduction

Consider the Volterra integro-differential equation

$$(1.1)\qquad y'(t) = f(t,y(t)) + \int_0^t (t-s)^{\nu}\, k(t,s,y(s))ds,\quad t \in I := [0,T],$$

together with the initial condition $y(0) = y_0$. Assume that the given functions $f(t,y)$ and $k(t,s,y)$ are smooth and such that the above initial-value problem possesses a unique solution $y \in C^1(I)$, and let the exponent ν be of the form $\nu = \rho-\alpha$, with $\rho \in \mathbb{N}_0$, $0 < \alpha < 1$. In view of practical applications the case $\rho = 0$ (i.e., $\nu = -\alpha$, $0 < \alpha < 1$) will be of particular interest; compare also, e.g., McKEE (1979), PROSPERETTI (1982), McKEE & STOKES (1983) for sources of integro-differential equations of the form (1.1) as well as of related forms.

For given $N \in \mathbb{N}$, let Π_N: $0 = t_0 < t_1 < \ldots < t_N = T$ denote a partition (or: mesh) for the interval I (here, $t_n = t_n^{(N)}$; for ease of notation the index N will be suppressed). Set $Z_N := \{t_n : n = 1,\ldots,N-1\}$ (the set of interior mesh points), $\sigma_n := [t_n, t_{n+1}]$, and $h_n := t_{n+1} - t_n$ $(n = 0,\ldots,N-1)$. The solution of (1.1) will be approximated by an element of the polynomial spline space

$$(1.2) \qquad S_m^{(o)}(Z_N) := \{u : u|_{\sigma_n} =: u_n \in \pi_m;\ u_n(t_n) = u_{n-1}(t_n) \text{ for } t_n \in Z_N\};$$

this space is a finite-dimensional subspace of C(I) whose dimension is given by Nm+1. Since (1.1) can be related to the given mesh Π_N by reformulating it as

$$(1.3a) \qquad y'(t) = f(t,y(t)) + \int_{t_n}^{t} (t-s)^{\nu}\, k(t,s,y(s))ds + F_n(t;y),\ t \in \sigma_n\ ,$$

with

$$(1.3b) \qquad F_n(t;y) := \sum_{i=0}^{n-1} \int_{t_i}^{t_{i+1}} (t-s)^{\nu}\, k(t,s,y(s))ds \quad (n = 0,\ldots,N-1),$$

the desired approximation $u \in S_m^{(o)}(Z_N)$ will be determined recursively by requiring that it satisfy (1.3) on a given finite subset

$$X_n := \{t = t_{n,j} := t_n + c_j h_n : 0 \leq c_1 < \ldots < c_m \leq 1\}$$

of σ_n $(n = 0,\ldots,N-1)$; i.e.,

$$(1.4a) \qquad u_n'(t) = f(t,u_n(t)) + \int_{t_n}^{t} (t-s)^{\nu}\, k(t,s,u_n(s))ds + \hat{F}_n(t;u),\ t \in X_n\ ,$$

with

$$(1.4b) \qquad \hat{F}_n(t;u) := \sum_{i=0}^{n-1} \int_{t_i}^{t_{i+1}} (t-s)^{\nu}\, k(t,s,u_i(s))ds \quad (n = 0,\ldots,N-1).$$

In other words, u is the collocation approximation from $S_m^{(o)}(Z_N)$ satisfying the given integro-differential equation (1.1) at the collocation points $X(N) := \bigcup_{n=o}^{N-1} X_n$.

It will be convenient to rewrite the collocation equation (1.4) in a somewhat different form. Using an obvious change of variable, we define

$$(1,5)\qquad \Phi_{n,i}^{(j)}[u_i;\nu] := \begin{cases} \int_0^1 \left(\frac{t_{n,j}-t_i}{h_i} - v\right)^{\nu} k(t_{n,j}, t_i+vh_i, u_i(t_i+vh_i))dv, & \text{if } 0 \leqq i \leqq n-1; \\ \int_0^{c_j} (c_j-v)^{\nu}\, k(t_{n,j}, t_n+vh_n, u_n(t_n+vh_n))dv, & \text{if } i = n \end{cases} \qquad (j = 1,\dots,m).$$

The collocation equation (1.4) defining the approximation $u \in S_m^{(o)}(Z_N)$ thus assumes the form

$$(1.6)\qquad u_n'(t_{n,j}) = f(t_{n,j}, u_n(t_{n,j})) + h_n^{1+\nu}\, \Phi_{n,n}^{(j)}[u_n;\nu] + \sum_{i=o}^{n-1} h_i^{1+\nu}\, \Phi_{n,i}^{(j)}[u_i;\nu] ,$$

$$j = 1,\dots,m \ (n = 0,\dots,N-1),$$

with $u_o(t_o) = y_o$. Since $u_n' \in \pi_{m-1}$, we have, setting $Y_{n,k} := u_n'(t_{n,k})$ and $y_n := u_n(t_n)$,

$$(1.7a)\qquad u_n'(t_n+vh_n) = \sum_{k=1}^{m} L_k(v) Y_{n,k} ,$$

and hence

$$(1.7b)\qquad u_n(t_n+vh_n) = y_n + h_n \sum_{k=1}^{m} a_k(v) Y_{n,k} , \quad t_n+vh_n \in \sigma_n ,$$

with

$$L_k(v) := \prod_{r\neq k}^{m} (v-c_r)/(c_k-c_r), \quad a_k(v) := \int_0^v L_k(z)dz \qquad (v \in [0,1]).$$

For each $n = 0,\dots,N-1$, (1.6) represents a nonlinear system in $\mathbb{R}^m$ for the vector $Y_n := (Y_{n,1},\dots,Y_{n,m})^T$; once Y_n has been determined, the collocation approximation and its derivative on the subinterval σ_n can be computed by means of the interpolation formulas (1.7b) and (1.7a). We note in passing that if the collocation parameters $\{c_j\}$ are such that $0 = c_1 < \dots < c_m = 1$ (i.e., if both endpoints of σ_n are collocation points), then, due to the continuity of f and k, the resulting collocation approximation u is an element of the smoother polynomial spline space

$$S_m^{(1)}(Z_N) := S_m^{(0)}(Z_N) \cap C^1(I).$$

If the exact solution y of (1.1) is in the space $C^{m+1}(I)$, then it is well known that the order of (global) convergence of the collocation approximation $u \in S_m^{(0)}(Z_N)$ on uniform (or: quasi-uniform) meshes is given by

$$(1.8) \qquad \|e^{(k)}\|_\infty = \mathcal{O}(N^{-m}),\ k = 0,1,$$

where $e := y-u$ (see, e.g., MAKROGLOU (1981), ABDALKHANI (1982); compare also BRUNNER (1984a) for the case $\nu = 0$). However, if $\nu = -\alpha$ $(0 < \alpha < 1)$, then y will in general only be in $C^1(I)$, with $y''(t) \sim t^{-\alpha}$ near $t = 0$ (LUBICH (1983), BRUNNER (1983)). In this case (1.8) will no longer hold: Collocation in $S_m^{(0)}(Z_N)$, with the underlying meshes being uniform (or: quasi-uniform), yields only

$$(1.9) \qquad \|e^{(k)}\|_\infty = \mathcal{O}(N^{-(1-\alpha)}),\ k = 0,1,$$

regardless of how one chooses the degree m of the approximating polynomial spline. Higher-order convergence can be obtained only by employing special graded meshes (BRUNNER (1984c)).

It is the aim of this paper to extend the results of BRUNNER (1984c) to integro-differential equations (1.1) with arbitrary $\nu = \rho - \alpha$ ($\rho \in \mathbb{N}_0$, $0 < \alpha < 1$), thus including, e.g., kernels of the form $(t-s)^{1/2}k(t,s,y)$.

2. Collocation on graded meshes: convergence results

Let Π_N: $0 = t_0 < t_1 < \ldots < t_N = T$ ($N \in \mathbb{N}$) be a given sequence of partitions for I, and define

$$h := \max\{h_n : n = 0,\ldots,N-1\}, \quad h' := \min\{h_n : n = 0,\ldots,N-1\};$$

the quantity h is usually referred to as the diameter of the mesh Π_N (as before, we again omit the index showing the dependence of h and h' on N, the number of subintervals generated by Π_N).

A sequence of meshes $\{\Pi_N\}$ is called quasi-uniform if there exists a finite constant γ not depending on N so that

$$(2.1) \qquad h/h' \leqq \gamma \quad \text{for all } N \in \mathbb{N}.$$

For $\gamma = 1$ the meshes are the uniform ones, and we have $h = TN^{-1}$. More generally, (2.1) implies $h \leqq \gamma\, TN^{-1}$, and hence $h = O(N^{-1})$, as $N \to \infty$.

A mesh Π_N is said to be graded if it is given by

$$(2.2) \qquad t_n := \left(\frac{n}{N}\right)^r \cdot T,\ n = 0,\ldots,N \quad (N \geqq 2);$$

in the present context the so-called grading exponent r will be assumed to satisfy $r > 1$. (For $r = 1$, (2.2) represents, of course, the uniform mesh.) For future reference we list a number of easily verified properties of graded meshes with $r > 1$.

(2.3a) $h' = h_0 < h_1 < \dots < h_{N-1} = h$.

(2.3b) $h' = TN^{-r}$ $(= t_1)$; $h < rTN^{-1}$.

(2.3c) $h/h' = rN^{r-1}\cdot(1-\theta N^{-1})^{r-1}$ $(0 < \theta < 1)$.

(2.3d) $t_n = n^r t_1$ $(n = 1,\dots,N)$.

(Property (2.3c) shows, incidentally, that a sequence of graded meshes with $r > 1$ is not quasi-uniform.)

<u>THEOREM 2.1.</u> Let $f(t,y)$ and $k(t,s,y)$ $(k \not\equiv 0)$ have continuous and bounded derivatives of order m $(m \geq 1)$, and assume that they are such that (1.1) does not possess the trivial solution. Moreover, let ν in (1.1) be of the form $\nu = \rho-\alpha$, with $0 < \alpha < 1$, $\rho \in \mathbb{N}_0$, $\rho \leq m-1$. If $u \in S_m^{(0)}(Z_N)$ denotes the collocation approximation defined by (1.6), (1.7), then the resulting error $e := y - u$ satisfies

(2.4) $$\|e^{(k)}\|_\infty = \mathcal{O}(N^{-(1+\nu)}),\ k = 0,1,$$

if the underlying mesh sequence $\{\Pi_N\}$ is <u>quasi-uniform</u>, or

(2.5) $$\|e^{(k)}\|_\infty = \mathcal{O}(N^{-m}),\ k = 0,1,$$

if the mesh sequence $\{\Pi_N\}$ is the <u>graded</u> one given by (2.2), with grading exponent

(2.6) $$r = m/(1+\nu) \quad (= m/(\rho+1-\alpha)).$$

The above estimates hold for all collocation parameters $\{c_j\}$ with $0 \leq c_1 < \dots < c_m \leq 1$ and are best possible.

If ρ in $\nu = \rho-\alpha$ satisfies $\rho \geqq m$, then we have $y \in C^{m+1}(I)$; hence, as remarked before, there is no need to employ graded meshes since optimal (global) convergence of the form (2.5) can be obtained on quasi-uniform meshes.

Graded meshes were introduced by RICE (1969) in the context of generating uniformly good approximations by polynomial spline functions to nonsmooth functions like $f(t) = t^{\beta}$ ($\beta > 0$, $\beta \notin \mathbb{N}$) on [0,1]. His theory was subsequently refined and generalized by, e.g., BURCHARD (1974), (1977), DE BOOR (1973), BURCHARD & HALE (1975); compare also DE BOOR (1978), SCHUMAKER (1981), and POWELL (1981). A brief survey of these results may be found in BRUNNER (1984b).

The use of graded meshes in the numerical solution (by product integration, Galerkin, and collocation methods) of second-kind Fredholm integral equations with weakly singular kernels has been studied by CHANDLER (1979), SCHNEIDER (1981), GRAHAM (1982), and VAINIKKO & UBA (1981); here, the exact solution exhibits nonsmooth behaviour at both endpoints (t = 0 and t = T) of the interval of integration, and hence the graded mesh (2.2) must be replaced by a symmetrical one,

$$t_n := \begin{cases} \left(\frac{2n}{N}\right)^r \cdot \frac{T}{2}, & \text{if } n = 0,\dots,[\frac{N}{2}], \\ T - t_{N-n}, & \text{if } n = [\frac{N}{2}]+1,\dots,N, \end{cases}$$

with suitably chosen grading exponent r.

BRUNNER (1984b) employed graded meshes (2.2) in the numerical solution by collocation methods of Volterra integral equations of the second kind with weakly singular kernels.

3. Convergence results: outline of proofs

The key to the proof of Theorem 2.1 is to be found in the structure of the exact solution of (1.1): if α in $\nu = \rho - \alpha$ is rational: $\alpha = p/q$, with $p, q \in \mathbb{N}$ coprime (which we shall, for ease of exposition, assume in the following), then the solution may be written as

$$(3.1) \qquad y(t) = w_0(t) + \sum_{s=1}^{q-1} w_s(t)\cdot t^{s(1+\nu)}, \quad t \in I,$$

with $w_s \in C^{m+1}(I)$ $(s = 0,\dots,q-1)$. (Compare BRUNNER (1982), (1984b) for the corresponding analysis of the linear version of (1.1): $f(t,y) = a(t)y+b(t)$ (with $a, b \in C^m(I)$), and $k(t,s,y) = K(t,s)y$ (with $K \in C^m(S)$, $S := \{(t,s): 0 \leqq s \leqq t \leqq T\}$); an analogous analysis for the nonlinear case is easily carried out by adapting the techniques used by LUBICH (1983) for nonlinear integral equations of the second kind with kernels as in (1.1).)

Hence, if $t = t_0 + vh_0 \in \sigma_0$, we obtain, setting

$$w_s(t_0+vh_0) = \sum_{\ell=0}^{m} c_{0,\ell}^{(s)} v^\ell + h_0^{m+1} R_{0,s}(v) \quad (s = 0,\dots,q-1),$$

with

$$c_{0,\ell}^{(s)} := w_s^{(\ell)}(t_0) h_0^\ell/\ell!,$$

and

$$R_{0,s}(v) := \frac{1}{m!} \int_0^v (v-z)^m \, w_s^{(m+1)}(t_0+zh_0)dz,$$

the expression

$$(3.2) \qquad y(t_0+vh_0) = \sum_{\ell=0}^{m} c_{0,\ell} v^\ell + h_0^{2+\nu} C_0(v) + h_0^{m+1} R_0(v), \quad v \in [0,1],$$

where we have set

$$c_{0,\ell} := \sum_{s=0}^{q-1} h_0^{s(2+\nu)} c_{0,\ell}^{(s)} ,$$

$$R_o(v) := \sum_{s=0}^{q-1} h_o^{s(2+\ )} R_{o,s}(v) v^{s(2+\nu)},$$

and

$$C_o(v) := \sum_{s=1}^{q-1} h_o^{(s-1)(2+\nu)} (v^{s(2+\nu)} - 1) \sum_{\ell=0}^{m} c_{o,\ell}^{(s)} v^{\ell} .$$

On any other subinterval σ_n with $1 \leq n \leq N-1$, we have $t_n > 0$; here, the solution may be written as

$$(3.3) \qquad y(t_n + vh_n) = \sum_{\ell=0}^{m} c_{n,\ell} v^{\ell} + h_n^{m+1} R_n(v), \ v \in [0,1],$$

with

$$c_{n,\ell} := y^{(\ell)}(t_n) h_n^{\ell} / \ell! ,$$

and

$$R_n(v) := \frac{1}{m!} \int_0^v (v-z)^m \, y^{(m+1)}(t_n + zh_n) dz .$$

The expression (3.1) shows, incidentally, that the solution of (1.1) corresponding to smooth $f(t,y)$ and $k(t,s,y)$, with $\nu = \rho - \alpha$ $(0 < \alpha < 1)$, satisfies $y \in C^{\rho+1}(I)$, $y^{(\rho+1)} \in Lip_{1-\alpha}(I)$; hence, $\rho \geq m$ implies $y \in C^{m+1}(I)$ (see also BRUNNER (1984b)).

Suppose now that the restriction u_n of $u \in S_m^{(0)}(Z_N)$ to the subinterval σ_n has the form

$$u_n(t_n + vh_n) = \sum_{\ell=0}^{m} \alpha_{n,\ell} v^{\ell} .$$

The restriction e_n of the error $e := y - u$ to this subinterval then becomes, setting $\beta_{n,\ell} := c_{n,\ell} - \alpha_{n,\ell}$,

$$(3.4) \qquad e_n(t_n + vh_n) = \begin{cases} \sum_{\ell=0}^{m} \beta_{o,\ell} v^{\ell} + h_o^{2+\nu} C_o(v) + h_o^{m+1} R_o(v), & \text{if } n = 0; \\ \sum_{\ell=o}^{m} \beta_{n,\ell} v^{\ell} + h_n^{m+1} R_n(v), & \text{if } 1 \leq n \leq N-1; \end{cases}$$

its derivative on σ_n is given by

$$(3.5)\qquad e_n'(t_n+vh_n) = \begin{cases} h_0^{-1}\{\sum_{\ell=1}^{m} \ell\beta_{0,\ell}\, v^{\ell-1} + h_0^{2+\nu}C_0'(v)+h_0^{m+1}R_0'(v)\}, & \text{if } n = 0; \\ h_n^{-1}\{\sum_{\ell=1}^{m} \ell\beta_{n,\ell}\, v^{\ell-1} + h_n^{m+1}R_n'(v)\}, & \text{if } 1 \leq n \leq N-1. \end{cases}$$

The error function e is continuous on I; thus, the continuity conditions for the knots Z_N: $e_n(t_n) = e_{n-1}(t_n)$ for $t_n \in Z_N$, yield, by (3.4), the relation

$$(3.6a)\qquad \beta_{n,0} = \beta_{0,0} + \sum_{i=0}^{n-1}\sum_{\ell=1}^{m} \beta_{i,\ell} + h_0^{2+\nu}C_0(1) + \sum_{i=0}^{n-1} h_i^{m+1}R_i(1)$$
$$(n = 1,\ldots,N-1).$$

Moreover, since $\beta_{0,0} = c_{0,0} - \alpha_{0,0}$, we obtain, by (3.2),

$$(3.6b)\qquad \beta_{0,0} = h_0^{2+\nu}\sum_{s=1}^{q-1} h_0^{(s-1)(2+\nu)}w_s(0).$$

If we subtract the collocation equation (1.4) from (1.1) (with t replaced by $t_{n,j}$), then, after linearization, we find

$$e_n'(t_{n,j}) = a(t_{n,j})e_n(t_{n,j}) + h_n^{1+\nu}\int_0^{c_j} (c_j-v)^{\nu}\, K_{n,j}(t_n+vh_n)e_n(t_n+vh_n)dv +$$
$$+ \sum_{i=0}^{n-1} h_i^{1+\nu}\int_0^1 \left(\frac{t_{n,j}-t_i}{h_i} - v\right)^{\nu} K_{n,j}(t_i+vh_i)e_i(t_i+vh_i)dv,$$
$$j = 1,\ldots,m\ (n = 0,\ldots,N-1),$$

with $e_0(t_0) = 0$. Here, $a(t_{n,j}) := \frac{\partial}{\partial y} f(t_n,j,\ \cdot\ )$, $K_{n,j}(t_i+vh_i) :=$ $\frac{\partial}{\partial y} k(t_{n,j},t_i+vh_i,\ \cdot\ )$, where the unspecified last arguments are determined through the application of the mean-value theorem.

Using (3.4), (3.5), and (3.6), we thus obtain a linear recurrence relation for the components of the vectors $\beta_n := (\beta_{n,1},\ldots,\beta_{n,m})^T \in \mathbb{R}^m$ $(n=0,\ldots,N-1)$ which, upon employing standard arguments (cf. BRUNNER (1984a), (1984c)), leads to a discrete Gronwall inequality for the ℓ_1-norms of these vectors:

$$\|\beta_n\|_1 \leq hC_o \sum_{i=o}^{n-1} \|\beta_i\|_1 + hC_1 \quad (n = 0,\dots,N-1),$$

with C_o and C_1 denoting finite constants not depending on n. It follows from the theory of discrete Gronwall inequalities (see DIXON & McKEE (1983) and the relevant references listed there) that $\|\beta_n\|_1 = \mathcal{O}(hC_1)$. Hence our principal task consists in estimating C_1 .

Consider first the case of <u>quasi-uniform</u> mesh sequences $\{\Pi_N\}$: here, it is readily seen (since $h_n = \mathcal{O}(N^{-1})$ for all n) that we obtain

$$\|\beta_n\|_1 = \mathcal{O}(N^{-(2+\nu)}) \quad (n = 0,\dots,N-1;\ Nh \leq \gamma T).$$

Since (3.6) implies

$$|\beta_{n,o}| = N \cdot \mathcal{O}(N^{-(2+\nu)}) = \mathcal{O}(N^{-(1+\nu)}),$$

it follows from (3.4) and (3.5) that the collocation error satisfies

$$\|e^{(k)}\|_\infty = \mathcal{O}(N^{-(1+\nu)}), \quad k = 0,1.$$

Suppose now that the underlying meshes are <u>graded</u>; i.e., that they are of the form (2.2), with grading exponent $r > 1$ as yet unspecified. Returning to (3.4) and (3.5) we observe that the crucial terms in the estimation of C_1 are $h_o^{2+\nu}|C_o(1)|$, $h_o^{1+\nu}|C_o'(1)|$, $h_n^{m+1}|R_n(v)|$, and $h_n^m|R_n'(v)|$. By definition (cf. (3.2) and (3.3)) the last two of these depend on $y^{(m+1)}(t)$ which, according to (3.1) and by the Leibniz product rule, has the form

$$y^{(m+1)}(t) = w_o^{(m+1)}(t) + \sum_{s=1}^{q-1} \sum_{k=o}^{m+1} \gamma_{m,k}^{(s)}(\nu)\cdot w_s^{(m+1-k)}(t)\cdot t^{s(2+\nu)-k}, \ t > 0,$$

with

$$\gamma_{m,k}^{(s)}(\nu) := \binom{m+1}{k}\cdot\binom{s(2+\nu)}{k}\cdot k! \quad .$$

This shows that the orders of the terms $h_n^{m+1}|R_n(v)|$ and $h_n^m|R_n'(v)|$ will be determined by those of the products $h_n^{m+\lambda} t_n^{s(2+\nu)-k}$ $(n = 1,\dots,N)$, where $\lambda \in \{0,1\}$ and $k = 0,\dots,m+1$.

LEMMA 3.1. Let $\nu = \rho - \alpha$, with $0 < \alpha < 1$, $\rho \in \mathbb{N}_0$, and assume that $\{\Pi_N\}$ is the sequence of graded meshes given by (2.2), with grading exponent

$$r = m/(1+\nu).$$

Then for $k = 0,\ldots,m+1$, for $s \geqq 1$, and for $\lambda \in \{0,1\}$, we have

$$h_n^{m+\lambda} \cdot t_n^{s(2+\nu)-k} = O(N^{-(m+\lambda)}) \quad (n = 1,\ldots,N), \text{ as } N \to \infty . \tag{3.7}$$

Note that (3.7) holds in particular for those values of s and k for which $s(2+\nu)-k$ is negative (for positive values of this expression the statement is, of course, trivial).

Proof: Let $s(2+\nu)-k$ be negative. Then, by (2.3) and (2.2),

$$h_n^{m+\lambda} t_n^{s(2+\nu)-k} < c \cdot n^{r[s(2+\nu)-(1-\lambda)]-(m+\lambda)} \cdot N^{-r[s(2+\nu)-(1-\lambda)]},$$

with

$$c := (r \cdot 2^{r-1}T)^{m+\lambda} \cdot T^{s(2+\nu)-k} .$$

Assume that $\mu \geqq 0$ is a real number such that

$$r[2+\nu-(1-\lambda)] - (m+\lambda) \geqq -\mu ,$$

or, equivalently,

$$r(1+\lambda+\nu) - (m+\lambda-\mu) \geqq 0.$$

It then follows that for $s \geqq 1$ and $k \leqq m+1$,

$$h_n^{m+\lambda} \cdot t_n^{s(2+\nu)-k} = O(N^{-(m+\lambda-\mu)}) \quad (n = 1,\ldots,N).$$

This result contains the desired information on how to choose the grading exponent r so as to achieve optimal order: we have

$$h_n^{m+\lambda} \cdot t_n^{s(2+\nu)-k} = O(N^{-(m+\lambda)}) \quad (n = 1,\ldots,N)$$

if, and only if, $\mu = 0$; i.e., if, and only if,

$$r \geqq (m+\lambda)/(1+\lambda+\nu)$$

for $\lambda \in \{0,1\}$. Since the largest value of this lower bound occurs for $\lambda = 0$, the smallest grading exponent r for which (3.7) holds is given by $r = m/(1+\nu)$. This completes the proof of Lemma 3.1. □

The above arguments reveal, incidentally, that the choice $r = 1$ (uniform meshes) leads to the value $\mu = m-(1+\lambda+\nu)$, and hence to

$$h_n^{m+\lambda} \cdot t_n^{s(2+\nu)-k} = \mathcal{O}(N^{-(m+\lambda-\mu)}) = \mathcal{O}(N^{-(1+\nu)}),$$

thus confirming the result indicated already before.

Recall now (3.4) and (3.5), particularly the terms $h_o^{2+\nu}C_o(v)$ and $h_o^{1+\nu}C_o'(v)$: if we use graded meshes of the type indicated in Lemma 3.1 (i.e., with grading exponent $r = m/(1+\nu)$), then, by (2.3b),

$$h_o^{1+\nu} = (TN^{-r})^{1+\nu} = T^{1+\nu} \cdot N^{-m} = \mathcal{O}(N^{-m}),$$

while both $C_o(v)$ and $C_o'(v)$ are bounded functions (cf. (3.2)). Using arguments analogous to those for the case of quasi-uniform mesh sequences it is then readily verified that the ℓ_1-norms of the vectors β_n satisfy

$$||\beta_n||_1 = \mathcal{O}(N^{-(m+1)}) \quad (n = 0,\ldots,N-1;\ Nh < rT),$$

and hence (3.6a) and (3.6b) imply

$$|\beta_{n,o}| = N \cdot \mathcal{O}(N^{-(m+1)}) \quad (n = 0,\ldots,N-1).$$

This leads immediately to assertion (2.5) of Theorem 2.1. □

4. Additional remarks and numerical examples

In practical applications a further discretization step will be necessary in the collocation equation (1.6) since the integrals (1.5) can, in general, not be evaluated analytically. The quadrature formulas approximating these integrals will be based on product-integration techniques; more precisely, these approximations will be of the form

$$(4.1)\quad \hat{\Phi}^{(j)}_{n,i}[u_i;\nu] := \begin{cases} \sum_{\ell=1}^{m} w^{(n,i)}_{j,\ell}(\nu)\cdot k(t_{n,j}, t_i + c_\ell h_i, u_i(t_i + c_\ell h_i)), & \text{if } 0 \leq i < n; \\ \sum_{\ell=1}^{m} w_{j,\ell}(\nu)\cdot k(t_{n,j}, t_n + c_j c_\ell h_n, u_n(t_n + c_j c_\ell h_n)), & \text{if } i = n \end{cases}$$

$(j = 1,\dots,m)$,

where the quadrature weights are given by

$$(4.2a)\qquad w^{(n,i)}_{j,\ell}(\nu) := \int_0^1 \left(\frac{t_{n,j}-t_i}{h_i} - v\right)^{\nu} L_\ell(v)dv,\ 0 \leq i < n,$$

and

$$(4.2b)\qquad w_{j,\ell}(\nu) := c_j^{1+\nu} \cdot \int_0^1 (1-v)^{\nu} L_\ell(v)dv \quad (j,\ell = 1,\dots,m),$$

with

$$L_\ell(v) := \prod_{k\neq\ell}^{m} (v-c_k)/(c_\ell - c_k) .$$

Since these quadrature approximations are based on m-point interpolation it is clear that the resulting collocation approximation $\hat{u} \in S_m^{(0)}(Z_N)$ (which, in general, will be different from u given by (1.6)) will still satisfy the convergence results of Theorem 2.1 (compare also BRUNNER (1984c) for details).

We illustrate the above analysis by two numerical examples.

Example 4.1.

$$y'(t) = a(t)y(t) + b(t) + \int_0^t (t-s)^{-\alpha} K(t,s)y(s)ds,\ t \in [0,1],\ y(0) = 1,$$

with $a(t) \equiv -1$, $K(t,s) \equiv -1$, and with $b(t)$ chosen so that $y(t) = 1 + t^{2-\alpha}$. The exact solution is approximated in $S_2^{(0)}(Z_N)$, with the collocation parameters given by $c_1 = (3-\sqrt{3})/6$, $c_2 = (3+\sqrt{3})/6$ (Gauss points for (0,1)); the fully discretized collocation equation is obtained by using (4.1), (4.2) (with m=2).

A sample of numerical results is displayed in Table 4.1a and Table 4.1b: here, values between parentheses correspond to r = 1 (uniform meshes), while the other values are obtained by using graded meshes (2.2) with $r = 2/(1-\alpha)$.

Table 4.1a. Error norms

N	α = 1/2		α = 2/3	
	$\|\|e\|\|_\infty$	$\|\|e'\|\|_\infty$	$\|\|e\|\|_\infty$	$\|\|e'\|\|_\infty$
5	1.23E-3 (1.99E-3)	2.29E-2 (7.46E-2)	4.96E-3 (2.67E-3)	4.65E-2 (9.89E-2)
10	2.38E-4 (7.28E-4)	5.93E-3 (5.41E-2)	1.04E-3 (1.11E-3)	1.34E-2 (8.14E-2)
20	4.67E-5 (2.61E-4)	1.45E-3 (3.87E-2)	1.93E-4 (4.52E-4)	3.32E-3 (6.57E-2)

Table 4.1b. Errors at t = T

N	α = 1/2		α = 2/3	
	$\|e(T)\|$	$\|e'(T)\|$	$\|e(T)\|$	$\|e'(T)\|$
5	1.23E-3 (4.38E-5)	2.29E-2 (1.17E-3)	4.96E-3 (9.97E-6)	4.65E-2 (1.19E-3)
10	2.23E-4 (1.12E-6)	5.93E-3 (2.12E-4)	1.04E-3 (2.73E-5)	1.34E-2 (2.19E-4)
20	3.98E-5 (2.82E-6)	1.45E-3 (3.33E-5)	1.93E-4 (1.55E-5)	3.32E-3 (3.56E-5)

Example 4.2.

$$y'(t) = a(t)y(t) + b(t),\ t \in [0,1],\ y(0) = 0,$$

with $a(t) \equiv -1$, and with $b(t)$ so that $y(t) = t^{2-\alpha}$. The setting for the approximate solution is the same as in Example 4.1. We note, however, that while in the case of a genuine integro-differential equation with weakly singular kernel (i.e., $k(t,s,y) \not\equiv 0$ in (1.1)) the qualitative behaviour of the solution near $t = 0$ is known (cf. (3.1)), the situation will in general be much more complex for ordinary differential equations, especially if they are nonlinear. We have added this example merely to show that, in the case of ordinary differential equations with nonsmooth solutions of known qualitative behaviour near t = 0, collocation in $S_m^{(0)}(Z_N)$ on graded meshes (which corresponds to an m-stage implicit Runge-Kutta method on graded meshes) restores the optimal convergence order. (The results shown in Table 4.2a and Table 4.2b correspond to $r = 2/(1-\alpha)$ and (between parentheses) to r = 1.)

Table 4.2a. Error norms

N	$\alpha = 1/2$		$\alpha = 2/3$	
	$\lVert e \rVert_\infty$	$\lVert e' \rVert_\infty$	$\lVert e \rVert_\infty$	$\lVert e' \rVert_\infty$
5	1.20E-3 (2.02E-3)	1.74E-2 (7.55E-2)	2.76E-3 (2.79E-3)	3.17E-2 (1.02E-1)
10	1.70E-4 (7.32E-4)	4.75E-3 (5.43E-2)	4.21E-4 (1.13E-3)	8.11E-3 (8.25E-2)
20	2.25E-5 (2.62E-4)	1.22E-3 (3.87E-2)	5.78E-5 (4.55E-4)	2.13E-3 (6.60E-2)

Table 4.2b. Errors at t = T

N	$\alpha = 1/2$		$\alpha = 2/3$	
	$\lvert e(T) \rvert$	$\lvert e'(T) \rvert$	$\lvert e(T) \rvert$	$\lvert e'(T) \rvert$
5	1.00E-4 (3.42E-4)	1.72E-2 (1.10E-3)	3.04E-4 (5.41E-4)	2.65E-2 (6.21E-4)
10	7.48E-6 (1.24E-4)	4.75E-3 (2.11E-4)	2.54E-5 (2.19E-4)	7.99E-3 (4.71E-5)
20	4.94E-7 (4.43E-5)	1.22E-3 (3.65E-5)	1.73E-6 (8.79E-5)	2.13E-3 (2.39E-5)

Although the above numerical examples confirm that the use of suitably graded meshes will lead to optimal orders of convergence, this approach is subject to severe practical limitations, especially if $\nu = -\alpha$ $(0 < \alpha < 1;$ i.e., $\rho = 0)$. Here, the grading exponent is given by $r = m/(1-\alpha)$, while the initial stepsize is h_0 (= h') = TN^{-r} (cf. (2.3b)). This means that for fixed values of m and α (in practical applications, α seems to be restricted to the set {1/3, 1/2, 2/3}), h_0 will assume very small positive values as N (the number of subintervals) increases; this, in turn, may lead to serious contamination of the numerical results due to rounding errors. The following table illustrates the behaviour of h_0 for the case $m = 2$; it also lists the mesh diameter h.

Table 4.3. Initial stepsize h_0 and mesh diameter h

N	$\alpha = 1/2$		$\alpha = 2/3$		$\alpha = 0.9$	
	h_0	h	h_0	h	h_0	h
5	1.60E-3	0.590	6.40E-5	0.738	1.05E-14	0.988
10	1.00E-4	0.344	1.00E-6	0.469	1.00E-20	0.878
20	6.25E-6	0.185	1.56E-8	0.265	9.54E-27	0.641

However, in many applications one is not so much interested in the uniform accuracy of the approximation u on I as in the accuracy at, or near, the right endpoint $t = T$ of the interval of integration. In this case the use of uniform meshes will usually be preferable: according to our experience collocation on uniform meshes will almost invariably lead to significantly more accurate approximations at $t = T$; hence, the results displayed in Table 4.1b indicate a typical behaviour.

References

ABDALKHANI, J. (1982) Collocation and Runge-Kutta-type methods for Volterra integral equations with weakly singular kernels. Ph.D. Thesis, Dalhousie University, Halifax. N.S.

De BOOR, C. (1973) Good approximation by splines with variable knots, in: Spline Functions and Approximation Theory (A. Meir & A. Sharma, eds.), Birkhäuser Verlag, Basel: pp. 57-72.

De BOOR, C. (1978) A Practical Guide to Splines (Springer-Verlag, New York).

BRUNNER, H. (1982) On collocation approximations for Volterra equations with weakly singular kernels, in: Treatment of Integral Equations by Numerical Methods (C.T.H. Baker & G.F. Miller, eds), Academic Press, London: pp. 409-420.

BRUNNER, H. (1984a) Implicit Runge-Kutta methods of optimal order for Volterra integro-differential equations. Math. Comp. 42, 95-109.

BRUNNER, H. (1984b) The approximate solution of Volterra equations with nonsmooth solutions. Utilitas Math. (to appear).

BRUNNER, H. (1984c) Polynomial spline collocation methods for Volterra integro-differential equations with weakly singular kernels. IMA J. Numer. Anal. (to appear).

BURCHARD, H.G. (1974) Splines (with optimal knots) are better. J. Applicable Anal. 3, 309-319.

BURCHARD, H.G. (1977) On the degree of convergence of piecewise polynomial approximation onoptimal meshes II. Trans. Amer. Math. Soc. 234, 531-559.

BURCHARD, H.G. & HALE, D.F. (1975) Piecewise polynomial approximation on optimal meshes. J. Approx. Theory 14, 128-147.

CHANDLER, I.G. (1979) Superconvergence of numerical methods to second kind integral equations. Ph.D. Thesis, Australian National University, Canberra.

DIXON, J. & McKEE, S. (1983) Singular Gronwall inequalities. Numerical Analysis Report NA/83/44, Hertford College, University of Oxford.

GRAHAM, I.G. (1982) Galerkin methods for second kind integral equations with singularities. Math. Comp. 39, 519-533.

LUBICH, CH. (1983) Runge-Kutta theory for Volterra and Abel integral equations of the second kind. Math. Comp. 41, 87-102.

MAKROGLOU, A. (1981) A block-by-block method for Volterra integro-differential equations with weakly singular kernels, Math. Comp. 37, 95-99.

McKEE, S. (1979) The analysis of a variable step, variable coefficient, linear multistep method for solving a singular integro-differential equation arising from the diffusion of discrete particles in a turbulent fluid. J. Inst. Math. Appl. 23, 373-388.

McKEE, S. & STOKES, A. (1983) Product integration methods for the nonlinear Basset equation. SIAM J. Numer. Anal. 20, 143-160.

POWELL, M.J.D. (1981) Approximation Theory and Methods (Cambridge University Press, Cambridge).

PROSPERETTI, A. (1982) A method for the solution of a class of singular Volterra integro-differential equations. J. Comput. Phys. 46, 462-468.

RICE, J.R. (1969) On the degree of convergence of nonlinear spline approximation, in: Approximation with Special Emphasis on Spline Functions (I.J. Schoenberg, ed.), Academic Press, New York: pp. 349-365.

SCHNEIDER, C. (1981) Product integration for weakly singular integral equations, Math. Comp. 36, 207-213.

SCHUMAKER, L.L. (1981) Spline Functions: Basic Theory (Wiley, New York).

VAINIKKO, G. & UBA, P. (1981) A piecewise polynomial approximation to the solution of an integral equation with weakly singular kernel. J. Austral. Math. Soc. Ser. B 22, 431-438.

Hermann Brunner
Institut de Mathématiques
Université de Fribourg
CH-1700 Fribourg
Switzerland

International Series of
Numerical Mathematics, Vol. 73

INCLUSION OF REGULAR AND SINGULAR SOLUTIONS OF CERTAIN TYPES OF INTEGRAL EQUATIONS

L. Collatz

Institut für Angewandte Mathematik
der Universität Hamburg

Abstract. In the functional equation u=Tu for a function $u(x)=u(x_1,\ldots,x_n)$ let the completely continuous (linear or nonlinear) operator T be "monotonically decomposible" in the sense of J. Schröder. We suppose, one has calculated, (for instance with an iteration procedure) an interval $J=[v_1,w_1]$, which contains under certain conditions at least one solution u (Schauders fixed point theorem). This is in many cases the only (easily calculable) possibility of an inclusion for u.

This method is also applicable for calculation of solutions with certain types of singularities. Recently three-dimensional singularities became more important. Numerical examples are given, also for distributed singularities in the three-dimensional space.

Zusammenfassung

Bei der Funktionalgleichung u=Tu für eine Funktion

$$u(x) = u(x_1,...,x_n)$$

sei der gegebene (lineare oder nichtlineare) vollstetige Operator T "monoton zerlegbar" im Sinne von J. Schröder. Man habe, etwa mit Hilfe eines Iterationsverfahrens, ein Intervall $J=[v_1,w_1]$ berechnet, in welchem unter gewissen Zusatzvoraussetzungen mindestens eine Lösung u existiert (Schauderscher Fixpunktsatz). In vielen Fällen ist dies die einzige praktisch brauchbare Möglichkeit einer Einschließung von u. Auch Lösungen mit gewissen Singularitäten können auf diese Weise berechnet werden. In neuerer Zeit sind insbesondere dreidimensionale Singularitäten zu Bedeutung gelangt. Es wird auf numerische Erfahrungen mit räumlich verteilten Singularitäten im R^3 berichtet.

We describe in no. 1 as survey the general concept for inclusion of wanted solutions and recent applications for singular boundary value problems.

1. The general scheme for theory and calculation

Let us consider a (linear or nonlinear) functional equation

(1.1) $$u = Tu$$

for a realvalued function $u(x)=u(x_1,...,x_n)$ of the independent real variables $x_1,...,x_n$ in a given bounded domain B of the pointspace R^n. Let C[B] be the Banachspace of continuous function f(x) with the classical maximum norm and T may be a completely continuous operator mapping the elements of C[B] into C[B]. Many types of boundary value problems for ordinary and partial differential equations can be transformed in integral equations of the form (1.1) with a completely continuous (linear or nonlinear) integral operator.

For such integral equations, two classical topological fixed point theorems are available, the contraction-mapping theorem (compare for instance Kantorowitsch-Akilov [64]) and the Schauder theorem with its variants. The second theorem (Schauder) is for many applications more suitable as the first one.

Theorem (Schauder [30]): Let T be a continuous operator, mapping a closed convex bounded set M of a Banach space R into a relatively compact set TM, which belongs to M. Then exists at least one fixed point u of T with $u = Tu$ and $u \in M$.

We take for equation (1.1) as R the space C[B] and suppose furthermore, that R is partially ordered. For simplicity we define the ordering for two functions f, g of R in the way:

(1.2) $\quad f \leqq g$ means: $f(x) \leqq g(x)$ for all $x \in B$.

Here $f(x) \leqq g(x)$ may be the classical ordering for real numbers. We introduce some definitions for operators T with the domain D of definition:

(1.3) $\quad$ T is syntone, if $v \leqq w$ implies $Tv \leqq Tw$ for all $v,w \in D$

(1.4) $\quad$ T is antitone, if $v \leqq w$ implies $Tv \geqq Tw$ for all $v,w \in D$

T is monotonically decomposible, if $T = T_1 + T_2$ where T_1 is syntone and T_2 is antitone.

Example: Nonlinear Hammerstein-Integral operator

$$(1.5) \qquad Hu(x) = \int_B K(x,t)\phi(u(t))dt \ .$$

We suppose the given kernel $K(x,t) = K(x_1,\dots,x_n,t_1,\dots,t_n)$ as real and the given realvalued function $\phi(x)$ as function of bounded variation. Every Hammerstein-Operator (1.5) with these assumptions is monotonically decomposible (Collatz [71], Bohl [74]):

$H = T_1 + T_2$, where T_1 is syntone and T_2 antitone.

An interval $J = [v,w]$ is in the case $v \leqq w$ defined as the set of all functions h with

(1.6) $$J = [v,w] = \{h,\ v \leqq h \leqq w\} .$$

Every interval [v,w] is closed, convex and bounded.

Suppose we have calculated an interval $M = [v,w]$ which is mapped by T into itself: $TM \subset M$. The Hammerstein-Operator (1.5) is under weak conditions completely continuous and maps every bounded set into a relatively compact set. Then the Schauder theorem is applicable and assures the existence of at least one solution u of $u = Hu$ and we have the inclusion theorem $u \varepsilon M$, or $v(x) \leqq u(x) \leqq w(x)$ for $x \varepsilon B$.

2. Iteration procedure and comparison of different fixed-point theorems.

The calculation of a suitable interval $M = [v,w]$ can be carried out by the iteration procedure

(2.1) $$v_1 = T_1 v_o + T_2 w_o; \quad w_1 = T_1 w_o + T_2 v_o .$$

If the conditions

(2.2) $$v_o \leqq v_1 \leqq w_1 \leqq w_o$$

are satisfied, one can easily see, that (Schröder [59]) $TM \subset M$. This gives an error estimation for the approximate solution

(2.3) $$\hat{u} = \frac{1}{2} (v_1 + w_1) .$$

One wishes to get good error bounds; for this purpose, let v_o, w_o depend on certain parameters a_ν, b_μ

(2.4) $v_o = v_o(x,a_1,\dots,a_p)$, $w_o = w_o\ (x,b_1,\dots,b_q)$

and determine the a_ν, b_μ from the optimization problems

(2.5) $0 \le w_1 - v_1 \le \delta$; $v_o \le v_1$; $w_1 \le w_o$; $\delta = \text{Min}$.

The described procedure was applied to many problems and tested for numerical examples on computers. Compare for instance for boundary value problems: Collatz [66], [81], for nonlinear vibrations: Reissig [69], Walter [70] a.o.

The Schauder theorem is often for numerical purposes more suitable as the well-known classical fixed point theorem of Banach for contractive mappings, for which one usually needs the knowledge of a Lipschitz-constant $K < 1$ (compare f.i. Collatz [66]).

Example: We consider a very simple nonlinear integral equation of Urysohn-type

(2.6) $$u(x) = Tu(x) = \lambda \int_0^1 \frac{dt}{1+x^2+[u(t)]^2}$$

λ is a given positive constant, and we ask for a nonnegative solution $u(x)$. The operator T is antitone: $Tf = T_2 f$; $T_1 f = 0$. Only for illustration we take in (2.1) v_0, w_0 as constants; also a may be constant:

$$Ta = \frac{\lambda}{1+x^2+a^2};$$

with $v_o = 0$ and formally $w_o = "\infty"$ we get from (2.1), fig 1

$$w_1 = Tv_o = \frac{\lambda}{1+x^2}, \quad v_1 = Tw_o = 0$$

and (2.2) is "formally" satisfied. One can avoid the symbol "∞" by using v_j, w_j instead of $\hat{v}_j, \hat{w}_j$:

(2.7) $$\hat{w}_0 = \lambda,\ \hat{v}_1 = T\hat{w}_0 = \frac{\lambda}{1+\lambda^2+x^2},\ \hat{v}_o = \frac{\lambda}{2+\lambda^2},$$

$$\hat{w}_1 = T\hat{v}_o = \frac{\lambda}{1+\left(\frac{\lambda}{2+\lambda^2}\right)^2+x^2} \quad \text{fig. 2}$$

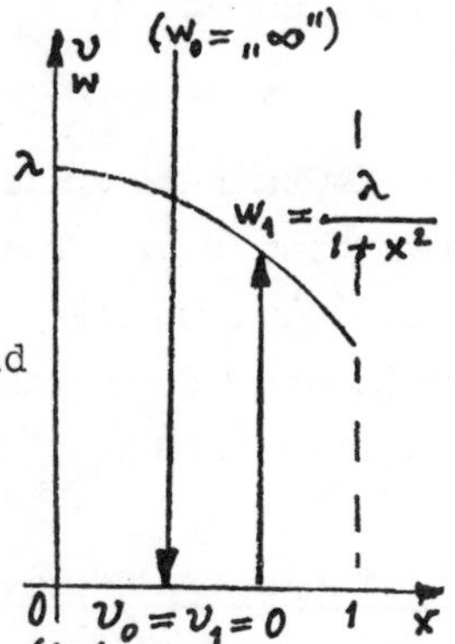

fig.1

and again (2.2) is satisfied. Therefore the Schauder-theorem gives the existence of a solution u(x) of (2.6) in the strip

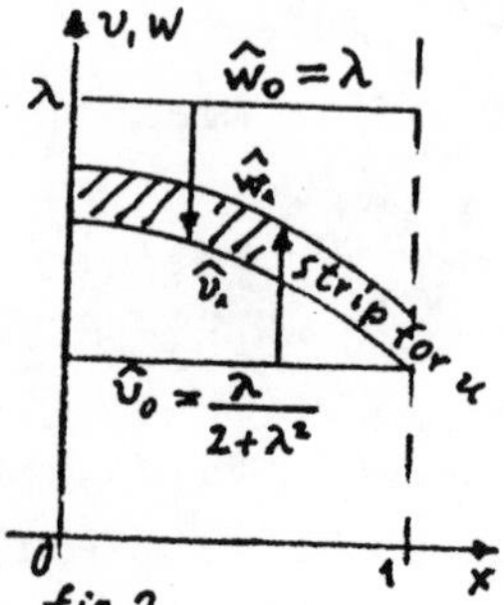

fig.2

(2.8) $\hat{v}_1 \leq u(x) \leq \hat{w}_1$

for every $\lambda > 0$; the contractive mapping-theorem insures the solution only for $\lambda > 0$ which are sufficiently small, for $\lambda < \lambda_0$, that means in a finite interval, otherwise the Lipschitz-constant K, which is proportional to λ, becomes > 1.

The bounds (2.7) (2.8) are very rough; here it was only the purpose to show that the Schauder-theorem is useful for arbitrarely large λ; of course it is easy to improve the accuracy and to get better bounds by introducing several parameters as in (2.4), for instance

$$v_0(x) = [a_0+a_1x^2]^{1/2}, \quad w_0(x) = [b_0+b_1x^2]^{1/2},$$

or to use the

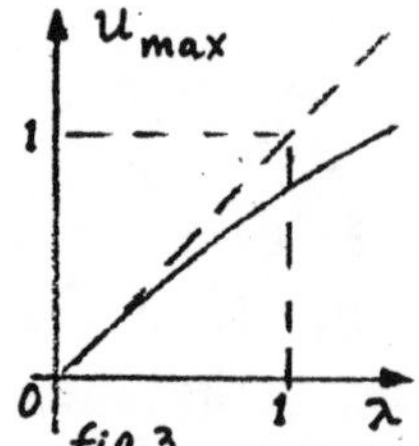

fig.3

Algorithm: Divide the interval B (of Nr.1) in to subdomains $B_1,\ldots,B_s$. Suppose: on has calculated approximate solutions v_j, w_j with (2.2). Take as new starting elements $\tilde{v}_0, \tilde{w}_0$ functions, constant in every subdomain B_σ:

$$\tilde{v}_o = (\operatorname*{Min}_{x\varepsilon B_\sigma} v_1(x)) \text{ for } x \varepsilon B_\sigma, \quad \tilde{w}_o = (\operatorname*{Max}_{x\varepsilon B_\sigma} w_1(x)) \text{ for } x \varepsilon B_\sigma$$

In certain cases it is easier to calculate $\tilde{v}_1, \tilde{w}_1$ with (2.1) (writing $\tilde{v}_j, \tilde{w}_j$ instead of v_j, w_j) as to use more parameters a_ν, b_μ in (2.4); on has then $\tilde{v}_1 \leq u \leq \tilde{w}_1$.
This procedure was used in the above example (2.6) fig. 3 shows the function u_{max} in dependence of λ.

3. Singularity in a threedimensional problem

The method of Nr.1 was applied also for different types of singular boundary value problems, f.i. for twodimensional problems, the ideal flow in a stream with breakwater, fig. 4, Collatz [81], the testproblem of Whiteman-Babuska "crack-problem" fig. 5 (Collatz [82]) and many other problems.

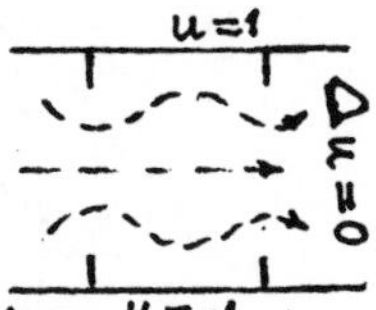

fig.4

Here we consider a problem with a singularity in the three-dimensional space. (Dobrowolski [83], Tolksdorf [83], Whiteman [83], Neta [84], Schnack [84] a.o.). The function u(x,y,z) in the x-y-z-space may satisfy the Laplace-equation

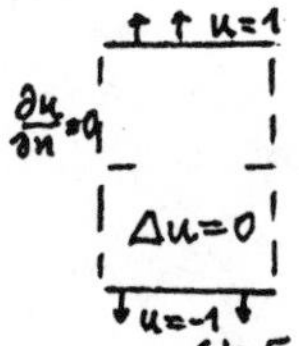

fig.5

$$(3.1)\quad \Delta u = \frac{\partial^2 u}{\partial x^2} + \frac{\partial^2 u}{\partial x^2} + \frac{\partial^2 u}{\partial z^2} = 0 \text{ in } B$$

and the boundary conditions on ∂B (fig. 6)

$$(3.2)\begin{cases} u = \frac{1}{2}(1-z^2)^2 & \text{for } x=-1 \quad \text{(boundary part } \Gamma_1) \\ u = 1 & \text{for } x=1 \quad \text{(boundary part } \Gamma_2) \\ u = 1 \text{ for } q \le x \le 1, & y=0,\ |z| \le 1 \quad \text{(boundary part } \Gamma_3) \\ \frac{\partial u}{\partial n} = 0 \text{ for } |y| = 1 & \text{and for } |z| = 1 \quad \text{(boundary part } \Gamma_4) \end{cases}$$

$B + \partial B$ is the closed cube $|x| \le 1$, $|x| \le 1$, $|z| \le 1$.
q = const. given, $0 \le q < 1$.

u(x,y,z) may be interpreted as temperature in a room B; the temperature u is given on the outer part Γ_1, Γ_2 and on the inner "wall" Γ_3. (In another paper Collatz [84], u=0 on Γ_1 is prescribed; then u depends only on x and y; but here u depends also on z, and therefore u is a threedimensional distribution of the temperature).

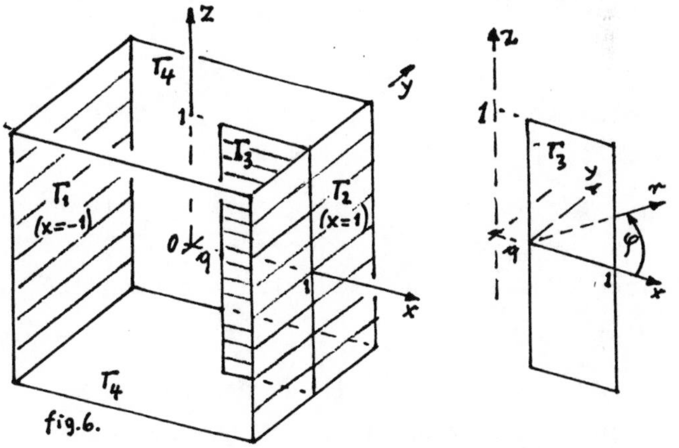

fig.6.

We write $v_o=\underline{v}$ and $w_o=\overline{v}$ as lower and upper bounds for u and take for both bounds the expression

$$(3.3)\qquad v = \sum_{j=1}^{n} \alpha_j\psi_j + \sum_{j=1}^{n} \beta_j\rho_j$$

with the singular functions

$$(3.4)\qquad \psi_j = r^{j-\frac{1}{2}} \sin\ [(j-\tfrac{1}{2})\phi], \qquad j=1,2,\ldots$$

here r,ϕ are polarcoordinates $[x=r(\cos\phi)+q,\ y=r \sin \phi]$. ρ_j are harmonic polynomials satisfying the symmetries of the problem

$$(3.5)\quad \rho_1=1,\ \rho_2=x,\ \rho_{2k-1}=\mathrm{Re}(x+iy)^k,\ \rho_{2k}=\mathrm{Re}(x+iz)^k,\ (k=2,3,\ldots);$$

We have $\Delta\psi_j=\Delta\rho_j=\Delta v=0$ $(j=1,2,\ldots)$ for arbitrary α_j,β_j. There are also other harmonic polynomials with the prescribed symmetry f.i.

$$y^4 - 8y^2z^2 + z^4 \quad \text{or} \quad 6xy^2z^2 - xy^4 - xz^4;$$

but calculation on the computer showed, that for all polynomials containing y and z, the corresponding coefficients β vanish (observation by Mr. U. Grothkopf).

The numerical bounds are for a small wall $q = \frac{1}{2}$ and for $s = 2$ and polynomials of degree ≤ 8 :

$$|\overline{v}-\underline{v}| \leq 0.015901$$

The bounds for the greater wall $q = 0$ (reaching to the midth of the cube) (fig. 6) were for $s = 2$ and

for polynomials of degree ≤ 8: $|\overline{v}-\underline{v}| \leq 0.022928$ and
for polynomials of degree ≤ 10 $|\overline{v}-\underline{v}| \leq 0.020402$

A discretization was used with the meshsize $h=0.05$.

The arithmetic mean $\hat{u} = \frac{1}{2}(\overline{v}-\underline{v})$ has the error bound

$$|\hat{u} - u| \leq 0.010201$$

The table gives the values of the coefficient a_ν, b_μ for $\overline{v}$ (for $\underline{v}$ are slight differences).

I thank Mr. Uwe Grothkopf very much for the careful computations on a computer.

a_1	-0.564108808
a_2	0.195211040
b_1	1.018408942
b_2	-0.054725185
b_3	0.013180856
b_4	0.050236776
b_5	0.004126114
b_6	-0.055438222
b_7	0.003645525
b_8	0.044080480
b_9	0.000599295
b_{10}	-0.025997838
b_{11}	-0.000734364
b_{12}	0.014285102
b_{13}	-0.000107276
b_{14}	-0.005278853
b_{15}	0.000020723
b_{16}	0.002301383

Prof. Dr. Lothar Collatz
Institut für Angewandte Mathematik
Universität Hamburg
Bundesstraße 55
D-2000 Hamburg 13
Germany

References

Bohl, E. [74] Monotonie, Lösbarkeit und Numerik bei Operatorglei- gleichungen, Springer, 1974, 255p.

Collatz, L. [66] Funktionalanalysis and Numerical mathematics, Academic Press, 1966, 473p.

Collatz, L. [71] Some applications of Functional analysis to Analysis particularly to Nonlinear Integral equations, Proc. Nonlin. Funct. Anal. Applic. Acad. Press, 1971, 1-43.

Collatz, L. [81] Anwendung von Monotoniesätzen zur Einschließung der Lösungen von Gleichungen; Jahrbuch Überblicke der Mathematik 1981, 189-225.

Collatz, L. [82] Some numerical Test Problems with Singularities; in: The Mathem. of Finite Elements and Applications, MAFELAP 4 (1982), ed. Whiteman, 65-76.

Collatz, L. [84] Approximation of solution of differential equations and of their derivatives, Proc. Construct. Th. of functions, Varna 1984, ed. Sendov.

Dobrowolski, M. [83] Vortrag Tagung: Singularities and Constructive Methods for their treatment. Proc. Oberwolfach 21.-26. November 1983.

Kantorowitsch, L.W. - G.P. Akilow [64] Funktionalanalysis in normierten Räumen, Acad. Verl. Berlin, 1964, 622p.

Neta, B. [84] Adaptive Method for the Numerical Solution of Fredholm Integral Equations of the Second Kind; Part II: Singular Kernels. Report No. INTT-29, March 1984, 16p. Dep. Math. Texas Techn. Univ. Lubbock, Texas 79409.

Reissig, R. [69] Anwendung von Fixpunktsätzen auf das Problem der periodischen Lösungen bei nichtautonomen Systemen, DLR Forschungsbericht 69-53 (1969), 63p.

Schauder, J. [30] Der Fixpunktsatz in Funktionenräumen, Studia Math. 2 (1930) 171-182.

Schnack, E. [84] Vortrag MAFELAP 1.-4. May 1984, Proc. ed. J.R. Whiteman

Schröder, J. [59] Anwendung von Fixpunktsätzen bei der numerischen Behandlung nichtlinearer Gleichungen in halbgeordneten Räumen, Arch.Rat.Mech.Anal. 4 (1959) 177-192.

Schröder, J. [80] Operator inequalities, Acad. Press, (1980) 367p.

Tolksdorf, P. [83] Vortrag Tagung: Singularities and Constructive Methods for their treatment. Proc. Oberwolfach 21.-26. Nov. 1983.

Walter, W. [70] Differential and Integral Inequalities, Springer (1970), 352p.

Whiteman, J.R. [83] Vortrag Tagung: Singularities and Constructive Methods for their treatment. Proc. Oberwolfach 21.-26. Nov. 1983, see also: E. Stephan - J.R. Whiteman: Singularities of the Laplacian at Corners and edges of three dimensional domains. Bicon 81/1 Institute of Computational Mathematics, Brunel University, Uxbridge, U.K.

International Series of
Numerical Mathematics, Vol. 73

TWO METHODS FOR SOLVING THE INVERSE SCATTERING PROBLEM FOR TIME-HARMONIC ACOUSTIC WAVES

David Colton*

Department of Mathematical Sciences
University of Delaware
Newark, Delaware 19716
U.S.A.

I. Introduction.

The inverse scattering problem we are considering in this paper is to determine the shape of an acoustically soft obstacle from a knowledge of the time-harmonic incident wave and the far field pattern of the scattered wave, where the frequency is assumed to be in the "resonant" region, i.e. high frequency asymptotic methods are not available. For a survey of the research done in this area, we refer the reader to the monograph of COLTON and KRESS [4] as well as the survey paper by COLTON [2]. Our aim is to provide methods that are numerically implementable, and the basic problem in trying to do this is the fact that the inverse scattering problem is both nonlinear and improperly posed ([2],[4]). In this paper, we shall present two methods for solving the inverse scattering problem. The first of these is based on the use of integral equations and has been numerically implemented by KIRSCH [7] (see also [2]). Our second method avoids the use of integral equations and is based on the theory of Herglotz wave functions (c.f. [6]). Numerical experiments using this method are presently being carried out, but as yet we have no results to report. Hence, the practicality of our second method has yet to be established.

Keeping the above comments in mind, we now turn to a precise mathematical formulation of the inverse scattering problem we are considering. Let D be a bounded, connected domain in the plane with Hölder continuous boundary

*This research was partially supported by AFOSR Grant 81-0103 and NSF Grant DMS-8320550.

∂D and let the incident field u^i be given by $u^i = \exp(ik\underset{\sim}{x}\cdot\underset{\sim}{\alpha})$ where $\underset{\sim}{x} \in \mathbb{R}^2$, $k > 0$ is the wave number and $\underset{\sim}{\alpha}$ is a fixed unit vector. If we denote the scattered field by u^s and define the total field u by $u = u^i + u^s$, then the direct scattering problem for an acoustically soft obstacle D is to find a solution $u \in C^2(\mathbb{R}^2\backslash\overline{D}) \cap C^\circ(\mathbb{R}^2\backslash D)$ of the Helmholtz equation

$$\Delta_2 u + k^2 u = 0 \tag{1.1}$$

in $\mathbb{R}^2\backslash\overline{D}$ such that

$$u = 0 \quad \text{on} \quad \partial D \tag{1.2}$$

and u^s satisfies the Sommerfeld radiation condition

$$\lim_{r\to\infty} r^{1/2} \left(\frac{\partial u^s}{\partial r} - iku^s\right) = 0 \tag{1.3}$$

uniformly in all directions where $r = |\underset{\sim}{x}|$. Under these conditions, it is easily shown ([4]) that u^s has the asymptotic behavior

$$u^s(r,\theta) = \frac{e^{ikr}}{\sqrt{r}} F(\theta;k,\underset{\sim}{\alpha}) + O(r^{-3/2}) \tag{1.4}$$

where (r,θ) denote polar coordinates and F is known as the <u>far field pattern</u> of the scattered wave u^s. The inverse scattering problem we are considering here is given F and u^i to determine ∂D.

From Green's formula and the asymptotic behavior of the Hankel function $H_0^{(1)}$ we can easily show ([4]) that

$$F(\theta;k,\underset{\sim}{\alpha}) = -\frac{e^{i\pi/4}}{\sqrt{8\pi k}} \int_{\partial D} \frac{\partial u}{\partial \nu}(\underset{\sim}{y}) \exp\left[-ik\rho\cos(\theta-\phi)\right] ds(\underset{\sim}{y}) \tag{1.5}$$

where $\underset{\sim}{x} = re^{i\theta}$, $\underset{\sim}{y} = \rho e^{i\phi}$, ν is the unit outward normal to ∂D, and $\partial u/\partial\nu$ is the unique solution of the Fredholm integral equation

$$\frac{\partial u}{\partial \nu}(\underset{\sim}{x}) + \frac{i}{2} \int_{\partial D} \frac{\partial u}{\partial \nu}(\underset{\sim}{y}) \frac{\partial}{\partial \nu(\underset{\sim}{x})} H_0^{(1)}(k|\underset{\sim}{x}-\underset{\sim}{y}|)\, ds(\underset{\sim}{y}) = 2\frac{\partial u^i}{\partial \nu}(\underset{\sim}{x}) \; ; \quad \underset{\sim}{x} \in \partial D \tag{1.6}$$

where for the sake of simplicity, we have assumed that k^2 is not an eigenvalue of the interior Neumann problem. The strong nonlinear nature of the inverse scattering problem is evident from (1.5) and (1.6). Furthermore, from (1.5), we see that the far field pattern F is an entire function of the angle θ, and hence arbitrarily small perturbations of F lead to a problem which has no solution at all, i.e. the inverse scattering problem is improperly posed. Hence, in order to arrive at a stable approximation scheme, it will be necessary to introduce certain a priori information in order to regularize our problem.

II. A Method for Solving the Inverse Scattering Problem

In this section, we shall outline a stable method for solving the inverse scattering problem as first presented by ANGELL, COLTON and KIRSCH [1]. Let $\underset{\sim}{T}: \partial D \to F$ denote the operator defined by (1.5) and (1.6). Our approach is to construct an optimal solution to the operator equation $\underset{\sim}{T}[\partial D] = F$ in the sense that $||\underset{\sim}{T}[\partial D]-F||$ is minimized where $||\cdot||$ denotes the norm on $L^2[0,2\pi]$. The existence of an optimal solution will be guaranteed if it can be shown that $\underset{\sim}{T}$ is continuous and we restrict ∂D to lie in a compact set of a suitable metric space. To this end, we assume that D is starlike with respect to the origin and ∂D is parameterized in the form $r = r(\theta)$, $\theta \in [0,2\pi]$, and let U be any compact subset of

$$\{r \in C^{1,\beta}[0,2\pi]: \ ||r||_{1+\beta} \leq M, \ r(\theta) \geq m \ \text{ for } \ \theta \in [0,2\pi]\}$$

where m and M are a priori known positive constants and $C^{1,\beta}[0,2\pi]$ denotes the space of Hölder continuously differentiable periodic functions with index β, $0 < \beta \leq 1$. Geometrically, this implies that we are assuming a priori that the unknown obstacle D is starlike with respect to the origin, contains a disk of radius m, is contained in a disk of radius M, and ∂D has a uniformly bounded Hölder continuous tangent. Under these conditions, it is possible to prove the following theorems [1]:

Theorem: The minimization problem $\min\limits_{\partial D \in U} ||\underset{\sim}{T}[\partial D]-F||$ has a solution.

Theorem: Let $\Phi(F)$ be the set of all solutions of the minimization problem $\min\limits_{\partial D \in U} ||\underset{\sim}{T}[\partial D]-F||$ where ∂D is parameterized by $r = r(\theta)$. Then if $F_n \to F$ in $L^2[0,2\pi]$, $r_n \in \Phi(F_n)$, there exists a convergent subsequence of $\{r_n\}$ and every limit point lies in $\Phi(F)$.

The numerical implementation of the above scheme has been carried out by KIRSCH [7]. The approach used is to compute the Fréchet derivative of $\underset{\sim}{T}$ and apply a Newton-like procedure. For technical reasons (the Fréchet derivative is easily computable) the given data is chosen to be the total scattering cross section σ instead of the far field pattern, where σ is defined by

$$\sigma(k;\underset{\sim}{\alpha}) = \int_0^{2\pi} |F(\theta;k,\underset{\sim}{\alpha})|^2 \, d\theta \quad .$$

Numerical computations using the modulus of the far field pattern as the given data have been carried out by ROGER [8]. The difficulties in the approach for numerically solving the inverse scattering problem as described in this section are that, except for the case of the total scattering cross section as given data, the Fréchet derivative is difficult to compute, and an integral equation has to be solved at each step of the iterative process. The approach to be described in the following section was designed in an attempt to avoid these difficulties.

III. A Second Method for Solving the Inverse Scattering Problem

Our second approach for solving the inverse scattering problem is based on the representation (1.5) for the far field pattern. In particular, if $g \in L^2[0,2\pi]$ and g is periodic of period 2π, then from (1.5) we have that

$$\int_0^{2\pi} F(\theta;k,\underset{\sim}{\alpha})g(\theta)d\theta = -\frac{e^{i\pi/4}}{\sqrt{8\pi k}} \int_{\partial D} \frac{\partial u}{\partial \nu}(\underset{\sim}{y})v(\underset{\sim}{y};k)ds(\underset{\sim}{y}) \tag{3.1}$$

where

$$v(\underset{\sim}{y};k) = v(\rho,\phi;k) = \int_0^{2\pi} g(\theta)\exp[-ik\rho\cos(\theta-\phi)] \, d\theta \quad . \tag{3.2}$$

From [6], we see that v is an entire <u>Herglotz wave function</u>, i.e. a solution of the Helmholtz equation defined in all of $\mathbb{R}^2$ such that

$$\lim_{r\to\infty} \frac{1}{r} \iint_{|\underset{\sim}{x}|\le r} |v(\underset{\sim}{x})|^2 \, d\underset{\sim}{x} < \infty \quad . \tag{3.3}$$

As in Section II, we shall reformulate the inverse scattering problem as a problem in constrained optimization, where now we base our approach on the observation that if v is an eigenfunction of D then the right hand side of (3.1) is identically zero. In particular, we note that the far field pattern F and scattering obstacle D are linked by the function g rather than by an integral equation as in our first method.

To be more precise, we assume that D is starlike with respect to the origin and ∂D is parameterized in the form $\rho = \rho(\phi)$ where $0 < a \le \rho(\phi) \le b$ for some positive constants a and b. Under this assumption, we can determine an interval $I = I(a,b)$ such that the first eigenvalue of the Laplacian is contained in I (c.f. [5]). On g, we impose the restriction

$$(g,1) = \int_0^{2\pi} g(\theta)\, d\theta = 1 \tag{3.4}$$

in order to guarantee that v is not identically zero and define the sets U_1 and U_2 by

$$U_1 = \{g \in L^2[0,2\pi]:\ g \text{ periodic},\ \|g\| \le M,\ (g,1) = 1\}$$
$$U_2 = \{\rho \in C[0,2\pi]:\ \rho \text{ periodic},\ 0 < a \le \rho(\phi) \le b \text{ for } \phi \in [0,2\pi]\}$$

where M is a positive constant. We can now define the minimization problem

$$\mu(F,M) = \min_{(k^2,g,\rho)\in U} \{ \left| \int_0^{2\pi} F(\theta;k,\alpha)g(\theta)d\theta \right| + \int_0^{2\pi} |v(\rho(\phi),\phi;k)|^2 d\phi \} \tag{3.5}$$

where U is a compact set of $I \times U_1 \times U_2$. From the compactness of U and the continuity of the integrals in (3.5) as a function of k, g and ρ, we can immediately deduce the following theorem, where continuity is meant in the sense of Section II:

<u>Theorem</u>: $\mu(F,M)$ exists and if (k^2,g,ρ) is a solution of (3.5) then ρ depends continuously on F.

In our first method, it was obvious that if $\partial D \in U$ was a solution of the inverse scattering problem with far field pattern F, then $\min_{\partial D \in U} \|T[\partial D]-F\| = 0$. In the present case, we have the following analogous result:

<u>Theorem</u>: Suppose ∂D: $\rho = \rho(\phi)$ is a solution of the inverse scattering problem with far field pattern F such that $\rho \in C^{1,\beta}[0,2\pi]$. Then $\lim_{M\to\infty} \mu(F,M) = 0$.

<u>Proof</u>: From the results of [9], we can approximate any eigenfunction of $\Delta_2 u + k^2 u = 0$ in D uniformly in $\bar{D}$ by an entire Herglotz wave function v. Expressing v in the form (3.2), we see from (3.1) that

$\mu(F,M)$ can be made arbitrarily small by approximating the eigenfunction to a sufficiently high degree of accuracy. In this procedure, M tends to infinity unless the eigenfunction is an entire Herglotz wave function. (For a detailed examination of this second situation, see [3].) In either case, the theorem is established.

We conclude by making several observations on the above method for solving the inverse scattering problem. To begin with, as already mentioned, this approach has yet to be numerically tested. As is well known, many reasonable analytic procedures can fail to meet the test of numerical practicality! Subject to this warning, the advantages of our second method are that the Fréchet derivative is easy to compute and the use of integral equations is avoided (in conflict with the spirit of this conference!). The obvious disadvantages are that it is now necessary to know the far field pattern F for an interval of k values and that $\mu(F,M)$ depends on the constant M which is not known a priori.

REFERENCES

[1] Angell, T. S., Colton, D., and Kirsch, A., The three dimensional inverse scattering problem for acoustic waves. J. Diff. Eqns. 46 (1982), 46-58.

[2] Colton, D., The inverse scattering problem for time-harmonic acoustic waves. SIAM Review, 26 (1984), 323-350.

[3] Colton, D., and Kirsch, A., Dense sets and far field patterns in acoustic wave propagation. SIAM J. Math. Anal., to appear.

[4] Colton, D., and Kress, R., Integral Equation Methods in Scattering Theory, John Wiley, New York, 1983.

[5] Garabedian, P., Partial Differential Equations, John Wiley, New York, 1964.

[6] Hartman, P., and Wilcox, C., On solutions of the Helmholtz equation in exterior domains. Math. Zeit. 75 (1961), 228-255.

[7] Kirsch, A., A numerical method for an inverse scattering problem. Tech. Report No. 127A, University of Delaware Applied Mathematics Institute, 1982.

[8] Roger, A., Newton-Kantorovich algorithm applied to an electromagnetic inverse problem. IEEE Trans. Ant. and Prop. AP-29 (1981), 232-238.

[9] Vekua, I. N., New Methods for Solving Elliptic Equations, North-Holland, Amsterdam, 1967.

David Colton
Department of Mathematical Sciences
501 Ewing Hall
University of Delaware
Newark, Delaware
USA

International Series of
Numerical Mathematics, Vol. 73

BEYOND SUPERCONVERGENCE OF COLLOCATION METHODS FOR VOLTERRA INTEGRAL EQUATIONS OF THE FIRST KIND

P. P. B. Eggermont

University of Delaware

We discuss superconvergence aspects of collocation methods for Volterra integral equations of the first kind. If piecewise polynomials of degree $\le p$ are used, then convergence of order $p + 2$ is best possible. We show here that one may perform some postprocessing on the collocation solution to obtain convergence of order $p + 3$. This possibility arises because of the oscillating error in the collocation solution. The relevance of superconvergence techniques to a third order Runge-Kutta method is also discussed.

1. Introduction

We consider Volterra integral equations of the first kind

(1.1) $$Vf(x) = \int_0^x k(x,y)f(y)dy = g(x) \ , \quad x \in [0,1] \ ,$$

where k is continuously differentiable on $T = \{(x,y): \ 0 \le y \le x \le 1\}$, and $k(x,x) = 1$. The collocation methods are as follows. Partition $[0,1]$ into n subintervals $\sigma_i = [i/n,(i+1)/n]$, $i = 0, 1, \ldots, n-1$, and choose $p + 1$ collocation points per subinterval σ_i,

(1.2) $$x_{iq} = (i+\theta_q)/n, \quad q = 0, 1, \ldots, p,$$

with $0 < \theta_0 < \theta_1 < \ldots < \theta_p \le 1$, and approximate (1.1) by

(1.3) $$\begin{cases} Vf_n(x_{iq}) = g(x_{iq}), & \forall i,q \ , \\ f_n \in S_n = \{\phi: \ \forall j(\phi|_{\sigma_j} \text{ is polynomial of degree} \le p)\} \ . \end{cases}$$

The following is known about the convergence of the above methods.

(i) If $\prod_q (1-\theta_q)/\theta_q < 1$ then $||f_n - f||_\infty = O(n^{-p-1})$, for $n \to \infty$, provided $f \in C^{p+1}$ (DeHoog and Weiss [3], Brunner [1]).

(ii) If $f \in C^{p+2}$, $\theta_p = 1$ and $u_0 < u_1 < \dots < u_p$ are defined by

$$\prod_r (x-u_r) = (p+2)^{-1} \frac{d}{dx} \{x \prod_q (x-\theta_q)\} \tag{1.4}$$

then

$$\max_{j,r} |f_n(y_{jr}) - f(y_{jr})| = O(n^{-p-2}), \quad n \to \infty \quad , \tag{1.5}$$

where $y_{jr} = (j+u_r)/n$, $r = 0, 1, \dots, p$; $j = 0, 1, \dots, n-1$. This is known as superconvergence (Brunner [2], Eggermont [4]).

(iii) Higher order convergence at selected points improving on (1.5) is in general impossible (Brunner [2]) despite the fact that we are free to choose $0 < \theta_0 < \theta_1 < \dots < \theta_{p-1} < 1$ any which way we want.

However, higher order approximations to f at selected points are obtainable from f_n alone, as follows. It turns out that for $f \in C^{p+3}$, and provided

$$\int_0^1 y \prod_q (y-\theta_q)dy = 0, \quad \text{or} \quad \int_0^1 y \prod_r (y-u_r)dy = 0 \ , \tag{1.6}$$

we have the asymptotic expansion

$$f_n(y_{jr}) - f(y_{jr}) = c(j/n)u_r \prod_q (u_r - \theta_q)n^{-p-2} + O(n^{-p-3}) \ , \tag{1.7}$$

where $c(x)$ is continuously differentiable. Since the u_r and θ_q interlace, by (1.4), this implies that the error in f_n is oscillating on each σ_j. By suitable Lagrange interpolation on at least $p+3$ points $(y_{jr}, f_n(y_{jr}))$ we then obtain approximations to f with error $O(n^{-p-3})$.

In this paper, we prove (1.7) for the simple case of numerical differentiation, and indicate the proof for the general case. The case where (1.3) is replaced by the "usual" quadrature scheme of DeHoog and Weiss [3] is given in [6]. We also show that the techniques used for proving (1.7) in the general case are useful in proving the optimal rate of convergence of Keech's Runge-Kutta method [7] under minimal smoothness conditions.

2. Numerical differentiation

We treat the case $k(x,y) \equiv 1$ in detail. Let $\mathcal{V}$ in this case be denoted by $\mathcal{W}$, and consider

(2.1) $\quad \mathcal{W}f_n(x_{iq}) = g(x_{iq}), \quad \forall i,q, \quad \text{with} \quad f_n \in S_n$.

We assume $\theta_p = 1$, and that (1.4) holds. To solve (2.1) for f_n, note that $\mathcal{W}f_n$ is a continuous, piecewise polynomial function of degree $\leq p + 1$, and that $\mathcal{W}f_n(0) = 0$. On each σ_i we know $\mathcal{W}f_n$ at $p + 2$ points, including the two endpoints, so we can just do Lagrange interpolation on each σ_i. We denote this by

(2.2) $\quad \mathcal{W}f_n = \mathcal{P}_n g$

and f_n is obtained by differentiation. To determine the accuracy, let $f \in C^{p+3}$, and let ψ_n be the unique element of S_n which interpolates f at the y_{jr}. Then

(2.3) $\quad f_n - \psi_n = n^{-p-1}\ \Phi_n + n^{-p-2}\ \Psi_n + R_n$,

where, for $y \in \sigma_j$,

(2.4) $\quad \Phi_n(y) = c_j\ \Phi(ny-j)$, $\quad \Psi_n(y) = d_j\ \Psi(ny-j)$

in which

(2.5) $\quad c_j = f^{(p+1)}((j+\alpha)/n)/(p+1)!$, $\quad d_j = f^{(p+2)}(j/n)/(p+2)!$,

with $\alpha = \sum_r u_r/(p+2)$, and

(2.6) $\quad \Phi(y) = \prod_r (y-u_r)$, $\quad \Psi(y) = y\ \Phi(y)$,

and

(2.7) $\quad ||R_n|| = \mathcal{O}(n^{-p-3}||f^{(p+3)}||)$.

Since for all collocation points x_{iq} ,

(2.8) $\quad [\mathcal{W}(f_n-\psi_n)](x_{iq}) = [\mathcal{W}(f-\psi_n)](x_{iq})$,

and since $f_n - \psi_n \in S_n$, we are again solving a problem of the form (2.1). First, we work out the right hand side of (2.8). We have

(2.9) $$\mathcal{W}\Psi_n(x_{iq}) = \sum_{j=0}^{i-1} d_j \int_{\sigma_j} \Psi(ny-j)dy + d_i \int_{i/n}^{x_{iq}} \Psi(ny-j)dy ,$$

and each of the integrals over σ_j vanishes by (1.4) and (1.6). Consequently

(2.10) $$\mathcal{W}\Psi_n(x_{iq}) = n^{-1} \int_0^{\theta_q} \Psi(y)dy , \quad q = 0, 1, \ldots, p .$$

Similarly, we have from (1.4) that $\mathcal{W}\Phi_n(x_{iq}) = 0$, $\forall i,q$. Thus we have

(2.11) $[\mathcal{W}(f_n-\psi_n)](x_{iq}) = n^{-p-3} d_i\, A(\theta_q) + [\mathcal{W}R_n](x_{iq})$,

where we may take $A(x)$ to be the unique polynomial of degree $\leq p+1$ for which

(2.12) $$\begin{cases} A(0) = 0 \\ A(\theta_q) = \int_0^{\theta_q} \Psi(y)dy\ , \quad q = 0, 1, \dots, p\ . \end{cases}$$

Then it is easily verified that for $x \in \sigma_i$,

(2.13) $[P_n\mathcal{W}(f_n-\psi_n)](x) = n^{-p-3} d_i A(nx-i) + P_n\mathcal{W}R_n(x)$,

and so after differentiation at the y_{jr} ,

(2.14) $f_n(y_{jr}) - \psi_n(y_{jr}) = n^{-p-2} d_i A'(u_r) + \frac{d}{dx} P_n\mathcal{W}R_n(y_{jr})$

In [4,§4.1] it has been shown that $\frac{d}{dx} P_n\mathcal{W}$ is bounded, uniformly in n, as a map from L^∞ onto S_n (as subspace of L^∞). Consequently, the second term in (2.14) is $\mathcal{O}(||R_n||)$. The verification of

(2.16) $A'(u_r) = -(p+3)^{-1}\ u_r \prod_q (u_r-\theta_q)$

is left to the reader. Together with (2.14), this then shows (1.7).

3. The general case

The treatment of the general case consists of two more or less independent parts, viz. the treatment of the consistency error, and the "projection method" aspects. These two parts combined yield the asymptotic expansion.

3.1 The consistency error

The result we now state concerns a special representation of the consistency error.

Lemma 3.1. Let $f \in C^{p+3}$ and ψ_n as before. Then

$$[\mathcal{V}(f-\psi_n)](x_{iq}) = n^{-p-2}\ \mathcal{V}\tilde{\Psi}_n(x_{iq}) + \mathcal{V}\tilde{R}_n(x_{iq})\ ,$$

with $\tilde{\Psi}_n(y) = e(j/n)\ \Psi(ny-j)$, $y \in \sigma_j$, where $e(x)$ is continuously differentiable, and $||\tilde{R}_n|| = \mathcal{O}(n^{-p-3})$, $n \to \infty$.

Proof outline. Using (1.4), (1.7) and (2.3), it is not hard to show that $\mathcal{V}\Phi_n(xiq) = n^{-1} \mathcal{U}_n\tilde{\Phi}_n(xiq)$ with $\tilde{\Phi}_n(y) = (ny-j)\Phi_n(y)$, $y \in \sigma_j$, and $\mathcal{U}_n$ is a Volterra integral operator with kernel $u_n(x,y) = (k(x,y)-k(x,j/n))/(y-j/n)$, $y \in \sigma_j$. Now note that $\tilde{\Phi}_n$ is of the same form as Ψ_n in (2.4). Writing $\mathcal{U}_n\tilde{\Phi}_n = \mathcal{V}\{\mathcal{V}^{-1}\mathcal{U}_n\tilde{\Phi}_n\}$ and working out $\mathcal{V}^{-1}\mathcal{U}_n\tilde{\Phi}_n$ using (1.7), and similarly for Ψ_n, then results in the lemma. For the full details, see [6].

3.2 Projection method aspects

If the equations (1.3) have a unique solution f_n, then the collocation method is equivalent to a projection method

$$\mathcal{V}f_n = \mathcal{P}_n(\mathcal{V})g \tag{3.1}$$

where $\mathcal{P}_n(\mathcal{V})$ is a projector of the set of Lipschitz continuous functions onto $\mathcal{V}(S_n)$, see, e.g. [4], or Phillips [8]. The projector $\mathcal{P}_n(\mathcal{W})$ coincides with the piecewise Lagrange interpolator $\mathcal{P}_n$ of (2.2). From (3.1), with $g = \mathcal{V}f$, we then have

$$f_n = \mathcal{Q}_n(\mathcal{V})f \tag{3.2}$$

where

$$\mathcal{Q}_n(\mathcal{V}) = \mathcal{V}^{-1}\mathcal{P}_n(\mathcal{V})\mathcal{V} \quad . \tag{3.3}$$

The following result is very useful.

Lemma 3.2. If $k \in C^2(T)$ then for n large enough

$$||\mathcal{Q}_n(\mathcal{V})-\mathcal{Q}_n(\mathcal{W})|| = \mathcal{O}(n^{-1}) \ , \quad n \to \infty \ .$$

This result is an instance of an abstract result of Witsch [9] concerning the stability of projections under compact perturbations. For the details, see [6].

3.3 The asymptotic expansion

Let f_n be the solution of (1.2). Then $f_n - \psi_n = \mathcal{Q}_n(\mathcal{V})(f-\psi_n)$ and by Lemma 3.1 we get

$$f_n - \psi_n = n^{-p-2}\mathcal{Q}_n(\mathcal{V})\tilde{\Psi}_n + \mathcal{O}(||\mathcal{Q}_n(\mathcal{V})|| \ ||R_n||) \ , \tag{3.4}$$

and the big $\mathcal{O}$ term is $\mathcal{O}(n^{-p-3})$. Now, by Lemma 3.2

$$\mathcal{Q}_n(\mathcal{V})\tilde{\Psi}_n = \mathcal{Q}_n(\mathcal{W})\tilde{\Psi}_n + \mathcal{O}(n^{-1}||\tilde{\Psi}_n||) \ , \tag{3.5}$$

and $\mathcal{Q}_n(\mathcal{W})\tilde{\Psi}_n$ has essentially been computed in Section 2, viz.

(3.6) $\mathcal{Q}_n(W)\tilde{\Psi}_n(y_{jr}) = a(j/n)A'(u_r)$,

for some continuously differentiable function $a(x)$. Together with (3.4) and (3.5) this results in the expansion (1.7).

4. Some numerical results

The equations (1.3) are equivalent to a block-triangular system of linear equations

(4.1) $V_n r_n f_n = \rho_n g$

where

(4.2)
$$(r_n f_n)_{j(p+1)+r} = f_n(y_{jr});(\rho_n g)_{i(p+1)+q} = g(x_{iq}) ,$$
$$(V_n)_{i(p+1)+q,j(p+1)+r} = \int_{\sigma_j} k(x_{iq},y)\ell_r(ny-j)dy ,$$

with $i,j = 0, 1, \ldots, n-1$; $q,r = 0, 1, \ldots, p$. Unfortunately, the elements of V_n have to be approximated in general. The asymptotic expansion (1.7) still holds if V_n is replaced by $\overline{V}_n$ with

$$(\overline{V}_n)_{i(p+1)+q,j(p+1)+r} = k(x_{iq},y_{jr}) \int \ell_r(ny-j)dy ,$$

where the integral is over $\sigma_j \cap [0,x_{iq}]$.

The asymptotic expansion (1.7) is now used to construct approximations to f with error $\mathcal{O}(n^{-p-3})$ as follows. Choose $p = 2$. Let the u_r be the Gaussian integration points for $[0,1]$, and let the θ_q be the Lobatto points. Then (1.4) and (1.6) are satisfied. Let $B(x)$ be the polynomial of degree 4 which satisfies $B(-1+u_r) = A'(u_r)$, $r = 1,2$; $B(u_r) = A'(u_r)$, $r = 0, 1, 2$. Its four zeroes are given by $v_0 = 0.307400315012218$, $v_1 = 0.839943478056940$, $v_2 = -v_0$, $v_3 = -v_1$. If $\overline{f}_n$ is the solution of $\overline{V}_n r_n \overline{f}_n = \rho_n g$, let F_{nj} be the polynomial of degree ≤ 4 for which

(4.7)
$$\begin{cases} F_{nj}(y_{jr}) = \overline{f}_n(y_{jr}), & r = 0, 1, 2 \quad , \\ F_{nj}(y_{j-1,r}) = \overline{f}_n(y_{j-1,r}), & r = 1, 2 \quad . \end{cases}$$

Finally, let $z_{js} = (j+v_s)/n$, and set

$$(4.8)\qquad \begin{cases} r_n^I = \max\{|F_{nj}(z_{js})-f(z_{js})|:\quad s=0,1;\ j=1,2,\dots,n-1\} \\ r_n^{II} = \max\{|F_{nj}(z_{js})-f(z_{js})|:\quad s=2,3;\ j=1,2,\dots,n-1\} \end{cases} .$$

Then both r_n^I and r_n^{II} are $\mathcal{O}(n^{-5})$.

We illustrate this numerically with the equation

$$\int_0^x (1+x-y)f(y)dy = -1 + x + e^{-x}, \qquad x \in [0,1],$$

with solution $f(x) = xe^{-x}$. The results are in Table I.

Table I. Improving the accuracy.

n	$\|\|r_n(\bar{f}_n-f)\|\|$	Ratio	r_n^I	Ratio	r_n^{II}	Ratio
10	.16E-6		.35E-8		.52E-6	
		16		29.2		30.6
20	.10E-7		.12E-9		.17E-7	
		15.6		32.4		30.4
40	.64E-9		.37E-11		.56E-9	
order		4		5		5

Observe that although both r_n^I and r_n^{II} exhibit $\mathcal{O}(n^{-5})$ convergence, the results for r_n^{II} are worse than for r_n^I. This is due to the fact that the interpolation at z_{j0} and z_{j1} is much more stable than at z_{j2}, z_{j3}. This is illustrated by the values of the Lebesgue function which equal 1.72, 2.06, 2.81 and 37.9, respectively!

5. Superconvergence and Runge-Kutta methods

In this section, we discuss a proof of the optimal asymptotic rate of convergence under minimal smoothness conditions of Keech's third order semi-implicit Runge-Kutta method [7]. In [5], this author gave a unifying analysis of quadrature methods, which when applied to Keech's method (only) gives second order convergence. Here we show that the third order convergence follows from (an analogue of) Lemma 3.2.

Keech's method is as follows. Let $p = 2$, $\theta_0 = \frac{1}{2}$, $\theta_1 = \frac{3}{4}$, $\theta_2 = 1$ and $u_0 = \frac{1}{4}$, $u_1 = \frac{1}{2}$, $u_2 = \frac{3}{4}$. Let

$$(5.1) \qquad A = \begin{bmatrix} 1/2 & 0 & 0 \\ 3/8 & 3/8 & 0 \\ 2/3 & -1/3 & 2/3 \end{bmatrix} , \quad B = \begin{bmatrix} 1 \\ 1 \\ 1 \end{bmatrix} [2/3 \quad -1/3 \quad 2/3] .$$

Equation (1.1) is approximated by

$$(5.2) \qquad \tilde{V}_n r_n \tilde{f}_n = \rho_n g ,$$

with r_n and ρ_n as in (4.2), and

$$(5.3) \qquad (\tilde{V}_n)_{3i+q,3j+r} = \begin{cases} n^{-1}k(x_{iq},y_{jr})B_{qr}, & i > j , \\ n^{-1}k(x_{iq},x_{ir})A_{qr}, & i = j , \\ 0 \quad , & i < j . \end{cases}$$

First, we interpret (5.2) as a discretized version of a collocation method. For a given continuous function f, we construct a piecewise polynomial function ψ_n for which $r_n\psi_n = r_n f$ and $\tilde{W}_n r_n \psi_n = \rho_n W\psi_n = \tilde{W}_n r_n f$. Let Ψ_j be the unique polynomial of degree ≤ 6 for which

$$(5.4) \qquad \begin{cases} \Psi_j(x_{jq}) = (\tilde{W}_n r_n f)_{3j+q} , & q = 0, 1, 2, \\ \Psi_j(x_{j-1,2}) = (\tilde{W}_n r_n f)_{3j-1} & (= 0 \text{ if } j = 0) \\ \Psi_j'(y_{jr}) = f(y_{jr}) , & r = 0, 1, 2 . \end{cases}$$

Now define $\psi_n = \tilde{p}_n r_n f$ by

$$(5.5) \qquad \psi_n(x) = \Psi_j'(x) , \quad x \in \sigma_j , \quad j = 0, 1, \ldots, n-1 ,$$

and we observe that

$$(5.6) \qquad (\tilde{V}_n r_n f)_{3i+q} = \int_0^{x_{iq}} [\tilde{p}_n r_n k(x_{iq},\cdot)f(\cdot)](y)\, dy .$$

Since $\Delta_n(\tilde{W}_n r_n f - \rho_n Wf) = O(n^{-3})$ for $f \in C^2$, where $(\Delta_n a)_{3i+q} = a_{3i+q} - a_{3i-1}$, $q = 0, 1, 2$ (with $a_{-1} = 0$), it follows that $||f-\tilde{p}_n r_n f|| = O(n^{-2})$, and even for $f \in C^3$,

$$(5.7) \qquad f(y) - \tilde{p}_n r_n f(y) = n^{-2}f''(j/n)\Phi(ny-j) + O(n^{-3}) ,$$

with a suitable polynomial Φ. In addition, we know that $[W(f-\tilde{p}_n r_n f)](x_{i2}) = O(n^{-3})$, since the last row of A is a third order quadrature rule, but this implies that

$$(5.8) \qquad \int_0^1 \Phi(y)\, dy = 0 .$$

After these preliminaries, we can more or less imitate Sections 2 and 3. If F_n is the solution of $\tilde{W}_n r_n F_n = \rho_n \mathcal{W} f$, then direct verification yields

$$F_n - \tilde{p}_n r_n f = n^{-2} A_n + \mathcal{O}(n^{-3}) \ , \qquad (5.9)$$

for suitable $A_n(x)$, continuous on each σ_j, and $A_n(y_{j2}) = 0$.

For the consistency error $\rho_n H = \rho_n \mathcal{V} f - \tilde{V}_n r_n f$ in the general case, we have

$$H(x) = \int_0^x m(x,y)\,dy \ , \qquad (5.10)$$

with $m(x,y) = k(x,y)f(y) - [\tilde{p}_n r_n k(x,\cdot)f(\cdot)](y)$. From (5.7), we have $m(x,y) = n^{-2}c(x,j/n)\Phi(ny-j) + \mathcal{O}(n^{-3})$, $y \in \sigma_j$, with suitable $c(x,y)$. Now for $x \in \sigma_i$ we thus get

$$H(x) = n^{-2} d(i/n) \int_{i/n}^{x} \Phi(ny-j)\,dy + \mathcal{V}\tilde{R}_n(x) \ , \qquad (5.11)$$

with $||\tilde{R}|| = \mathcal{O}(n^{-3})$, and $d(x) = c(x,x)$. Now, once more using (5.8), we finally get

$$H(x) = n^{-2}\, \mathcal{V}\Phi_n(x) + \mathcal{V}R_n(x) \ , \qquad (5.12)$$

with $||R_n|| = \mathcal{O}(n^{-3})$, and $\Phi_n(y) = d(j/n)\Phi(ny-j)$, $y \in \sigma_j$. We thus get, for the error in the solution of (5.2),

$$\tilde{f}_n - \tilde{p}_n r_n f = \tilde{p}_n \tilde{V}_n^{-1} \rho_n H = n^{-2} \mathfrak{Q}_n(\mathcal{V})\Phi_n + \mathcal{O}(n^{-3}) \ , \qquad (5.13)$$

where $\mathfrak{Q}_n(\mathcal{V}) = \tilde{p}_n \tilde{V}_n^{-1} \rho_n \mathcal{V}$. By the analogue of Lemma 3.2, see [6, Theorem 6.4], $\mathfrak{Q}_n(\mathcal{V})\Phi_n = \mathfrak{Q}_n(\mathcal{W})\Phi_n + \mathcal{O}(n^{-1})$, and $\mathfrak{Q}_n(\mathcal{W})\Phi_n$ is a multiple of $A_n(x)$ on each σ_j. Consequently, $\tilde{f}_n(y_{j2}) - f(y_{j2}) = \mathcal{O}(n^{-3})$, thus proving the third order convergence of Keech's method under minimal smoothness assumptions.

Acknowledgement. This research was sponsored by the United States Army under Contract No. DAAG 29-83-K-0109.

References

[1] H. Brunner, Discretization of Volterra integral equations of the first kind. II. Numer. Math. 30, 117-136 (1978).

[2] H. Brunner, Superconvergence of collocation methods for Volterra integral equations of the first kind. Computing 21, 151-157 (1979).

[3] F. deHoog, and R. Weiss. High order methods for Volterra integral equations of the first kind. SIAM J. Numer. Anal. 10, 647-664 (1973).

[4] P. P. B. Eggermont, Collocation as a projection method and superconvergence for Volterra integral equations of the first kind. In: Treatment of integral equations by numerical methods (C. T. H. Baker, and G. F. Miller, editors) London: Academic Press, 1982.

[5] P. P. B. Eggermont, Approximation properties of quadrature methods for Volterra integral equations of the first kind. Math. Comp., October 1984.

[6] P. P. B. Eggermont, Improving the accuracy of collocation solutions of Volterra integral equations of the first kind. Submitted, 1984.

[7] M. S. Keech, A third order, semi-explicit method in the numerical solution of first kind Volterra integral equations. BIT 17, 312-320 (1977).

[8] J. L. Phillips, The use of collocation as a projection method for solving linear operator equations. SIAM J. Numer. Anal. 9, 14-28 (1972).

[9] K. Witsch, Konvergenzaussagen fur Projektions methoden bei linearen Operatoren. Numer. Math. 27, 339-354 (1977).

P. P. B. Eggermont, Department of Mathematical Sciences, University of Delaware, Newark, Delaware 19716 U.S.A.

International Series of
Numerical Mathematics, Vol. 73

OPTIMAL DISCREPANCY PRINCIPLES FOR THE TIKHONOV REGULARIZATION OF INTEGRAL EQUATIONS OF THE FIRST KIND

Heinz W. Engl and Andreas Neubauer
Johannes-Kepler-Universität
Linz, Austria

1. Introduction

Throughout this paper, let X and Y be real Hilbert spaces, T be a bounded linear operator on X into Y, $y \in Y$. We look for the "best-approximate solution" of

(1.1) $\quad Tx = y,$

i.e., the unique element that has minimal norm among all minimizers of the residual $\|Tx-y\|$. The best-approximate solution is actually given by $T^{\dagger}y$, where $T^{\dagger}$ is the Moore-Penrose generalized inverse of T (see e.g. [15], [7]).

The problem of computing $T^{\dagger}y$ is well-posed iff the range of T, R(T), is closed. For compact operators T, this is in turn equivalent to R(T) being

---

This paper is in final form and no version of it will be submitted for publication elsewhere.
The research that lead to this paper was supported by the Austrian Fonds zur Förderung der wissenschaftlichen Forschung under project number S32/o3.

finite-dimensional.

We are interested in the ill-posed case, so that we assume that $R(T)$ is non-closed. This assumption is fulfilled if T is an integral operator with square-integrable non-degenerate kernel from, say, $L^2([0,1])$ into itself, so that the integral equation of the first kind

$$(1.2) \qquad \int_0^1 k(t,s)x(s)ds = y(t)$$

can be taken as an illustration for everything that will be said below about the ill-posed case of (1.1).

By y_δ we will always denote an element of Y fulfilling

$$(1.3) \qquad \|y-y_\delta\| \le \delta;$$

y_δ will symbolize the perturbed data which are used during the computations, while y stand for the (non-accessible) exact data. Because of the ill-posedness of (1.1), $T^\dagger y_\delta$ is not an approximation for $T^\dagger y$. Moreover, $T^\dagger y_\delta$ need not even exist, since the domain $D(T^\dagger)$ is the dense, but proper subset $R(T)\dot{+}R(T)^\perp$ of Y. Because of these facts, one has to use "regularization methods" for obtaining approximate solutions of (1.1). The most widely used regularization method seems to be Tikhonov regularization. There, one uses the "regularized solution"

$$(1.4) \qquad x_\alpha^\delta := (T^*T+\alpha I)^{-1}T^*y_\delta$$

as an approximation for $T^\dagger y$, where the "regularization parameter" α has to be chosen appropriately (in dependence of the "noise-level" δ). For a thorough overview over Tikhonov regularization see [8]. There one can find the following well-known facts:

If $\alpha = \alpha(\delta)$ is chosen such that $\lim_{\delta\to 0} \alpha(\delta) = 0$ and $\lim_{\delta\to 0}(\delta^2.\alpha(\delta)^{-1}) = 0$, then $\lim_{\delta\to 0} \|x_{\alpha(\delta)}^\delta - T^\dagger y\| = 0$. These conditions are also necessary for convergence (see [2] for details).

If

$$(1.5) \qquad T^\dagger y \in R(T^*T),$$

then $\|x^{\delta}_{\alpha(\delta)} - T^{\dagger}y\| = O(\delta^{2/3})$ is the fastest rate of convergence that can be obtained; it is obtained for an "a-priori choice" of α as $\alpha(\delta) = C.\delta^{2/3}$ (with $C > 0$ arbitrary).

If

$$(1.6) \qquad T^{\dagger}y \in R(T^{*}),$$

the optimal rate of convergence is $\|x^{\delta}_{\alpha(\delta)}-T^{\dagger}y\| = O(\delta^{1/2})$, which is achieved if $\alpha(\delta) = C.\delta$.

See [8] for the exact statement of these results. Note that (1.5) and (1.6) can be thought of as a-priori smoothness assumptions about the (unknown) exact solution.

In contrast to the a-priori choices of α mentioned above, many authors, especially in the Soviet literature, advocate a-posteriori choices of α, where results occuring during the computations are used to compute a reasonable value of α. A widely used a-posteriori choice of α is the so-called "discrepancy principle" due to MOROZOV [14], where α is chosen as the unique solution of

$$(1.7) \qquad \|Tx^{\delta}_{\alpha} - y_{\delta}\|^{2} = \delta^{2},$$

where x^{δ}_{α} is given by (1.4). A related method is due to ARCANGELI [1]; he proposes to choose α as the unique solution of

$$(1.8) \qquad \|Tx^{\delta}_{\alpha} - y_{\delta}\|^{2} = \delta^{2}.\alpha^{-1}.$$

It is shown in [9] and [1o] that both these methods do not yield the optimal convergence rates mentioned above. In this paper, we propose variants of these discrepancy principles that lead to optimal convergence rates. We do this for classical Tikhonov regularization in Section 2, for variants in Sections 3 and 4.

2. Classical Tikhonov Regularization

In this section, we review the results obtained in [3]; see there for proofs and further details.
The key for obtaining optimal convergence rates is to use a different "discrepancy measure", namely the residual of the normal equation instead of the residual in (1.1); let for all $\alpha > 0$ and $y_\delta \in Y$ fulfilling (1.3)

$$\rho(\alpha,y_\delta) := \|T^*Tx_\alpha^\delta - T^*y_\delta\|^2, \tag{2.1}$$

where x_α^δ is given by (1.4). An easy computation shows that

$$\rho(\alpha,y_\delta) = \alpha^2 . \|x_\alpha^\delta\|^2, \tag{2.2}$$

so that $\rho(\alpha,y_\delta)$ can actually be computed easily.
To avoid trivialities, which nevertheless would have to be treated separately, we always assume that

$$T^*y \neq 0 \text{ and } T^*y_\delta \neq 0. \tag{2.3}$$

Theorem 2.1: a) For each $r,s > 0$, $\delta > 0$ and $y_\delta \in Y$ fulfilling (1.3), there is a unique $\alpha > 0$ with

$$\rho(\alpha,y_\delta) = \delta^r . \alpha^{-s}. \tag{2.4}$$

b) Assume that (1.5) holds and that $\alpha > 0$ is chosen according to (2.4) with $\frac{3r}{2} - 2 = s \geq 1$. Then $\|x_\alpha^\delta - T^\dagger y\| = O(\delta^{2/3})$.

c) Assume that (1.6) holds and that $\alpha > 0$ is chosen according to (2.4) with $r-2 = s \geq 2$. Then $\|x_\alpha^\delta - T^\dagger y\| = O(\delta^{1/2})$.

Theorem 2.1 provides us with a one-parameter family of discrepancy principles that lead to optimal convergence rates under both types of smoothness assumptions. One possible choice under assumption (1.5) is $r=2$, $s=1$, so that the optimal convergence rate is achieved if α solves

(2.5) $\|T^*Tx_\alpha^\delta - T^*y_\delta\|^2 = \delta^2.\alpha^{-1}$,

which closely resembles (1.8) and can thus be thought of as a variant of ARCANGELI's method. For an order-optimal version of MOROZOV's method see [3, Rem. 2.2].

The results of Theorem 2.1 remain true if in (2.4), $\delta^r.\alpha^{-s}$ is replaced by $C.\delta^r.\alpha^{-s}$ with $C > 0$. The choice of an appropriate C turned out to be crucial in our computations; for some theoretical discussion about good choices of C see Section 4.

There remains the question how the nonlinear equation (2.4) can be solved efficiently. We show that this can be achieved by Newton's method, which converges globally in this case. To this end, let

(2.9) $f(\alpha) := \alpha^s.\rho(\alpha, y_\delta) - \delta^r$

for $\alpha > 0$ with $y_\delta \in Y$, $s, r > 0$. For any $\alpha_0 > 0$, let for all $n \in \mathbb{N}$

(2.1o) $\alpha_n := \alpha_{n-1} - \frac{f(\alpha_{n-1})}{f'(\alpha_{n-1})}$.

Then we have

Proposition 2.2: For $s \geq 1$, the sequence defined by (2.1o) converges to the unique solution of (2.9) for all $\alpha_0 > 0$.

Proof: By (2.9) and (2.2) we have
$f'(\alpha) = (s+2)\alpha^{s+1}. \|x_\alpha^\delta\|^2 + 2\,\alpha^{s+2} \langle x_\alpha^\delta, \frac{dx_\alpha^\delta}{d\alpha}\rangle$. Because of (1.4) we have

$\frac{dx_\alpha^\delta}{d\alpha} = -(T^*T+\alpha I)^{-2}\, T^*y_\delta = -(T^*T+\alpha I)^{-1}\, x_\alpha^\delta$.

Thus

(2.11) $f'(\alpha) = \langle x_\alpha^\delta, [(s+2)\alpha^{s+1}\, I - 2\alpha^{s+2}(T^*T+\alpha I)^{-1}]\, x_\alpha^\delta\rangle$.

Let $\{E_\lambda\}$ be the spectral family induced by T^*T. Then (2.11) implies that

$f'(\alpha) = \int_0^\infty [(s+2)\alpha^{s+1} - \frac{2\alpha^{s+2}}{\alpha+\lambda}]\, d\langle E_\lambda x_\alpha^\delta, x_\alpha^\delta\rangle = \int_0^\infty (s.\alpha^{s+1} + 2\alpha^{s+1}.\frac{\lambda}{\alpha+\lambda}) d\langle E_\lambda x_\alpha^\delta, x_\alpha^\delta\rangle \geq$

$\geq s.\alpha^{s+1}.\ \|x_\alpha^\delta\|^2 > 0$. Thus $\frac{f(\alpha)}{f'(\alpha)} \leq \frac{\alpha^{s+2}\|x_\alpha^\delta\|^2-\delta^r}{s.\alpha^{s+1}\|x_\alpha^\delta\|^2} < \frac{\alpha}{s} \leqslant \alpha$, so that (2.1o) is well-defined.

Analogous computations yield that

$$f''(\alpha) = \int_0^\infty \alpha^s\ [(s+2)(s+1) - \frac{4(s+2)}{\alpha+\lambda} + \frac{6\alpha^2}{(\alpha+\lambda)^2}]\ d <E_\lambda x_\alpha^\delta, x_\alpha^\delta> =$$

$$= \int_0^\infty \frac{\alpha^s}{(\lambda+\alpha)^2} [\lambda^2(s^2+ 3s + 2) + 2\alpha\lambda(s^2+s-2) + \alpha^2(s^2-s)]d <E_\lambda x_\alpha^\delta, x_\alpha^\delta> \geq\ 0 \text{ for } s \geq 1.$$

Now let $\bar{\alpha}$ be the unique solution of (2.9). By Taylor expansion we see that with a suitable $\vartheta = \vartheta(\alpha) \in]0,1[$ we have for all $\alpha > 0$: $0 = f(\bar{\alpha}) =$

$= f(\alpha) + f'(\alpha).(\bar{\alpha}-\alpha) + f''(\alpha+\vartheta(\alpha).(\bar{\alpha}-\alpha)).(\bar{\alpha}-\alpha)^2 \geq f(\alpha) + f'(\alpha).(\bar{\alpha}-\alpha)$, so that

$$\text{(2.12)} \qquad \bar{\alpha} \leq \alpha - \frac{f(\alpha)}{f'(\alpha)} \text{ for all } \alpha > 0.$$

Thus, $\alpha_n \geq \bar{\alpha}$ for all $n \in \mathbb{N}$ no matter what α_0 was. But then,

$\alpha_{n+1} = \alpha_n - \frac{f(\alpha_n)}{f'(\alpha_n)} \leq \alpha_n$, since f is strictly monotonic, so that $f(\alpha_n) \geq 0$.

Hence, $(\alpha_1, \alpha_2, \alpha_3,\ldots)$ is monotonically decreasing and bounded below by $\bar{\alpha}$ and thus convergent. Since f is continuously differentiable, the limit is a zero of f and hence a solution of (2.9), which is unique by Theorem 2.1.

□

It follows from the proof of Proposition 2.1 that after the first iteration, Newton's method (2.1o) converges monotonically from above. Since f' is strictly positive, the convergence is locally quadratic. Also,the proof shows how the iterates in (2.1o) can be computed (cf. (2.11)).

3. Regularization with Differential Operators

The approximate solution obtained from classical Tikhonov regularization according to (1.4) can be characterized as the unique minimizer of the functional

$$(3.1) \qquad x \to \|Tx-x_\delta\|^2 + \alpha\|x\|^2.$$

Thus, the regularized solution will tend to have small norm. This might be desirable in some situations, but probably not in others, where a-priori knowledge about the solution might suggest to keep $\|x''\|$ small instead of $\|x\|$. This can be achieved by a variant of Tikhonov regularization using the functional

$$(3.2) \qquad x \to \|Tx-y_\delta\|^2 + \alpha\|Lx\|^2$$

instead of (3.1), where L is a differential operator. To make things precise, let L be a closed, densely defined linear operator from X into Y (or another Hilbert space) which is assumed to have the following properties: $N(T) \cap N(L) = \{0\}$, where N(L) denotes the null-space of L; R(L) is closed; with a suitable $\beta > 0$, $\|Tx\| \geq \beta.\|x\|$ holds for all $x \in N(L)$. The latter condition is certainly fulfilled in the (most interesting) case that $\dim N(L) < \infty$. Usually, L will be a differential operator (see [12], [8]).
Under these assumptions, the functional (3.2) will have a unique minimizer, which we will denote by x_α^δ:

$$(3.3) \qquad \|Tx_\alpha^\delta-y_\delta\|^2+\alpha\|Lx_\alpha^\delta\|^2= \inf\{\|Tx-y_\delta\|^2 +\alpha\|Lx\|^2 \,/\, x \in X\}.$$

As in classical Tikhonov regularization, x_α^δ can of course be characterized by a regularized normal equation in the following obvious way:

<u>Proposition 3.1:</u> Let x_α^δ be as in (3.3). Then

$$(3.4) \qquad T^*T\, x_\alpha^\delta + \alpha L^*Lx_\alpha^\delta = T^*y_\delta.$$

For a detailed treatment of this variant of Tikhonov regularization see [12], [8], [19]. The key of this treatment is the following relation with classical Tikhonov regularization:
Let

$$(3.5) \qquad \begin{aligned} &\langle x,y\rangle_*: = \langle Tx,Ty\rangle + \langle Lx,Ly \rangle, \\ &\|x\|_*: = \sqrt{\langle x,x\rangle_*} \qquad \text{for } x,y \in D(L). \end{aligned}$$

Then $(D(L),\langle,\rangle_*)$ is a Hilbert space. The restriction of T to D(L) will again be denoted by T, since this will not lead to confusion. By $T^\#$ and $L^\#$ we denote the adjoints of T and L with respect to the inner product defined in (3.5). Then the following result holds (see [12], [8]):

<u>Proposition 3.2:</u> Let x_α^δ be as in (3.3). Then for $\alpha < 1$,

$$x_\alpha^\delta = \frac{1}{1-\alpha}[T^{\#}T + \frac{\alpha}{1-\alpha} I]^{-1} T^{\#}y. \tag{3.5}$$

Because of this Proposition, Tikhonov regularization with differential operators is closely connected with classical Tikhonov regularization in the space $(D(L), \langle\ ,\ \rangle_*)$, so that all results about classical Tikhonov regularization can be translated into the new setting, e.g:

If $y \in R(T|_{D(L)}) \dotplus R(T)^{\perp}$ (which will be assumed throughout this section), $y_\delta \in Y$ fulfills (1.3), and if $\alpha = \alpha(\delta)$ is chosen in such a way that $\lim_{\delta\to 0} \alpha(\delta) = 0$ and $\lim_{\delta\to 0} (\delta^2.\alpha(\delta)^{-1}) = 0$, then $\lim_{\delta\to 0} \|x_{\alpha(\delta)}^\delta - T_L^{\dagger}y\|_* = 0$, where x_α^δ is defined by (3.3) and $T_L^{\dagger}y$ is defined to be the minimizer of the residual $\|Tx-y\|$ for which $\|Lx\|$ is minimal.

Convergence now holds in the norm $\|\ \|_*$, which also implies convergence in the original norm, since $\|\ \|_*$ is equivalent to the graph-norm of L (see [12]).

Also, the results about rates of convergence quoted in Section 1 can be carried over. It turns out that if

$$T_L^{\dagger}y \in R(T^{\#}T) \tag{3.6}$$

then $\|x_{\alpha(\delta)}^\delta - T_L^{\dagger}y\|_* = O(\delta^{2/3})$ is again the fastest rate of convergence, which is obtained by $\alpha(\delta) = C.\delta^{2/3}$, while if

$$T_L^{\dagger}y \in R(T^{\#}), \tag{3.7}$$

then $\|x_{\alpha(\delta)}^\delta - T_L^{\dagger}y\|_* = O(\delta^{1/2})$ is the fastest rate of convergence, which is again obtained by $\alpha(\delta) = C.\delta$. See [17] for detailed proofs.

Here, the a-priori assumptions (3.6) and (3.7) seem to be quite complicated, since they involve $T^{\#}$. But the following result gives more insight into their meaning:

Lemma 3.3: a) (3.6) holds iff

(3.8) $T_L^\dagger y \in D(L^*L)$ and $L^*L\ T_L^\dagger y \in R(T^*T)$.

b) (3.7) holds iff

(3.9) $T_L^\dagger y \in D(L^*L)$ and $L^*L\ T_L^\dagger y \in R(T^*)$.

Proof: follows immediately from the fact that $T^\# = (T^*T+L^*L)^{-1}T^*$.

□

We are now in the position to formulate a discrepancy principle for the choice of $\alpha = \alpha(\delta)$ that gives rise to the optimal convergence rates discussed above.

The discrepancy measure used will be

(3.10) $$\rho_L(\alpha,y_\delta) := \|(1-\alpha)\ T^\# T x_\alpha^\delta - T^\# y_\delta\|_*^2 \quad (\alpha < 1),$$

where x_α^δ is given by (3.3). Because of Proposition 3.2, we obtain that

(3.11) $$\rho_L(\alpha,y_\delta) = \alpha^2 \| x_\alpha^\delta\|_*^2,$$

which is the form of ρ_L that is used in computations. As in Section 2, we always assume that (1.3) and (2.3) hold.

Proposition 3.4: Let $2s \geq r > 0$. Then for δ sufficiently small there is a unique $\alpha = \alpha(\delta) \in \,]0,1[$ such that

(3.12) $$\rho_L(\alpha,y_\delta) = \delta^r . \left(\frac{\alpha}{1-\alpha}\right)^{-s}.$$

If $\alpha = \alpha(\delta)$ is chosen as in (3.12), then

(3.13) $$\lim_{\delta\to 0} \|x_{\alpha(\delta)}^\delta - T_L^\dagger y\|_* = 0.$$

Proof: For any $\alpha < 1$, let $\beta = \beta(\alpha) := \frac{\alpha}{1-\alpha}$ and $\bar{x}_\beta^\delta := (T^\# T+\beta I)^{-1} T^\# y_\delta$. Because of Proposition 3.2, $\bar{x}_\beta^\delta = (1-\alpha)x_\alpha^\delta$, so that $\rho_L(\alpha,y_\delta) = \|T^\# T\bar{x}_\beta^\delta - T^\# y_\delta\|_*^2 =: \rho(\beta,y_\delta)$. Because of (2.3) and the fact that

$T^{\#} = (T^*T + L^*L)^{-1} T^*$, we have $T^{\#}y \neq 0$ and $T^{\#}y_\delta \neq 0$. Thus it follows from [3, Lemma 2.1], applied to the Hilbert space $(D(L), <,>_*)$, that there is a unique $\beta = \beta(\delta)$ with $\rho(\beta(\delta), y_\delta) = \delta^r . \beta(\delta)^{-s}$. Hence $\alpha(\delta) := \frac{\beta(\delta)}{1+\beta(\delta)}$ is the (unique) solution of (3.12).

Because of [3, Lemma 2.4], we have $\lim\limits_{\delta\to 0} \|\bar{x}^\delta_{\beta(\delta)} - T^\dagger_L y\|_* = 0$. Since $\lim\limits_{\delta\to 0} \beta(\delta) = 0$ (cf. [3, Lemma 2.2]) and hence $\lim\limits_{\delta\to 0} \alpha(\delta) = 0$, this implies (3.13).

□

The following result shows how one has to choose r and s in (3.12) in order to achieve the optimal convergence rates:

<u>Theorem 3.5:</u> Let $\alpha = \alpha(\delta)$ be chosen according to (3.12).

a) If (3.8) holds and $\frac{3r}{2} - 2 = s \geq 1$, then $\|x^\delta_\alpha - T^\dagger_L y\|_* = O(\delta^{2/3})$.

b) If (3.9) holds and $r-2 = s \geq 2$, then $\|x^\delta_\alpha - T^\dagger_L y\|_* = O(\delta^{1/2})$.

<u>Proof:</u> Using the notation of the proof of Proposition 3.4, it follows from Theorem 2.1, applied to $(D(L), <,>_*)$ instead of X, that

$$(3.14) \qquad \|\bar{x}^\delta_{\beta(\alpha)} - T^\dagger_L y\|_* = O(\delta^k),$$

where $k = \frac{2}{3}$ in case a), $k = \frac{1}{2}$ in case b). Theorem 2.1 is applicable because of Lemma 3.3.

Now, $\lim\limits_{\delta\to 0} [\delta^r . (\frac{\alpha(\delta)}{1-\alpha(\delta)})^{-s} . \alpha(\delta)^{-2}] = \lim\limits_{\delta\to 0} [\rho_L(\alpha(\delta), y_\delta) . \alpha(\delta)^{-2}] =$

$= \lim\limits_{\delta\to 0} \|x^\delta_{\alpha(\delta)}\|_*^{\,2} = \|T^\dagger_L y\|^2 > 0$ because of (3.11), (3.13) and **(2.3)**. Since $\lim\limits_{\delta\to 0} \alpha(\delta) = 0$, this implies that $C_1 \leq \delta^r . \alpha(\delta)^{-s-2} \leq C_2$ with suitable $C_1, C_2 > 0$. Thus $\alpha(\delta) = O(\delta^{\frac{r}{s+2}})$ and hence $\alpha(\delta) = O(\delta^{2/3})$ in case a), $\alpha(\delta) = O(\delta)$ in case b). This implies that $\|\bar{x}^\delta_{\beta(\alpha)} - x^\delta_\alpha\|_* = \alpha\|x^\delta_\alpha\|_* = O(\delta^{2/3})$, which implies the asserted convergence rates together with (3.14).

□

These results show that with the same choices of r and s as in classical Tikhonov regularization, one obtains the optimal convergence rates also for Tikhonov regularization with differential operators, if α is chosen from the discrepancy principle (3.12). Similarly to Proposition 2.2, one can show ([17]) that (3.12) can again be solved by Newton's method, which converges globally and locally quadratically.

4. Regularization in Hilbert Scales

This variant of Tikhonov regularization goes back to NATTERER ([16]) and can be described as follows:

Let $\{X_\beta\}_{\beta\in\mathbb{R}}$ be a Hilbert scale induced by a densely defined self-adjoint strictly positive operator L on X that fulfills $\|Lx\| \geq \|x\|$ on its domain (see [11]), i.e., X_β is the completion of $\bigcap_{k=0}^{\infty} D(L^k)$ with respect to the Hilbert space norm $\|x\|_\beta := \|L^\beta x\|$. Let $T: X \to Y$ be a bounded linear injective operator and $a > 0$ be such that with suitable $M,m > 0$,

$$(4.1) \qquad m.\|x\|_{-a} \leq \|Tx\| \leq M.\|x\|_{-a}$$

holds for all $x \in X$; this number a can be interpreted as one ingredient to a "degree of ill-posedness" of equations involving T, the other part being a-priori information about the exact solution, which is here assumed to be of the form

$$(4.2) \qquad x_0 \in X_q \text{ and } \|x_0\|_q \leq \rho,$$

where x_0 is defined as the exact solution of (1.1), which is assumed to be solvable here (the latter assumption could easily be dispensed with). If $L = \|T^*T\|.(T^*T)^{-1}$, then $a = \frac{1}{2}$, and (4.2) reduces to (1.5) (and an estimate for the element w with $T^*Tw = T^\dagger y$) if $q = 1$ and to (1.6) if $q = \frac{1}{2}$. Thus, in NATTERER's setting, both ingredients for the degree of ill-posedness are measured via the operator L, while in classical Tikhonov regularization, one is fixed ($a = \frac{1}{2}$) and the other is measured via the operator $(T^*T)^{-1}$, which

gives much less flexibility.
As regularized solution x_α^δ, NATTERER takes the minimizer of the functional

$$(4.3) \qquad \|Tx-y_\delta\|^2 + \alpha\|x\|_p^2 \qquad (x \in X_p)$$

with $p \in \mathbb{R}$ (we only consider $p \geq 0$ here); he shows that if

$$(4.4) \qquad p \geq \frac{q-a}{2}$$

and

$$(4.5) \qquad \alpha = C.\delta^{2(a+p)/(a+q)}$$

with $C > 0$, then

$$(4.6) \qquad \|x_\alpha^\delta - x_0\| = O(\delta^{q/(a+q)}),$$

which is optimal in the sense that the rate in (4.6) is of the same order as the best possible worst case error for recovering x_0 from (1.1) using y_δ instead of y and the information provided by (1.3) and (4.2). If $(T^*T)^{1/2}$ and L commute, these results hold also if (4.4) is weakened to

$$(4.7) \qquad p \geq \frac{q}{2} - a,$$

which explains the saturation result of [6, Prop. 2.2]: Since $p = 0$ there, (4.7) is fulfilled only for $q \leq 1$; if $q > 1$, this information can only be utilized to obtain the optimal rate (4.6) if also the order of regularization, namely p, is increased; e.g., if $x_0 \in R((T^*T)^2)$, i.e., $q = 2$, and the regularized solution were obtained by minimizing $\|Tx-y\|^2 + \alpha\|(T^*T)^{-1/2}x\|^2$, then the optimal convergence rate $O(\delta^{4/5})$ could be obtained. But since $(T^*T)^{-1/2}$ will not be easy to evaluate, it seems to be crucial to be able to choose L independent of T^*T, as it is done in NATTERER's setting.
We proceed by presenting two versions of a discrepancy principle for choosing the regularization parameter that lead to the optimal convergence rates (4.6) under certain conditions. Again we assume that (2.3) holds.
First, let

(4.8) $\rho_1(\alpha,y_\delta) := \alpha^2 . \|x_\alpha^\delta\|_p^2$,

where x_α^δ minimizes the functional in (4.3). Then we have

<u>Theorem 4.1:</u> For any $r,s > 0$ and $y_\delta \in Y$ fulfilling (1.3) and (2.3), there is a unique $\alpha = \alpha(\delta)$ fulfilling

(4.9) $\rho_1(\alpha,y_\delta) = \delta^r . \alpha^{-s}$.

If moreover $q > p \geq \max\{0, \frac{q-a}{2}\}$, $r \geq 4 . \frac{a+p}{q-p}$ and $s = r . \frac{a+q}{2(a+p)} - 2$, then $\|x_{\alpha(\delta)}^\delta - x_0\| = O(\delta^{q/(a+q)})$ holds.

<u>Proof:</u> The restriction of T to X_p is bounded; let $T^\#$ be its adjoint. One can easily show that $T^\# = L^{-2p}T^*$. Since x_α^δ can be characterized by

(4.1o) $(T^*T+\alpha L^{2p})x_\alpha^\delta = T^*y_\delta$

(see [16]), this implies: $\rho_1(\alpha,y_\delta) = \|L^{-2p}T^*T\, x_\alpha^\delta - L^{-2p}T^*y_\delta\|_p^2 =$

$= \|T^\# T x_\alpha^\delta - T^\# y_\delta\|_p^2$. By (2.3), $T^\# y \neq 0$ and $T^\# y_\delta \neq 0$. Since by (4.1o), $x_\alpha^\delta = (T^\# T + \alpha I)^{-1}\, T^\# y_\delta$, Theorem 2.1a can be applied (with X replaced by X_p) and yields the unique solvability of (4.9). Now let the additional assumptions about p,q,r,s be fulfilled. Then $x_0 \in X_p \subseteq X_q$, so that the results of [3] can be applied with X replaced by X_p. Since $r \leq 2s$ follows from the assumptions, [3, Lemma 2.5] yields

(4.11) $C_1 \leq \delta^r . \alpha(\delta)^{-s-2} \leq C_2$

for $\delta > 0$ sufficiently small with suitable $C_1, C_2 > 0$. Together with the proof of [16, Theorem 1] we obtain with suitable constants k,K and $d := \frac{a}{2(a+p)}$, $b := \frac{q}{2(a+p)}$: $\|x_{\alpha(\delta)}^\delta - x_0\| \leq k . \alpha(\delta)^{-d}\, \delta + K . \alpha(\delta)^b \leq$

$\leq k .\, C_2^{d/(s+2)} . \delta^{1-dr/(s+2)} + K . C_1^{-b/(s+2)} . \delta^{rb/(s+2)} = O(\delta^{q/(a+q)})$. □

The result of Theorem 4.1 applies only to the case where the order of regularization is less than the a-priori assumed smoothness order of the exact solution, i.e., $p < q$. This is not surprising, since the discrepancy measure ρ_1 contains the X_p-norm of the regularized solution, which would not seem appropriate if $x_0 \notin X_p$. We now present another discrepancy principle that leads to the optimal convergence rates also if $p \geq q$. We use the following discrepancy measure:

$$(4.12) \qquad \rho_2(\alpha,y_\delta) := \alpha^2 . \|x_\alpha^\delta\|^2,$$

where x_α^δ is again the minimizer of the functional in (4.3). As opposed to (4.8), the norm in X is used in (4.12), not the X_p-norm.

<u>Lemma 4.2:</u> As a function of α, ρ_2 is continuous and bounded. Furthermore, $\lim_{\alpha\to 0} \rho_2(\alpha,y_\delta) = 0$ and $\lim_{\alpha\to\infty} \rho_2(\alpha,y_\delta) = \|T^* y_\delta\|_{-2p}^2 > 0$.

<u>Proof:</u> We use the notation and the results of the proof of Theorem 4.1. It follows that

$$(4.13) \qquad \rho_2(\alpha,y_\delta) = \|T^\# T x_\alpha^\delta - T^\# y_\delta\|^2,$$

hence $\rho_2(\alpha,y_\delta) \leq \rho_1(\alpha,y_\delta)$. Thus it follows from [5,Lemma 3.1] that $\lim_{\alpha\to 0} \rho_2(\alpha,y_\delta) = 0$ and that ρ_2 is bounded. Let $\{E_\lambda\}$ be the spectral family induced by $T^\# T$, $\gamma \geq \frac{\alpha}{2}$. Then $\|x_\alpha^\delta - x_\gamma^\delta\|_p^2 = \int_0^\infty (\frac{1}{\alpha+\lambda} - \frac{1}{\gamma+\lambda})^2 d< E_\lambda T^\# y_\delta, T^\# y_\delta >_p \leq$

$\leq \frac{(\alpha-\gamma)^2}{\alpha^2\gamma^2} . \|T^\# y_\delta\|_p^2$. This implies that $\lim_{\gamma\to\alpha} \|x_\alpha^\delta - x_\gamma^\delta\| \leq \lim_{\gamma\to\alpha} \|x_\alpha^\delta - x_\gamma^\delta\|_p = 0$, which implies the continuity of ρ_2.

Since $x_\alpha^\delta = (T^\# T+\alpha I)^{-1} T^\# y_\delta$, we have $\|x_\alpha^\delta\| \leq \|x_\alpha^\delta\|_p \leq \alpha^{-1} . \|T^\# y_\delta\|_p$, so that $\lim_{\alpha\to\infty} \|x_\alpha^\delta\| = 0$, which implies together with (4.13) and (2.3) that $\lim_{\alpha\to\infty} \rho_2(\alpha,y_\delta) = \|T^\# y_\delta\|^2 = \|L^{-2p} T^* y_\delta\|^2 = \|T^* y_\delta\|_{-2p}^2 > 0$. $\square$

Proposition 4.3: For any $r,s > 0$ and $y_\delta \in Y$ fulfilling (1.3) and (2.3), the equation

$$(4.14) \qquad \rho_2(\alpha,y_\delta) = \delta^r.\alpha^{-s}$$

has a solution α. We have:

a) $\underline{\alpha}(\delta) := \inf\{\alpha > 0/\alpha \text{ solves } (4.14)\} > 0$ solves (4.14).

b) $\bar{\alpha}(\delta) := \sup\{\alpha > 0/\alpha \text{ solves } (4.14)\} < +\infty$ solves (4.14).

Proof: Because of Lemma 4.2, we have $\lim_{\alpha\to 0} (\alpha^s.\rho_2(\alpha,y_\delta)) = 0$ and $\lim_{\alpha\to\infty} (\alpha^s\rho_2(\alpha,y_\delta)) = +\infty$. Because of the Intermediate Value Theorem, this implies the solvability of (4.14).

It follows from the proof of Lemma 4.2 that $\rho_2(\alpha,y_\delta) \le \|T^\# y_\delta\|_p^2$. Hence, for any solution α of (4.14) we have $\alpha \ge (\delta^r.\|T^\# y_\delta\|_p^{-2})^{1/s}$, which implies that $\underline{\alpha}(\delta) > 0$. If $\bar{\alpha}(\delta) = +\infty$, there exists a sequence $(\alpha_n) \to +\infty$ of solutions of (4.14). This implies $0 = \lim_{n\to\infty} (\delta^r.\alpha_n^{-s}) = \lim_{n\to\infty} \rho_2(\alpha_n,y_\delta) =$ $= \|T^* y_\delta\|_{-2p}^2 > 0$ because of Lemma 4.2, which is a contradiction. Hence $\bar{\alpha}(\delta) < +\infty$. The fact that $\bar{\alpha}(\delta)$ and $\underline{\alpha}(\delta)$ solve (4.14) follows from continuity arguments.

□

Lemma 4.4: Let $\underline{\alpha}(\delta)$ and $\bar{\alpha}(\delta)$ be defined as in Proposition 4.3. Then $\lim_{\delta\to 0} \bar{\alpha}(\delta) = 0$. If furthermore $0 < r < \frac{s}{d}$, where $d := \frac{a}{2(a+p)}$, then $\lim_{\delta\to 0} (\delta.\underline{\alpha}(\delta)^{-d}) = 0$.

Proof: The first assertion follows as in the proof of [3, Lemma 2.2] (with T^* replaced by $T^\#$; cf. (4.13)).

It follows from the proof of Lemma 4.2 that for all $\alpha > 0$, $\rho_2(\alpha,y_\delta) \le \|T^\# y_\delta\|_p^2 \le (\|T^\#\|.\delta + \|T^\# y\|_p)^2$. Hence $\rho_2(\underline{\alpha}(\delta),y_\delta)$ remains bounded as $\delta \to 0$. (Note that we cannot follow the proof of [3, Lemma 2.4] here unless

$p \le q$.) This implies that $\lim_{\delta\to 0} (\delta^r . \underline{\alpha}(\delta)^{-dr}) = \lim_{\delta\to 0} [\rho_2(\underline{\alpha}(\delta),y_\delta).\underline{\alpha}(\delta)^{s-dr}] = 0$, since $s-dr > 0$ and $\lim_{\delta\to 0} \underline{\alpha}(\delta) \le \lim_{\delta\to 0} \bar{\alpha}(\delta) = 0$. Hence $\lim_{\delta\to 0} (\delta . \underline{\alpha}(\delta)^{-d}) = 0$.

□

<u>Proposition 4.5:</u> Let $p \ge \max\{0, \frac{q-a}{2}\}$, $d := \frac{a}{2(a+p)}$, $0 < r < \frac{s}{d}$. Let $\alpha(\delta)$ be any solution of (4.14). Then $\lim_{\delta\to 0} \|x^\delta_{\alpha(\delta)} - x_0\| = 0$.

<u>Proof:</u> Because of Lemma 4.4, we have $\lim_{\delta\to 0} \alpha(\delta) = 0$ and $\lim_{\delta\to 0} (\delta.\alpha(\delta)^{-d}) = 0$. The assertion follows now from the proof of [16, Theorem 1].

□

<u>Lemma 4.6:</u> Under the assumptions of Proposition 4.5, there are constants C_1, $C_2 > 0$ such that for sufficiently small $\delta > 0$

(4.15) $\quad C_1 \le \delta^r . \alpha(\delta)^{-s-2} \le C_2$

holds.

<u>Proof:</u> Because of Proposition 4.5., $\lim_{\delta\to 0} (\delta^r . \alpha(\delta)^{-s-2}) =$
$= \lim_{\delta\to 0} (\alpha(\delta)^{-2} . \rho_2(\alpha(\delta),y_\delta)) = \lim_{\delta\to 0} \|x^\delta_{\alpha(\delta)}\|^2 = \|x_0\|^2 > 0$ because of (2.3). Hence, the assertion holds e.g. with $C_1 := \frac{1}{2}\|x_0\|^2$, $C_2 := \frac{3}{2}\|x_0\|^2$.

□

<u>Theorem 4.7:</u> In addition to the general assumptions, let $p \ge \max\{0, \frac{q-a}{2}\}$, $r > 4.\frac{a+p}{q}$, $s = r.\frac{a+q}{2(a+p)} - 2$. For any $\delta > 0$ and $y_\delta \in Y$ fulfilling (1.3), let $\alpha(\delta)$ by any solution of (4.14). Then

(4.16) $\quad \|x^\delta_{\alpha(\delta)} - x_0\| = O(\delta^{q/(a+q)})$.

Proof: For this choice of r and s, we have $s-dr > 0$, so that Lemma 4.6 is applicable. Now we proceed as in the last part of the proof of Theorem 4.1 with (4.11) replaced by (4.15).

□

Remark 4.8: As Theorem 4.7 shows, the optimal rate of convergence can also be obtained from the discrepancy principle (4.14) without the restriction "$p < q$" that was needed in Theorem 4.1. But as opposed to the discrepancy principle (4.9), we were not able to show that (4.14) is uniquely solvable; nevertheless, the conclusions of (4.14) hold for any solution of (4.14). If L^{-p} and T^*T commute, (e.g.: $L = \|T^*T\|.(T^*T)^{-1}$, see above), then the solution of (4.14) is unique. This can be seen as follows:
$T^{\#}T = L^{-2p}T^*T = L^{-p}T^*TL^{-p} = (TL^{-p})^*\ (TL^{-p})$, hence $\|(T^{\#}T+\alpha I)^{-1}\| \leq \alpha^{-1}$, so that

$$\frac{d\rho_2}{d\alpha}(\alpha,y_\delta) = 2\alpha\|x_\alpha^\delta\|^2 + 2\alpha^2 <x_\alpha^\delta, \frac{d}{d\alpha}x_\alpha^\delta> = 2\alpha\|x_\alpha^\delta\|^2 + 2\alpha^2 <x_\alpha^\delta, -(T^{\#}T+\alpha I)^{-1}x_\alpha^\delta> \geq$$

$\geq 2\alpha\|x_\alpha^\delta\|^2.\ [1-\alpha.\|(T^{\#}T+\alpha I)^{-1}\|] \geq 0$. Hence $\alpha \to \alpha^s.\rho_2(\alpha,y_\delta)$ is strictly monotonically increasing, which implies the unique solvability of (4.14).

5. Concluding Remarks

In the last three sections, we gave discrepancy principles for choosing the regularization parameter for three variants of Tikhonov regularization that have the property that they lead to optimal convergence rates. Of course these results are of asymptotic character. They remain true as far as convergence rates are concerned if the right-hand sides of each discrepancy principle are multiplied by a positive constant, say, if (4.14) is replaced by

$$(5.1) \qquad \rho_2(\alpha,y_\delta) = C.\delta^r.\alpha^{-s}.$$

The important question remains how to choose C. A comparison with [16, Theorem 1] shows that (provided that r,s are chosen as in Theorem 4.7)

$$(5.2) \qquad C = \|x_0\|^2.\ \left(\frac{aL}{qK\rho}\right)^r$$

is optimal in the sense that with this choice, $\alpha(\delta)$ as determined by (5.1) comes arbitrarily close to the optimal α of [16, Theorem 1] as $\delta \to 0$. In (5.2), x_0,a,q, and ρ are as in Section 4, while L and K are as in [16]. For the discrepancy principle of Theorem 4.1, the optimal constant is as in (5.2) with $\|x_0\|^2$ replaced by $\|x_0\|_p^2$. If $L = \|T^*T\|.(T^*T)^{-1}$ and (1.5) holds with $x_0 = T^\dagger y = T^*Tw$, then the optimal constant of (5.2) reduces to

$$(5.3) \qquad C = \|T^\dagger y\|^2.(4.\ \|T\|^4.\ \|w\|)^{-r}$$

with r chosen according to Theorem 2.1b. Thus we can also obtain optimal constants for the discrepancy principles of Section 2.
Our results can also be used in connection with superconvergence results (see [18]), e.g. as follows: If instead of (1.5), we have only

$$(5.4) \qquad T^\dagger y \in R((T^*T)^\mu)$$

with $0 < \mu < 1$, then we cannot expect that $\|x^\delta_{\alpha(\delta)} - T^\dagger y\| = 0(\delta^{2/3})$ for any choice of α; but $< x^\delta_{\alpha(\delta)} - T^\dagger y, w > = 0(\delta^{2/3})$ for any

$$(5.5) \qquad w \in R((T^*T)^{1-\mu}),$$

if $\alpha(\delta) = C.\delta^{2/3}$. From this one can conclude that Theorem 2.1b holds with (1.5) replaced by (5.4) and $\|x^\delta_\alpha - T^\dagger y\|$ replaced by $<x^\delta_\alpha - T^\dagger y, w>$,where w fulfills (5.5).

Another possible extension of our result is a discrepancy principle for constrained Tikhonov regularization; we will report about this later.

Finally, our results can be applied to give a variant of MARTI's method (cf. [13]) that converges faster than his original method. The key to this is the connection between MARTI's method and the discrepancy principle that is pointed out in [8]; details will be published in [4].

6. Numerical Examples

The following results were obtained from the Locker-Prenter-method (see [12]) with linear splines in the case of classical Tikhonov regularization, with piecewise cubic Hermite splines in the case of regularization with a differential operator of order 2 (see Section 3). The regularization parameter was obtained from the discrepancy principles of Theorem 2.1b and Theorem 3.5a (for the latter, the right-hand side of (3.12) was multiplied by 10^{-4}), respectively, with $r = 2$ and $s = 1$; it was calculated using Newton's method (cf. Proposition 2.2). For details about the calculations and for more examples see [17]. All examples are integral equations of the form (1.2) with different kernels k; the perturbed data y_δ were always obtained by randomly perturbing y such that (1.3) is fulfilled. All examples were chosen in such a way that an exact solution x_0 was known. By e_δ we will denote $\|x^\delta_{\alpha(\delta)}-x_0\|$ or $\|x^\delta_{\alpha(\delta)}-x_0\|_*$ (the latter for regularization with a differential operator). The fourth row, if present, in the tables below will contain $e_\delta \cdot \delta^{-2/3}$, which should become nearly constant for small δ according to the theory.

Example 1: $k(t,s) = \begin{cases} t(1-s) & \text{if } t \le s \\ s(1-t) & \text{if } t > s \end{cases}$;

$y(t) = \frac{1}{30}(3t-5t^3+3t^5-t^6)$, $x_0(s) = s-2s^3+s^4$ (cf.[13]). Classical Tikhonov regularization gives the following results, if the splines are (as always in Examples 1 - 3) based on 5 knots:

δ	10^{-3}	10^{-4}	10^{-5}	10^{-6}
$\alpha(\delta)$	0.265	0.0094	0.0014	0.0003
e_δ	0.215	0.112	0.029	0.0068
$e_\delta \cdot \delta^{-2/3}$	21.5	51.9	62.6	68.2

With more knots, the results were not very different.
If k is as above, but $y(t) = \frac{1}{6}(t-t^3)$, $x_0(s) = s$, then classical Tikhonov regularization gave the following result for $\delta = 10^{-3}$: $\alpha(\delta) = 0.075$, $e_\delta = 0.539$, which is as bad as in [13]. If regularization with the differential operator $Lx := x''$ was used, we obtained

δ	10^{-1}	10^{-2}	10^{-3}
$\alpha(\delta)$	0.045	0.017	0.0036
e_δ	2.81	0.134	0.0121

which is significantly better for $\delta = 10^{-3}$; cf. MARTI's "Open Problem" in this volume.

Example 2: $k(t,s) := \begin{cases} t(s-1)(s^2+t^2-2s) & \text{if } t \le s \\ s(t-1)(s^2+t^2-2t) & \text{if } t > s, \end{cases}$

$y(t) = \frac{1}{4}(t-2t^3+t^4)$, $x_0(s) = 1$. Regularizing with $Lx := x''$, we obtained

δ	0.00125	0.000625	0.0003125	0.000156
$\alpha(\delta)$	0.0037	0.0023	0.0015	0.0009
e_δ	0.000317	0.000255	0.000214	0.0001
$e_\delta \cdot \delta^{-2/3}$	0.027	0.035	0.046	0.035

Again, the use of more knots did not change the results significantly.

Example 3: $k(t,s) := \exp(ts)$, $y(t) := \frac{1}{t}(e^t-1)$, $x_0(s) \equiv 1$. Classical Tikhonov regularization yielded

δ	10^{-1}	10^{-2}	10^{-3}
$\alpha(\delta)$	0.224	0.048	0.01
e_δ	0.159	0.127	0.075

while the use of the differential operator $Lx := x''$ resulted in

δ	10^{-1}	10^{-2}	10^{-3}
$\alpha(\delta)$	0.008	0.0018	0.0004
e_δ	0.524	0.0081	0.0011

Example 4: $k(t,s) := t.s$; $y(t) = \frac{t}{6}$, $x_0(s) = \frac{s}{2}$. Classical Tikhonov regularization with linear splines based on 9 knots yielded

δ	10^{-3}	10^{-4}	10^{-5}	10^{-6}
$\alpha(\delta)$	0.0264	0.0051	0.0011	0.0002
e_δ	0.056	0.013	0.0028	0.0006
$e_\delta.\delta^{-2/3}$	5.58	5.92	5.96	5.96

Although the integral operator of this example has a closed range, the convergence rate predicted by the theory is clearly seen in this example.

References:

[1] Arcangeli, R. (1966) Pseudo-solution de l'équation Ax=y, Comptes Rendus des Seances de l'Academie des Sciences, Paris, Sér. A, 263, 282-285

[2] Engl, H.W. (1981) Necessary and sufficient conditions for convergence of regularization methods for solving linear operator eouations of the first kind, Numer.Funct.Analysis and Optim. 3, 2o1-222

[3] Engl, H.W. (1983) Discrepancy principles for Tikhonov regularization of ill-posed problems leading to optimal convergence rates, submitted

[4] Engl, H.W. and Neubauer, A. (1984) A variant of Marti's method for solving ill-posed linear integral equations that leads to optimal convergence rates, submitted

[5] Groetsch, C.W. (1979) The parameter choice problem in linear regularization, to appear in M.Z.Nashed (ed.), Ill-posed problems, theory and practice

[6] Groetsch, C.W. (1983) On the asymptotic order of accuracy of Tikhonov regularization, J. of Optim. Theory and Appl. 41, 293-298

[7] Groetsch, C.W. (1977) Generalized inverses of linear operators, Dekker, New York

[8] Groetsch, C.W. (1984) The theory of Tikhonov regularization for Fredholm equations of the first kind, Pitman, Boston

[9] Groetsch, C.W. (1983) Comments on Morozov's discrepancy principle, in: G.Hämmerlin and K.H.Hoffmann (eds.), Improperly posed problems and their numerical treatment, Birkhäuser, Basel, 97-1o4

[1o] Groetsch, C.W. and Schock, E. (1983) Asymptotic convergence rate of Arcangeli's method for ill-posed problems, submitted

[11] Krein, S.G. and Petunin, J.I. (1966) Scales of Banach spaces, Russian Math. Surveys 21, 85-16o

[12] Locker, J. and Prenter, P.M. (198o) Regularization with differential operators; I: J.Math.Anal.Appl. 74, 5o4-529; II: SIAM J.Numer.Anal. 17, 247-267

[13] Marti, J.T. (1978) An algorithm for computing minimum norm solutions of Fredholm integral equations of the first kind, SIAM J.Numer.Anal. 15, 1o71-1o76

[14] Morozov, A. (1966) On the solution of functional equations by the method of regularization, Soviet Math.Dokl. 7, 414-417

[15] Nashed, M.Z. (ed.) (1976) Generalized inverses and applications, Academic Press, New York

[16] Natterer, F. (1984) Error bounds for Tikhonov regularization in Hilbert scales, Applic.Analysis (to appear)

[17] Neubauer, A. (1984) Zur Tikhonov-Regularisierung von linearen Operatorgleichungen, Diplomarbeit, Univ.Linz

[18] Schock, E. (1984) Approximate solution of ill-posed equations: arbitrarily slow convergence vs. superconvergence, this volume

[19] Trummer, M.R. (1983) Parameterwahl bei der Regularisierung schlecht gestellter Probleme mit Differentialoperatoren, Dissertation, ETH Zürich

Authors' address:

Institut für Mathematik, Johannes-Kepler-Universität, A-4o4o Linz, Austria

International Series of
Numerical Mathematics, Vol. 73

SPLINE-GALERKIN METHOD FOR SOLVING SOME QUANTUM MECHANIC INTEGRAL EQUATIONS

D Eyre[1] and M Brannigan[2]

[1]National Research Institute for Mathematical Sciences of the CSIR, Pretoria, South Africa.

[2]Department of Statistics and Computer Sciences, University of Georgia, Athens, USA.

1. Introduction

The Schrodinger equation is the fundamental equation that describes the nonrelativistic motion of particles in quantum mechanics. The Schrodinger equation, together with appropriate boundary conditions, can be written as an integral equation of the second kind. In this article we shall be concerned with the integral equation that describes the collision between three mutually interacting particles; the three-body problem. In the FADDEEV approach the integral equation for the three-body problem is multidimensional, with a kernel that is singular, and a non-smooth (C_1 discontinuity) in the solution function. In most cases of physical interest this equation can be solved only by using approximate numerical methods. Apart from the physical insight to be gained from such numerical solutions, the numerical treatment of the integral equation, in itself, poses an interesting mathematical problem. One seeks a method that is both flexible enough to respond to any rapidly varying structure in the solution to the integral equation, and, at the same time, is simple enough so that the integral of the kernel can be accurately and easily evaluated.

The final version of this paper has been submitted for publication elsewhere.

This article gives an outline of the Galerkin method with cubic spline approximants for solving the integral equations that arise in the quantum three-body problem. The numerical procedure is an extension of the method employed by BRANNIGAN and EYRE.

2. Spline-Galerkin Method

2.1 Description of the Integral Equation

Before addressing any particular problem that arises in quantum mechanics, we shall first consider the general problem of finding a solution to the inhomogeneous equation

$$(I-K)f = y \ ,$$

where $f,y \in C[a,b]$, and I is the identity operator. The integral operator K is given by

$$Kf = \int_a^b K(\cdot,t)f(t)dt \ .$$

The equations that we consider here have three properties:- first the kernel K is of the Cauchy principal value type and has the form

$$K(\cdot,t) = \tilde{K}(\cdot,t)/(u-t)$$

for some $u \in [a,b]$; second this kernel will contain weak logarithmic singulari= ties; thirdly it is known that the solution to the equation, namely $f(\cdot)$, has C_1 discontinuity at a given value $\eta \in [a,b]$.

It should be borne in mind that the integral equation described above may also be generalized to more than one dimension. Such equations are typical of those that arise in the quantum three-body problem.

2.2 Spline Approximation

In order to solve the integral equation numerically, we choose an approximation which satisfies the properties of f. For such an approximation a linear space of cubic splines form an ideal setting (see DE BOOR).

We partition the interval [a,b] by knots $\{t_i\}_1^N$. On this partition we construct the cubic B-splines $\{B_i \, ; \, i=0,\ldots,N+1\}$ using the stable method of COX and DE BOOR. The solution f is now approximated by the linear combination

$$\sum_{i=0}^{N+1} \alpha_i B_i \,,$$

where it remains to determine the coefficients $\{\alpha_i\}$.

For simple knots, $t_{i-1} < t_i$, the cubic spline is twice differentiable. The solution of the integral equation, on the other hand, has C_1 discontinuity at some value $\eta \in [a,b]$. One way to reduce continuity of the spline is to combine knots, i.e. use multiple knots. By combining three knots at $t_\nu = \eta$, the cubic spline has C_1 discontinuity at η.

2.3 The Galerkin Method

We must now obtain the coefficients $\{\alpha_i\}$. For this purpose we define a residual function

$$f = \sum_{i=0}^{N+1} \alpha_i (I-K) B_i - y \,.$$

We choose to calculate the coefficients $\{\alpha_i\}$ by solving the linear system of equations given by

$$(r,B_j) = 0 \;,\; j=0,\ldots,N+1 \,,$$

where $(\cdot,\cdot)$ denotes the usual inner product on $C[a,b]$. This is the classical Galerkin technique (see ATKINSON).

2.4 Iterative Galerkin

A useful device to improve the solution is the Neumann iteration scheme. Given an initial approximation f_1, which in this case is the spline approximation, a sequence of functions $\{f_\mu\}$ is constructed from the relation

$$f_\mu = y - Kf_{\mu-1} \,.$$

Note that for the first iterate

$$Kf_1 = \sum_{i=0}^{N+1} \alpha_i KB_i \ .$$

The coefficients $\{\alpha_i\}$ are known from the Galerkin solution, and the integrals KB_i do not require much additional computational effort.

3. Physical Example

As a concrete example we consider a special case of a one-dimensional integral equation taken from the three-body problem. This problem is described by the solution $T(p;E+i0)$ of the integral equation

$$T(p;E+i0) = v(p,k;E+i0) - \int_0^\infty K(p,p';E+i0)T(p';E+i0)p'^2dp' \ ,$$

over the semi-infinite interval $p \in [0,\infty)$. The energy E is a constant in this equation.

The kernel K is given by

$$K(p,p';E+i0) = v(p,p';E+i0)S(\tfrac{3}{4}p'^2 - E - i0) \ \frac{p'^2}{p'^2 - k^2 - i0} \ .$$

Here the momentum $k = \sqrt{\frac{4}{3}\ (E+\varepsilon)}$, and $\varepsilon > 0$ is the binding energy of the two-particle subsystem. The potential v is defined by the integral

$$v(p,p';E+i0) = -\frac{1}{2\pi}\int_{-1}^{1} \frac{\phi(q_1)\phi(q_2)}{p^2+p'^2+pp'y-E-i0}\, dy \ ,$$

where

$$q_1 = (\tfrac{1}{4}p^2 + p'^2 + pp'y)^{\frac{1}{2}} \ , \ q_2 = (p^2 + \tfrac{1}{4}p'^2 + pp'y)^{\frac{1}{2}} \ .$$

Finally, the functions ϕ and S are defined by

$$\phi(q) = \frac{C}{q^2+\beta^2} \ , \qquad C = [2\alpha\beta(\alpha+\beta)^3]^{\frac{1}{2}} \ ,$$

and

$$S(\xi^2) = \frac{(\xi + \beta)^2}{\alpha(\alpha + \beta)} [1 + 2\beta/(\alpha + \xi)]^{-1} ,$$

with $\alpha = \sqrt{\varepsilon}$ and $\xi = \sqrt{\frac{3}{4}p'^2 - E}$.

We may perform the integration for v. In this case we arrive at logarithmic singular terms of the form

$$\ell n|p^2 + p'^2 \pm pp' - E| .$$

The solution function $T(p;E + i0)$ has a square root singularity $(p - p_c)^{\frac{1}{2}}$ at $p_c = \sqrt{\frac{4}{3}E}$.

4. Numerical Procedure

In order to construct the spline basis, we first map the variable $p \in [0,\infty)$ onto a finite interval $[-1,+1]$, using

$$p(x) = (\frac{1+x}{1-x}) .$$

We partition the interval $[-1,+1]$ by points $\{x_i\}$. Three knots are placed in coincidence at the point $p(x_\nu) = p_c$.

In practice it is found that the most difficult and time consuming part of the problem is to evaluate moment integrals of the kernel K. On the finite interval $[-1,+1]$ we must evaluate the double integral

$$A_{ij} = \int_{-1}^{1} \int_{-1}^{1} K(p(x),p'(x');E + i0)B_i(x)B_j(x') \frac{2dx'}{(1 - x')^2} dx .$$

The numerical evaluation of this integral is made complicated by the presence of singularities in the integrand. For integration over the logarithmic singularities, we break up the region of integration and use a standard Gauss-Legendre quadrature formula. A method of subtracting the singularity is used to integrate over the Cauchy singularities.

5. Numerical Results

For our numerical results we take $\beta = 1.4498\ \mathrm{fm}^{-1}$, $\varepsilon = 0.05366\ \mathrm{fm}^{-2}$, and $E = 4\varepsilon$.

In order to get an impression of the robustness of the algorithm we have tried several distributions of knots. In each case three knots are placed in coincidence at the position of the C_1 discontinuity, $t_\nu = \eta$.

We first consider spacing the knots uniformly in the intervals $(-1,\eta)$ and $(\eta,+1)$ with an equal number of knots in each interval.

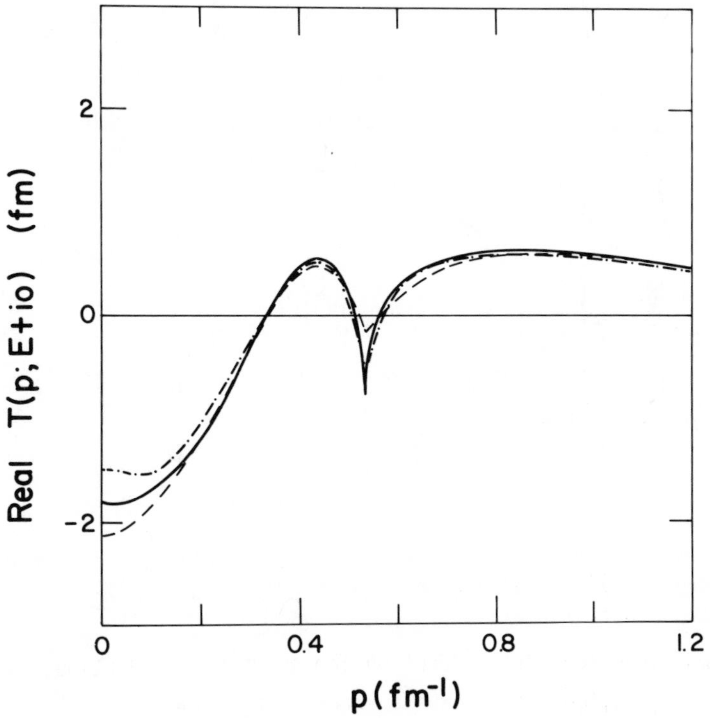

Fig. 1. Solid curve is the reference solution, the broken curve is for N=9, and dotted curve is for N=19.

The solid line in Fig. 1 shows the solution for the real part of T as a function of p. Of course, an exact solution of this problem is not available. The reference solution is obtained from a [6,6] Padé approximant, and agrees with the spline-Galerkin solution of the integral equation for a sufficiently large number of B-splines, at least to the accuracy that is shown in the figure.

Also shown in Fig. 1 is the approximate spline solution with N=9 and N=19, which are indicated by the broken and dotted lines respectively. It is noteworthy that with N=9 we have only two knots in each of the intervals $(-1,\eta)$ and $(\eta,+1)$.

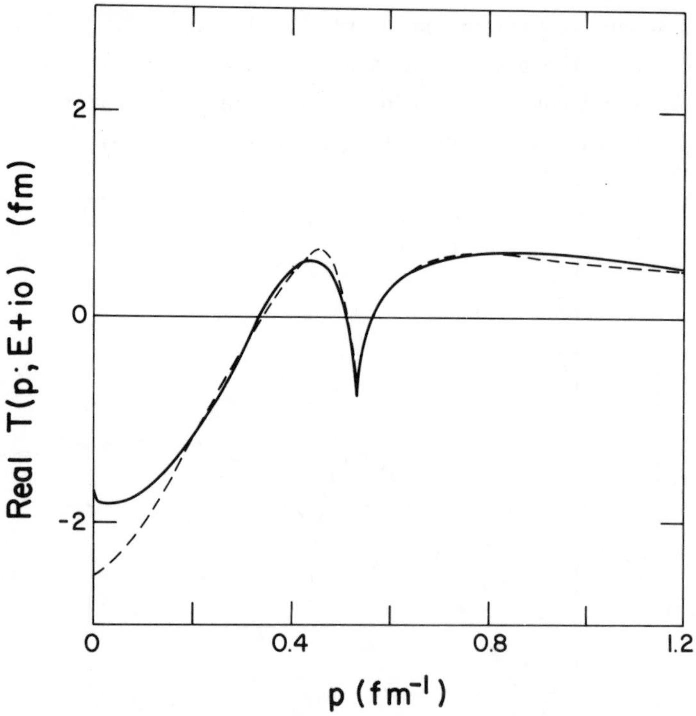

Fig. 2. Solid curve is the reference solution, the broken curve is for N=9. Knots are placed near the square root singularity.

We investigate the effect on the solution of changing the mesh. We know that the solution should have a square root term $\sqrt{p-p_c}$. Fig. 2 illustrates the real part of the solution obtained by packing the knots into a region close to the singularity at $p = p_c$. The approximate spline solution with N=9 is indicated by the broken line. The result with N=19 is indistinguishable from the reference solution on this figure. It is seen that the square root singu= larity is more accurately reproduced with the non-uniform mesh.

Table I. The L_2 error norm for several choices of knots with both uniform and non-uniform spacing

N	uniform		non-uniform	
	$\|T_1-T\|$	$\|T_2-T\|$	$\|T_1-T\|$	$\|T_2-T\|$
9	0.865	0.339	0.230(1)	0.185
11	0.500	0.277	0.155(1)	0.994(-1)
13	0.297	0.202	0.938	0.384(-1)
15	0.193	0.150	0.498	0.446(-1)
17	0.152	0.128	0.201	0.333(-1)
19	0.140	0.126	0.299(-1)	0.244(-1)
21	0.137	0.126	0.120	0.186(-1)

Table I shows the convergence behaviour of the solution in the L_2 norm as the number of knots N is increased. Here we compare the Galerkin solution T_1 with the once iterated Galerkin solution T_2. For a given number of knots the iterated Galerkin performs better and in the case of non-uniform spacing much better, than the Galerkin solution.

6. References

Atkinson, K.E. (1976) A survey of numerical methods for the solution of Fredholm integral equations of the second kind (SIAM, Philladelphia).

Brannigan, M. and Eyre, D. (1983) Splines and the Galerkin method for solving the integral equations of scattering theory, J. Math. Phys. 24, 1548-1554; (1984) E 25, 187.

Cox, M.G. (1972) The numeircal evaluation of B-splines, J. Inst. Math. Applic. 10, 134-149.

de Boor, C. (1972) A practical guide to splines (Springer, New York)

de Boor, C. (1972) On calculating with B-splines, J. Approx. Th. 6, 50-62.

Faddeev, L.D. (1963) Mathematical aspects of the three-body problem in quantum scattering theory, Steklov Math. Institute 69.

Dr David Eyre, Theoretical Physics Division, National Research Institute for Mathematical Sciences of the CSIR, P O Box 395, Pretoria 0001, Republic of South Africa.

International Series of
Numerical Mathematics, Vol. 73

INTEGRAL TREATMENT OF O.D.E WITH SPLINES

Tharwat Fawzy

Faculty of Sci. Math. Dept., Ismailia, Egypt.

1. Introduction

A spline approximation for the initial value problem $y'=f(x,y)$ was obtained by F.R. LOSCALZO and T.D. TALBOT [5],[6]. Then, following the method of LOSCALZO and TALBOT, G. MICULA, [7] presented a spline method for approximating the solution of $y''=f(x,y)$ with y' abscent. Recently, TH. FAWZY [1]-[4] introduced several local spline methods, using g-splines and non-polynomial splines, for approximating the solution of some initial value problems.

The purpose of this paper is to construct a spline approximation for the initial value problem $y''=f(x,y,y')$ for functions $f \in C^r$ such that the approximation is $0(h^{2+r+\alpha})$ in $y^{(i)}(x)$, $i=0,1,\ldots,r+2$, where h is the step size and $0<\alpha\leq 1$. The spline function approximating the solution is not necessarily polynomial spline.

This paper is in final form and no version of it will be submitted for publication elsewhere.

2. Assumptions and Description of The Method.

Consider the initial value problem:

(2.1) $y''=f(x,y,y'),\ y(x_0)=y_0,\ y'(x_0)=y'_0,\ 0=x_0\le x\le 1.$

Let $\Delta:\left\{x_k=kh\right\}_{k=0}^{n}$, where $x_n=1$. If $T=\{(x,y,y')\,|\,0\le x\le 1\}$, then we assume that f and its j-th possible derivatives, $j=0,1,\ldots,r$, are defined and continuous in:

$$D: |x-x_0|<\alpha,\quad |y-y_0|<\beta,\quad |y'-y'_0|<\gamma$$

where $T \subseteq D$. We also assume for all (x,y,y'), (x,y_1,y'_1) and (x,y_2,y'_2) in D,

(2.2) $|f^{(j)}(x,y,y')| \le M$ and

(2.3) $|f^{(j)}(x,y_1,y'_1)-f^{(j)}(x,y_2,y'_2)| \le L\{|y_1-y_2|+|y'_1-y'_2|\}$

where L is the Lipschitz constant, $f^{(j)}(x,y,y')$ denotes the j-th derivative D^jf in terms of x,y,y' and $j=0,1,\ldots,r$. If $M^*=\max(||y'||_\infty, ||f^{(j)}||_\infty)$, $j=0,1,\ldots,r$, then we also assume

(2.4) $M^*(e^h-1) < \min(\beta,\gamma)$.

Finally, we assume that $y^{(r+2)}(x) = f^{(r)}(x,y(x),y'(x))$ has the modulus of continuity $\omega(f^{(r)};h) = \omega_r(h)$.

Let $x_k\le x\le x_{k+1}$ and $k=0,1,\ldots,n-1$. Then under the above assumptions, we define the spline function approximating the solution of (2.1) as $S_\Delta(x)$ given by

(2.5) $$S_\Delta(x) = S_k(x) = S_{k-1}(x_k) + S'_{k-1}(x_k)(x-x_k) + \int_{x_k}^{x}\int_{x_k}^{t} f\{u,Q_k(u),Q_k^*(u)\}\,du\,dt$$

where $x_k\le u\le t\le x\le x_{k+1}$ and $S_{-1}(x_0)=y_0$, $S'_{-1}(x_0)=y'_0$, while for $j=0,1,\ldots,r$ we define

(2.6) $$S_k^{(j+2)}(x) = f^{(j)}(x,S_k(x),S_k'(x))$$

and in (2.5), the functions Q_k and Q_k^* are given by

(2.7) $$Q_k(x)=S_{k-1}(x_k)+S'_{k-1}(x_k)(x-x_k)+\sum_{j=0}^{r}\frac{\bar{f}_k^{(j)}}{(j+2)!}(x-x_k)^{j+2},$$

(2.8) $$Q_k^*(x)=S'_{k-1}(x_k)+\int_{x_k}^{x} f\{t,Q_k(t),Q_k'(t)\}dt \quad \text{and}$$

(2.9) $$\bar{f}_k^{(j)}=f^{(j)}(x_k,S_{k-1}(x_k),S'_{k-1}(x_k)), \quad j=0,1,\ldots,r.$$

Obviously, such spline function $S_\Delta(x)$ given in (2.5)-(2.9) exists and is unique. Moreover, by the construction it is clear that

(2.10) $$S_\Delta(x)\in C^1[0,1].$$

3. Error Bounds.

We first prove the boundness of $S_\Delta(x)$ and $S'_\Delta(x)$, such that the Lipschitz condition (2.3) could be applicable for $f^{(j)}(x,S_k(x),S_k'(x))$.

Lemma 3.1. Let $\Psi=\{(x,S_\Delta(x),S'_\Delta(x))\,|\,0\le x\le 1\}$. If $h<\ell n2$, then $\Psi\subseteq D$.

Proof. Using (2.7) and (2.4) we easily get

$$|Q_0(x)-y_0|<\beta,\ |Q_0'(x)-y_0'|<\gamma \Rightarrow |f(x,Q_0(x),Q'(x)|\le M.$$

Using the above result with (2.8) and (2.4), we get

$$|Q_0^*(x)-y_0'|<\gamma \Rightarrow |f(x,Q_0(x),Q_0^*(x))|\le M.$$

So, for $x_0 \le x \le x_1$ we get

$$|S_0(x)-y_0| \le h|y_0'| + \frac{h^2}{2} M < M^*(h + \frac{h^2}{2}) < B \quad \text{and}$$

$$|S_0'(x)-y_0'| \le \int_{x_0}^{x} |f(t,Q_0(t),Q_0^*(t))|dt \le Mh < \gamma.$$

Thus, we have proved that $S_0(x)$ and $S_0'(x)$ are bounded and in D. Using the induction, then it is easy to complete the proof.

Theorem 3.1. Let y(x) be the exact solution of (2.1) and let $S_\Delta(x)$ given in (2.5)-(2.9) be the approximate solution. If $f \in C^r$ and $h < \ell n 2$, then we have

$$||D^j(y-S_\Delta)||_\infty \le c\ h^{2+r}\ \omega_r(h)$$

where c is a constant independent of h.

Proof. The exact solution of (2.1) can be written for $x_k \le x \le x_{k+1}$ and $k=0,1,\dots,n-1$ in the form

$$y(x)=y_k+y_k'(x-x_k) + \int_{x_k}^{x} \int_{x_k}^{t} f\{u,y_k(u),y_k^*(u)\}dudt, \tag{3.1}$$

where $x_k \le u \le t \le x \le x_{k+1}$ and

$$y_k(u) = y_k+y_k'(u-x_k) + \sum_{j=0}^{r-1} \frac{f_k^{(j)}}{(j+2)!} (u-x_k)^{j+2} + \tag{3.2}$$

$$+ \frac{1}{(r+2)!} f^{(r)}(\xi_k,y(\xi_k),y'(\xi_k))(u-x_k)^{r+2},\ x_k<\xi_k<u, \quad \text{and}$$

$$y_k^*(u) = y_k' + \int_{x_k}^{u} f\{v,y_k(v),y_k'(v)\}dv. \tag{3.3}$$

Let us use the following notations for $j=0,1$ and $x_k \le x \le x_{k+1}$,

$$e^{(j)}(x) = |y^{(j)}(x)-S_k^{(j)}(x)| \qquad \text{and}$$

$$e_k^{(j)} = |y_k^{(j)}-S_{k-1}^{(j)}(x_k)| = |y_k^{(j)}-S_k^{(j)}(x_k)|.$$

Then using (2.5)-(2.9), (3.1)-(3.3) and Lemma 3.1, we get

(3.4) $\quad e(x) \le e_k(1+c_0h)+c_1he_k'+c_2h^{r+4}\ \omega_r(h) \quad$ and

(3.5) $\quad e'(x) \le e_k'(1+c_3h)+c_4he_k+c_5h^{r+3}\ \omega_r(h)$

where c_i, $i=0,1,\dots,5$, are constants independent of h. Using the definition of matrix inequality (see [3]) then (3.4) and (3.5) can be written in the form

(3.6) $\quad E(x) = \begin{bmatrix} e(x) \\ e'(x) \end{bmatrix} \le (I_r+hA)E_k+h^{r+3}\ \omega_r(h)B, \quad$ where

$$A = \begin{bmatrix} c_0 & c_1 \\ c_4 & c_3 \end{bmatrix},\ E_k = \begin{bmatrix} e_k \\ e_k' \end{bmatrix} \text{ and } B = \begin{bmatrix} c_2 \\ c_5 \end{bmatrix}.$$

Using the iteration, then (3.6) with $E_0=(0\ 0)^T$ becomes

$$E(x) \le h^{r+3}\ \omega^r(h)(\sum_{j=0}^{k} (I_2+hA)^j)B$$

$$\le h^{r+2}\ \omega_r(h)(e^A-I_2)B \le h^{r+2}\ \omega_r(h)C$$

where $C=(c_6\ c_7)^T$, and c_6 and c_7 are constants independent of h. Finally we have for $j=0,1,\dots,r$

$$|y^{(j+2)}(x)-S_k^{(j+2)}(x)|=|f^{(j)}(x,y(x),y'(x))-f^{(j)}(x,S_k(x),S_k'(x))| \le$$

$$\le L\{|y(x)-S_k(x)|+|y'(x)-S_k'(x)|\} \le$$

$$\le L(c_6+c_7)h^{r+2}\ \omega_r(h).$$

We take $c=\max(c_6,c_7,L(c_6+c_7))$ and this completes the proof.

4. Numerical Results.

The following results are obtained at x=1 for the D.E. y"=y, y(0)=2, y'(0)=0 where h=0.1:

Num. Results (r=2):	3.086161255	2.35042339
Exact Results:	y(1) = 3.086161270	y'(1) = 2.35042387
Num. Results (r=4):	3.086161270	2.35042387

References

1. Fawzy, Th. Spline Functions and Cauchy Problems, I,III. Annales Univ. Sci. Budapest. Sec.Comp. Tom I. (1978), 81-98, 35-46
2. Fawzy, Th. Spline Functions and Cauchy Problems, II, IV. Acta Math. Acad. Sci. Hungar, Tom 29,30 (3-4) (1977). 259-271, 219-226
3. Fawzy, Th. and A. Al-Mutib. Error of an arbitrary order for the approximate solution of y'=f(x,y) with spline functions. Proceeding of BAIL I Conference, Dublin 1980.
4. Fawzy, Th. Spline Functions and Cauchy Problems, VII. Annales Univ. Sci. Budapest Sec. Math. Tom 24(1981), 57-62.
5. Loscalzo, F.R. and Talbot, T.D. Spline function approximation for solutions of ordinary diff. equations. Siam J. Num. Anal. 3, (1967), 433-445.
6. Loscalzo, F.R. and Talbot, T.D. Spline function approximation for solution of ordinary diff. equations. Bull. Am. Math. Soc. 73 (1967), 438-442
7. Micula, Gh. Approximate solution of the differential equation y'=f(x,y) with spline functions. Math. of Computation. Vol 27 No. 4 (1973). 807-816.

Dr. Tharwat Fawzy, Math. Dept., Faculty of Science, Suez-Canal University. ISMAILIA, EGYPT.

International Series of
Numerical Mathematics, Vol. 73

PRODUCT INTEGRATION FOR WEAKLY SINGULAR INTEGRAL EQUATIONS IN $\mathbb{R}^m$

Ivan G. Graham
School of Mathematics,
University of Bath, U.K.

Claus Schneider
Fachbereich Mathematik
Johannes Gutenberg-Universität Mainz
West Germany

1. Introduction

In this note we discuss the numerical solution of the second kind Fredholm integral equation :

$$y(t) = f(t) + \lambda\int_{\Omega}\psi_\alpha(|t-s|)g(t,s)y(s)ds \ , \ t\in\bar{\Omega}, \tag{1}$$

where $\lambda\in\mathbb{C}\setminus\{0\}$, the functions f,g are given and continuous, $|.|$ denotes the Euclidean norm, and ψ_α, $0<\alpha\leqq m$, is a given function on $[0,\infty)$ which satisfies

$$|\psi_\alpha^{(j)}(r)| \leqq C_j \begin{cases} r^{\alpha-m-j} \ , & j\geqq 0, \ m>\alpha>0 \\ \begin{Bmatrix} \ln(r) & , \ j=0 \\ r^{-j} & , \ j>0 \end{Bmatrix} , & \alpha=m, \end{cases}$$

with C_j not depending on r. Here $\bar{\Omega}$ is the closure of a bounded domain $\Omega\subset\mathbb{R}^m$.

This paper is in final form and no version of it will be submitted for publication elsewhere.

With K denoting the integral operator in (1), we can abbreviate that equation by writing $y = f + \lambda Ky$. We assume that $1/\lambda$ is not an eigenvalue of K. It is then a standard result that (1) has a unique continuous solution y. We also assume that each point x of $\partial\Omega$ (the boundary of Ω) should have a neighbourhood U_x such that $\partial\Omega \cap U_x$ is the graph of a Lipschitz continuous function of m-1 variables. (In two dimensions, for example, this allows polygonal boundaries, but excludes boundaries with cusps.)

For $n \in \mathbb{N}$, intoduce a mesh Π_n by choosing $N=N(n)$ open simply connected pairwise disjoint subsets of Ω, $\{\Omega_i\}_{i=1}^N$ with the property that $\bar{\Omega} = \bigcup_{i=1}^N \bar{\Omega}_i$. Let $h:=\max\{h_i : i=1,..,N\}$, where h_i is the diameter of Ω_i and assume that $h \to 0$ as $n \to \infty$. Moreover, assume that the meshes Π_n are regular, i.e. that each Ω_i contains a sphere of diameter γh_i, where $\gamma > 0$ is independent of i and n. Then, if V_i denotes the volume of Ω_i, a constant C exists such that

$$V_i \geqq Ch_i^m . \tag{2}$$

We set $S_n := \text{span}\{u_i : i=1,...,N\}$, where u_i is the function on $\bar{\Omega}$ which is 1 on Ω_i and 0 elsewhere. For each i, let t_i denote the centroid of Ω_i. We then define a <u>product integration</u> solution y_n of (1) by the equation

$$y_n(t) = f(t) + \lambda \int_\Omega \phi_\alpha(|t-s|)[P_n(g_t y_n)](s)ds \ , \ t \in \bar{\Omega}, \tag{3}$$

where P_n is the interpolation operator $P_n \Phi := \sum_{i=1}^N \Phi(t_i)u_i$ and $g_t(s) := g(t,s)$. We abbreviate (3) by writing $y_n = f + \lambda K_n y_n$. Well known arguments (cf. [1]) show that, for n large enough, (3) is uniquely solvable and that $y_n \to y$ with

$$\|y - y_n\|_\infty = O(\|(K - K_n)y\|_\infty). \tag{4}$$

In this note we describe some recent results (given precisely in Theorems 4 and 6 below) on the rate of convergence of y_n to y.

2. Preliminaries

For $\nu \in \mathbb{N}$, we let C^ν denote the usual Banach space of functions which have partial derivatives of order $\leqq \nu$ bounded and uniformly continuous on Ω. For $t\in\bar{\Omega}$, let $\rho(t) := \inf\{\ |t-s|: s\in\partial\Omega\ \}$. Throughout the paper we will let C denote a generic constant which may vary from instance to instance.

Now return to equation (1). For the rest of the paper assume $f\in C^{\infty}$ and that g is infinitely continuously differentiable on $\mathbb{R}^m\times\mathbb{R}^m$. Also, define $\beta>0$, $\beta\notin\mathbb{N}$ by choosing $\beta=\alpha$ if $\alpha\notin\mathbb{N}$ and $0<\beta<\alpha$ if $\alpha\in\mathbb{N}$. Then set

$$p := \min\{\beta,2\}\ ,\qquad q := \min\{\beta,1\}\ .$$

Lemma 1. (Cf. [6]). (i) Let $\beta=\nu+\sigma$, where $\nu\in\mathbb{N}$ and $0<\sigma<1$. Then $y\in C^{\nu}$ and for $|\mu|=\nu$ we have $|D^{\mu}y(t) - D^{\mu}y(t')| \leqq C|t-t'|^{\sigma}$, for $t,t'\in\Omega$.
(ii) For $|\mu|\geqq\beta$ we have $|D^{\mu}y(t)| \leqq C_{\mu}[\rho(t)]^{\beta-|\mu|}$, for $t\in\Omega$, with C_{μ} not depending on t.

For further results on the regularity of y cf. the doctoral thesis [3].

Lemma 2.
$$\inf_{x_n\in S_n} \|g_t y - x_n\|_{\infty} = O(h^q)\ .$$

Proof: This follows from Lemma 1 (i).

Lemma 3. For $t\in\bar{\Omega}$, define $\phi_{\alpha,t}(s) := \phi_{\alpha}(|t-s|)$ and define $u_{\alpha,t,n}\in S_n$ by setting $u_{\alpha,t,n}$ equal to the constant $V_i^{-1}\int_{\Omega_i}\phi_{\alpha,t}(s)ds$ on each Ω_i. Then

(i) $\|u_{\alpha,t,n}\|_{\infty,\Omega_i} \leqq Ch_i^{\beta}V_i^{-1}$

(ii) $\|\phi_{\alpha,t} - u_{\alpha,t,n}\|_1 \leqq Ch^q$.

Proof: Part (i) is straightforward.
(ii): For $\varphi: \mathbb{R}^m \to \mathbb{C}$, $x,\eta\in\mathbb{R}^m$ let $\Delta_{\eta}\varphi(x) := \varphi(x+\eta) - \varphi(x)$.

Let $\Omega_i - x := \{y-x : y\in\Omega_i\}$. Then $\int_{\Omega_i - x}\Delta_{\eta}\varphi(x)d\eta = \int_{\Omega_i}\varphi(s)ds - V_i\varphi(x)$, and so

$$\|V_i^{-1}\int_{\Omega_i}\varphi(s)ds - \varphi\|_{1,\Omega_i} \leqq V_i^{-1}\int_{\Omega_i}\int_{\Omega_i - x}|\Delta_{\eta}\varphi(x)|d\eta dx.$$

When $x\in\Omega_i$, $\Omega_i - x\subset B(0,h_i) :=\{\ x\in\mathbb{R}^m\ :\ |x| < h_i\}$.

Hence, setting $\varphi=\psi_{\alpha,t}$, changing the order of integration in the right hand side and summing over i, we obtain

$$\| \psi_{\alpha,t} - u_{\alpha,t,n} \|_1 \leq \sum_{i=1}^{N} V_i^{-1} \int_{B(0,h_i)} \|\Delta_\eta \psi_{\alpha,t} \|_{1,\Omega_i} d\eta . \tag{5}$$

Now the methods of [5] show that

$$\| \Delta_\eta \psi_{\alpha,t} \|_{1,\Omega_i} \leq |\eta|^q |\psi_{\alpha,t}|_{q,1,\Omega_i} , \tag{6}$$

where $|.|_{q,1,\Omega_i}$ are certain Nikol'skii space seminorms which have the property that $\sum_{i=1}^{N} |\psi_{\alpha,t}|_{q,1,\Omega_i}$ is bounded independently of N. Substituting (6) into (5), integrating with respect to η and using (2) completes the proof.

3. Main theorems

Using the approximation theory developed above we now have :

Theorem 4. Under the conditions already imposed $\|y-y_n\|_\infty = O(h^p)$.

Proof: By definition we have

$$\begin{aligned} |(K-K_n)y(t)| \leq\ & |(\overline{\psi}_{\alpha,t}-\overline{u}_{\alpha,t,n} , (I-P_n)(g_t y))| + \\ & |(\overline{u}_{\alpha,t,n} , (I-P_n)(g_t y))| \end{aligned} \tag{7}$$

where (.,.) denotes the $L^2(\Omega)$ inner product. Now Lemmas 2 and 3 imply that the first term is $O(h^{2q})$. The second term can be shown to be $O(h^p)$ by the method described in [4, Section 4]. (Note that product integration is a simple generalisation of the iterated collocation considered in [4].) Then, since $2q \geq p$, the result follows.

Remark. The different orders for the first and second terms of the right hand side of (7) raise the question of whether the result of Theorem 4 is actually sharp. We shall show below that in the case of tensor product meshes over two dimensional rectangular regions we can prove that both the first and second terms are actually $O(h^{2q})$. It remains an open question as to whether this tighter result holds in more general cases.

The results described here have found practical application in the solution of the current distribution problem ($\alpha=m=2$, cf. [4]). The methods of analysis are generalisations of techniques developed for analogous one-dimensional equations, see [2] and [7].

From now on we restrict attention to the case $\overline{\Omega} = [0,1]\times[0,d] \subset \mathbb{R}^2$. We define a mesh Π_n on $\overline{\Omega}$ as follows. For $n \in \mathbb{N}$, let $r_1(n)$, $r_2(n) \in \mathbb{N}$ and choose meshes

$$0=x_0<x_1<\ldots<x_{r_1(n)}=1 \;, \quad 0=z_0<z_1<\ldots<z_{r_2(n)}=d$$

on [0,1] and [0,d]. For $1\leqq i\leqq r_1(n)$, $1\leqq j\leqq r_2(n)$, let Ω_{ij} denote the rectangle $(x_{i-1},x_i)\times(z_{j-1},z_j)$, and let Π_n be the mesh on $\overline{\Omega}$ composed of all possible Ω_{ij}. Let $\tau_i:=x_i-x_{i-1}$, $\sigma_j:=z_j-z_{j-1}$, and $\tau:=\min\{\tau_i\}$, $\sigma:=\min\{\sigma_j\}$. For each Ω_{ij}, let h_{ij} denote its diameter and V_{ij} denote its area. Then as before we set $h:=\max\{h_{ij}\}$ and we assume that $h\to 0$ as $n\to\infty$. Corresponding to (2), we assume $V_{ij} \geqq Ch_{ij}^2$. Under these assumptions we can prove by elementary arguments :

Lemma 5. There exist constants C_1, C_2, C_3 such that

(i) $C_1^{-1} \leqq \tau_i/\sigma_j \leqq C_1$; (ii) $\tau_i/\tau_l \leqq C_2$; (iii) $\sigma_j/\sigma_m \leqq C_3$, for all i,j,l,m.

Now we are ready to prove

Theorem 6. In the case $\overline{\Omega} = [0,1]\times[0,d]$ with the meshes as described above, we have $\| y - y_n \|_\infty = O(h^{2q})$.

Proof: The proof of Theorem 4 (cf. formula (7)) has shown that we have only to study $|(\overline{u}_{\alpha,t,n} \;, (I-P_n)(g_t y))|$:

$$|(\overline{u}_{\alpha,t,n} \;, (I-P_n)(g_t y)| \leqq \sum_{i,j} \Big| \int_{\Omega_{ij}} u_{\alpha,t,n}(I-P_n)(g_t y)(s)ds\Big| \leqq$$

$$\leqq \sum_{\overline{\Omega}_{ij}\cap\partial\Omega\neq\emptyset} \underbrace{\|u_{\alpha,t,n}\|_{1,\Omega_{ij}} \, \|(I-P_n)(g_t y)\|_{\infty,\Omega_{ij}}}_{=:\,F_{ij}} \; +$$

$$+ \sum_{\bar{\Omega}_{ij} \cap \partial\Omega = \emptyset} \underbrace{\|u_{\alpha,t,n}\|_{\infty,\Omega_{ij}} \left| \int_{\Omega_{ij}} (I-P_n)(g_t y)(s)ds \right|}_{=: E_{ij}}$$

$=: F + E$.

Analysis of $F = \sum_{i=2}^{r_1(n)-1} (F_{i1} + F_{ir_2(n)}) + \sum_{j=1}^{r_2(n)} (F_{1j} + F_{r_1(n),j})$:

Lemma 2 implies $\|(I-P_n)(g_t y)\|_{\infty,\Omega_{ij}} \leqq Ch^q$, furthermore $\|u_{\alpha,t,n}\|_{1,\Omega_{ij}} \leqq C\int_{\Omega_{ij}} |t-s|^{\alpha-2}ds$. Now pick $t^* \in \bigcup_{j=1}^{r_2(n)} \bar{\Omega}_{1j}$ such that $|t^*-t| \leqq |s-t|$ for all $s \in \bigcup_j \Omega_{1j}$. Then $|t-s|^{\alpha-2} \leqq C|t^*-s|^{\alpha-2}$ for all $s \in \bigcup_j \Omega_{1j}$. Thus $\sum_{j=1}^{r_2(n)} F_{1j} \leqq Ch^q \sum_{j=1}^{r_2(n)} \int_{\Omega_{1j}} |t^*-s|^{\alpha-2}ds$. Now certainly $t^* \in \bar{\Omega}_{1J}$ for some $J \in \{1,\dots,r_2(n)\}$. Then, with obvious modification if $J=1$ or $J=r_2(n)$, we have $\sum_{j=J-1}^{J+1} \int_{\Omega_{1j}} |t^*-s|^{\alpha-2}ds \leqq Ch^\alpha$. Also, for $s \in \Omega_{1j}$ with $j=1(1)J-2$, we have $|t^*-s| \geq (J-1-j)\sigma$ and thus $|t^*-s|^{\alpha-2} \leqq (J-1-j)^{\alpha-2}\sigma^{\alpha-2}$. Hence

$$\sum_{j=1}^{J-2} \int_{\Omega_{1j}} |t^*-s|^{\alpha-2}ds \leqq \sum_{j=1}^{J-2} V_{1j}\sigma^{\alpha-2}(J-1-j)^{\alpha-2} \leqq h^\alpha \sum_{j=1}^{J-2} \tau_1\sigma_j(J-1-j)^{\alpha-2}/\sigma^2 \leqq$$

$\leqq Ch^\alpha \sum_{j=1}^{J-2} j^{\alpha-2}$ (by Lemma 5). Therefore we obtain

$\sum_{j=1}^{r_2(n)} F_{1j} \leqq Ch^{\alpha+q} + Ch^q h^\alpha \sum_{j=1}^{r_2(n)} j^{\alpha-2}$. For $0<\alpha<1$ $\sum_{j=1}^{r_2(n)} j^{\alpha-2} = O(1)$, $n\to\infty$, and hence $\sum_{j=1}^{r_2(n)} F_{1j} = O(h^{2q})$, $h\to 0$. If $1<\alpha<2$ then $h \sum_{j=1}^{r_2(n)} (jh)^{\alpha-2} \leqq \int_0^1 t^{\alpha-2}dt + o(1)$.

Thus, $\sum_{j=1}^{r_2(n)} F_{1j} = O(h^2)$, $h\to 0$, in this case. Applying similar arguments to the remaining parts of F we obtain $F \leqq Ch^{2q}$. (The cases $\alpha=1$ or $\alpha=2$ are included by appropriately substituting β for α).

Analysis of $E = \sum_{i=2}^{r_1(n)-1} \sum_{j=2}^{r_2(n)-1} E_{ij} =: \sum_{(i,j)\in\Lambda} E_{ij}$:

If $y\in C^2(\Omega_{ij})$ then $\int_{\Omega_{ij}} y(t)dt - V_{ij}y(\frac{x_{i-1}+x_i}{2},\frac{z_{j-1}+z_j}{2}) =$

$= \frac{V_{ij}}{24}\{ \tau_i^2 y^{(2,0)}(\zeta_{ij},\xi_{ij}) + \sigma_j^2 y^{(0,2)}(\frac{x_{i-1}+x_i}{2},\mu_{ij}) \}$, ξ_{ij}, $\mu_{ij}\in[z_{j-1},z_j]$, $\zeta_{ij}\in[x_{i-1},x_i]$ (cf. [8] p.65). With this remainder formula for the midpoint--rule and with Lemma 1 we obtain

$$| \int_{\Omega_{ij}} (I-P_n)(g_t y)(s)ds \; | \leqq \frac{V_{ij}}{24}\{ \tau_i^2 \, ||(g_t y)^{(2,0)}||_{\infty,\Omega_{ij}} + \sigma_j^2 \, ||(g_t y)^{(0,2)}||_{\infty,\Omega_{ij}} \}$$

$$\leqq \frac{CV_{ij}}{24}\{ \tau_i^2 + \sigma_j^2 \} \max_{t\in\Omega_{ij}} [\rho(t)]^{\beta-2} \leqq CV_{ij} \, ||\rho^{\beta-2}||_{\infty,\Omega_{ij}} (\tau_i^2 + \sigma_j^2) \text{ . Hence}$$

$$E_{ij} \leqq C(\tau_i^2 + \sigma_j^2) \, ||\rho^{\beta-2}||_{\infty,\Omega_{ij}} \int_{\Omega_{ij}} |t-s|^{\alpha-2} ds \tag{8}$$

Obviously, $||\rho^{\beta-2}||_{\infty,\Omega_{ij}}$ depends on the position of Ω_{ij} in Ω which may be characterized with the boundary of Ω :

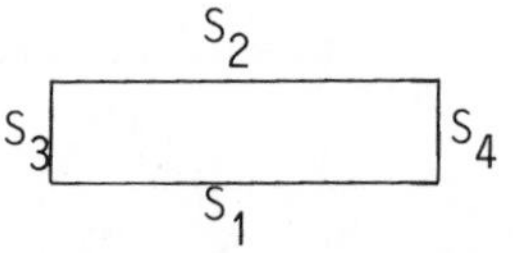

and the sets of indices $\Lambda_\nu := \{ (i,j)\in\Lambda : \sup_{s\in\Omega_{ij}} \inf_{t\in S_\nu} |t-s| \leqq \sup_{s\in\Omega_{ij}} \inf_{t\in S_\mu} |t-s|$ for all $\mu=1,2,3,4,\ \mu\neq\nu \}$, $\nu=1(1)4$. Thus, Λ_ν is the set of indices $(i,j)\in\Lambda$ such that the distance of the farthest point in Ω_{ij} from S_ν is not greater than the distance of the farthest point in Ω_{ij} from any of the other S_μ, $\nu\neq\mu$. Clearly it may be the case that $\Lambda_\nu \cap \Lambda_\mu \neq \emptyset$, for some $\nu\neq\mu$, but we certainly have $\bigcup_{\nu=1}^{4} \Lambda_\nu = \Lambda$.

Now we will study (8) for $(i,j)\in\Lambda_1$ (the remaining three cases may be discussed in the same way). We have $[\rho(s)]^{\beta-2} = \inf_{t\in S_1} |t-s|^{\beta-2} \leqq (j-1)^{\beta-2}\sigma^{\beta-2}$. Substituting into (8) yields

$$E_{ij} \leqq C\int_{\Omega_{ij}} |t-s|^{\alpha-2}ds\cdot(j-1)^{\beta-2}\sigma^{\beta-2}(\tau_i^2+\sigma_j^2) \leqq Ch^\beta(j-1)^{\beta-2}\int_{\Omega_{ij}}|t-s|^{\alpha-2}ds$$

- by Lemma 5. Now let t^* be the nearest point of $\bigcup_{(i,j)\in\Lambda_1}\Omega_{ij}$ to t. Then $C|t^*-s|^{\alpha-2} \geqq |t-s|^{\alpha-2}$ for all $s\in\bigcup_{(i,j)\in\Lambda_1}\Omega_{ij}$ and so for $(i,j)\in\Lambda_1$ we have

$$E_{ij} \leqq Ch^\beta(j-1)^{\beta-2}\int_{\Omega_{ij}} |t^*-s|^{\alpha-2}ds .$$

Assume $t^*\in\Omega_{I,J}$ for some $(I,J)\in\Lambda_1$ and let $\Lambda_{IJ}:=\{I-1,I,I+1\}\times\{J-1,J,J+1\}$. Then

$$\sum_{(i,j)\in\Lambda_1\cap\Lambda_{IJ}} E_{ij} \leqq Ch^{\alpha+\beta} .$$

Now consider $s\in\Omega_{ij}$ for $(i,j)\in\Lambda_1$ but $i\notin\{I-1,I,I+1\}$. Then $|t^*-s|\geqq(|I-i|-1)\tau$ and so

$$\sum_{\substack{(i,j)\in\Lambda_1\\ i\notin\{I-1,I,I+1\}}} E_{ij} \leqq Ch^\beta \sum_{\substack{(i,j)\in\Lambda_1\\ i\notin\{I-1,I,I+1\}}} V_{ij}(|I-i|-1)^{\alpha-2}\tau^{\alpha-2}(j-1)^{\beta-2} \leqq$$

$\leqq Ch^{\alpha+\beta}\sum_{i=1}^{r_1(n)}\sum_{j=1}^{r_2(n)} i^{\alpha-2}j^{\beta-2}$. For $0<\alpha<1$, $0<\beta<1$ this double sum is $O(1)$, $n\to\infty$, for $1<\alpha,\beta<2$ $h\sum_{i=1}^{r_1(n)}(ih)^{\alpha-2}\cdot h\sum_{j=1}^{r_2(n)}(jh)^{\beta-2} \leqq \int_0^1 t^{\alpha-2}dt\cdot\int_0^1 t^{\beta-2}dt + o(1)$ leading to $O(h^{2q})$ in both cases for this sum over E_{ij}. Finally consider $s\in\Omega_{ij}$ for $(i,j)\in\Lambda_1\cap\{I-1,I,I+1\}\times\{2,3,..,J-2,J+2,..,r_2(n)-1\} =: \Lambda_{1IJ}$. We have

$|t^*-s|^{\alpha-2} \leq C(|J-j|-1)^{\alpha-2}\sigma^{\alpha-2}$ and so

$$\sum_{(i,j)\in\Lambda_{1IJ}} E_{ij} \leq Ch^{\beta} \sum_{i=I-1}^{I+1} \sum_{\substack{j=2 \\ j\notin\{J-1,J,J+1\}}}^{r_2(n)-1} (j-1)^{\beta-2} V_{ij}(|J-j|-1)^{\alpha-2}\sigma^{\alpha-2} \leq$$

$$\leq Ch^{\alpha+\beta} \sum_{j=1}^{r_2(n)} j^{\beta-2} \leq Ch^{2q} .$$

Combining the results ensures $\sum_{(i,j)\in\Lambda_1} E_{ij} \leq Ch^{2q}$.

Similarly $\sum_{(i,j)\in\Lambda_\nu} E_{ij} \leq Ch^{2q}$ for $\nu=2,3,4$ and so $E \leq Ch^{2q}$, the required result.

Remark. For an analysis of the iterated Galerkin method for integral equations of the kind discussed here, see [9].

4. References

1. Anselone, P.M. (1971) Collectively compact operator approximation theory. (Prentice-Hall, Englewood Cliffs, New Jersey).
2. Chandler, G.A. (1979) Superconvergence of numerical solutions to second kind integral equations. Ph.D. thesis, Australian National University, Canberra.
3. Eschenbach, D. (1984) Zur numerischen Behandlung schwachsingulärer homogener Integralgleichungen in einer und in mehreren Dimensionen. Doctoral thesis, Ludwig-Maximilians-Universität, München.
4. Graham, I.G. (1984) Numerical methods for multidimensional integral equations. In: Noye, J. and Fletcher, C. (eds.) Computational techniques and applications. (North Holland, New York).
5. Graham, I.G. (to appear) Estimates for the modulus of smoothness. J.Approx.Th.
6. Pitkäranta, J. (1980) Estimates for the derivatives of solutions to weakly singular Fredholm integral equations. SIAM J.Math.Anal. 11, 952-968.
7. Schneider, C. (1981) Product integration for weakly singular integral equations. Math.Comp. 36, 207-213.
8. Schneider, C. (1983) Error analysis for numerical integration - an algorithmic approach. Habilitation thesis, Johannes Gutenberg-Universität, Mainz.

9. Sloan, I.H. (1984) The iterated Galerkin method for integral equations of the second kind. In: Jefferies, B. and McIntosh, A. (eds.) Proceedings of the Canberra Mini-Conference on operator theory and p.d.e.'s, Proceedings of C.M.A. 5, Australian National University.

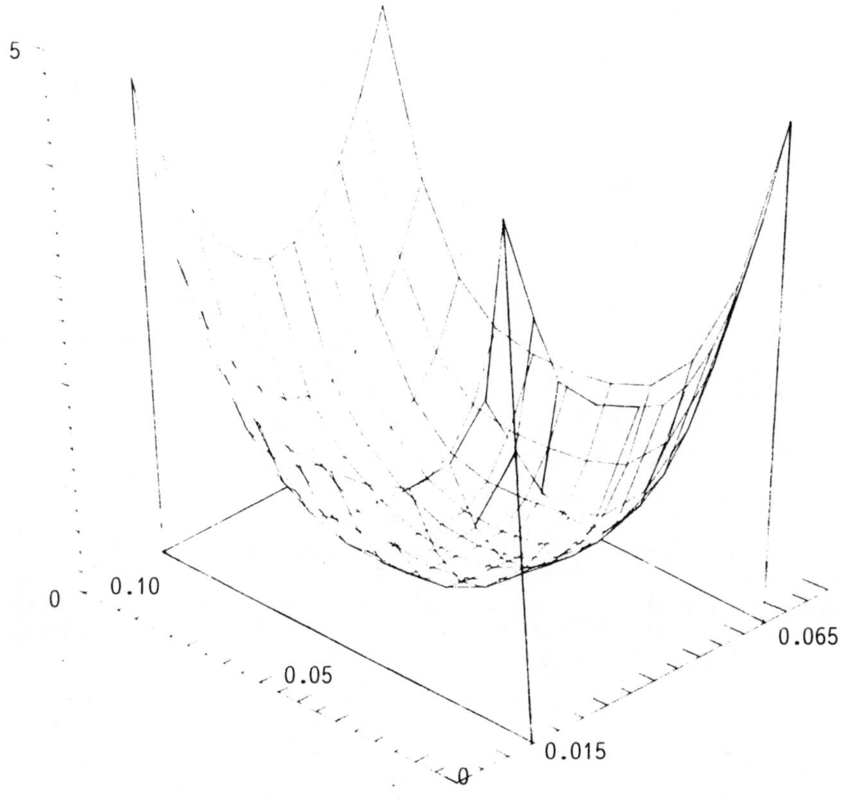

Sketch of a product integration solution of an integral equation over a rectangular region ($m=\alpha=2$, for details see [4]).

Dr. Claus Schneider, Johannes Gutenberg-Universität Mainz, Fachbereich 17 - Mathematik, Postfach 3980, D 6500 Mainz, Germany (FRG).

International Series of
Numerical Mathematics, Vol. 73

STABILITY RESULTS FOR DISCRETE VOLTERRA EQUATIONS: NUMERICAL EXPERIMENTS

P.J. van der Houwen and J.G. Blom

Centre for Mathematics and Computer Science, Department of Numerical Mathematics, Amsterdam, the Netherlands.

In this paper we formulate a local stability criterion for linear multistep discretizations of first- and second-kind Volterra integral equations with finitely decomposable kernel. In a large number of numerical experiments this criterion is tested. We did not find examples which behaved unstable while the stability criterion predicted stability. However, we found several examples which behaved stable while the stability criterion predicted instability. A possible explanation may be the fact that the stability criterion is independent of the decomposition of the kernel, that is, it holds for the most ill-conditioned decomposition and consequently it may be rather pessimistic.

1. Introduction

We consider Volterra equations of the form

$$\theta y(t) = g_0(t) + \int_0^t k(t,s,y(s))ds, \quad t \in I := [0,T] \tag{1.1}$$

where θ is either 0 (*first-kind* equations) or 1 (*second-kind* equations).

It is well known that applying direct quadrature methods to the *first-kind equation* may give unsatisfactory results (cf.LINZ [5,p.67]). An often applied remedy (cf. [1,p.898] and also [5]) consists of differentiating equation (1.1) to obtain the (implicit) second-kind equation (assuming that g' and k_t exist)

$$0 = k(t,t,y(t)) + g_0'(t) + \int_0^t k_t(t,s,y(s))ds. \tag{1.2}$$

If the derivatives occurring in (1.2) cannot be evaluated analytically, g_0' and k_t may be replaced by a difference approximation [5].

When we apply direct quadrature methods to the *second-kind equation* ($\theta=1$ in (1.1)), we again may obtain poor results, particularly when $\partial k/\partial y$ is large. As in the case of first-kind equations, let us differentiate the equation to obtain the integro-differential equation

$$\theta y'(t) = k(t,t,y(t)) + F_t(t,t), \qquad \theta = 1 \tag{1.3a}$$

where we have introduced the so-called *lag term*

$$F(t,s) := g_0(t) + \int_0^s k(t,x,y(x))dx. \tag{1.3b}$$

Again, the derivative F_t may be approximated by finite differences.

Let $\tilde{F}_n(t)$ denote the numerical lag term approximating $F(t,t_n)$:

$$\tilde{F}_n(t) := g_0(t) + h\sum_{\ell=0}^{\tilde{n}} w_{n,\ell}k(t,t_\ell,y_\ell),\ t_\ell = \ell h,\ \tilde{n} = \begin{cases}\tilde{\kappa}-1, n<\tilde{\kappa}\\ n, n\geq\tilde{\kappa}\end{cases}, \tag{1.4}$$

where $\tilde{\kappa}$ is sufficiently large to obtain the required order of accuracy. Let $\{a_i,b_i\}_{i=0}^{\kappa}$ define a linear multistep method $\{\rho,\sigma\}$ for ODEs and let $\tau(\zeta)$ define a κ-step difference formula, i.e.

$$g_0'(t_n) \approx h^{-1}\tau(E)g_0(t_n), \quad \tau(\zeta) = \sum_{i=0}^{\kappa} d_i\,\zeta^{\kappa-i-q},\ q \geq 0, \tag{1.5}$$

where E is the forward shift operator; here, q is an integer which we should choose 0 (*forward* differences) if the kernel is only defined for $s \leq t$, and which may be chosen such that $\tau(\zeta)$ defines a *symmetric* difference formula if the kernel is defined for all (t,s). In this paper we will use *forward differences*. Approximating $F_t(t,t)$ in (1.3) by the κ-step difference formula and applying the linear multistep method, we obtain the formula

$$\theta\rho(E)y_n = h\sigma(E)k(t_n,t_n,y_n) + \sigma(E)\tau(E)\tilde{F}_n(t_n), \quad n \geq \kappa, \tag{1.6}$$

where $\tau(E)$ only affects the index n of the argument t_n in $\tilde{F}_n(t_n)$.

The method {(1.4),(1.6)} will be called an *indirect linear multistep* (ILM) method [3]. Let $\tilde{p}$ be the order of the lag term approximation, let the starting values be sufficiently accurate, and let k and g_0 be sufficiently smooth. Then it can be proved that the ILM method is of order $\min\{\tilde{p},\kappa\}$ if $\theta = 0$ with $\sigma(\zeta)$ a Schur polynomial, and of order $\min\{p,\kappa,\tilde{p}\}$ if $\theta = 1$ with $\{\rho,\sigma\}$ being of order p.

It is the purpose of this paper to test the stability of the ILM method. In the particular case where $g_0(t)$ = constant and k is the *linear convolution* kernel

$$k(t,s,y) = [\xi + \eta(t-s)]y \tag{1.7}$$

the equation (1.3) reduces to the stability test equation investigated by BRUNNER and LAMBERT [2] and MATTHIJS [7]:

$$y'(t) = \xi y(t) + \eta \int_0^t y(s)ds; \tag{1.3'}$$

for $\theta = 1$ the ILM method then falls into the class of linear multistep methods studied by these authors so that their stability results apply. It was shown by MATTHIJS that for $\{\tilde{\rho},\tilde{\sigma}\}$-reducible lag term approximations, the application of a linear multistep method $\{\rho,\sigma\}$ to (1.3') is stable if the characteristic polynomial

$$\zeta^{\kappa-\tilde{\kappa}}[\rho(\zeta)\tilde{\rho}(\zeta) - h\xi\sigma(\zeta)\tilde{\rho}(\zeta) - h^2\eta\sigma(\zeta)\tilde{\sigma}(\zeta)] \tag{1.8}$$

is a Schur polynomial.

In Section 2 we show that an analogous characteristic equation is obtained in the case of *finitely decomposable* kernels, by associating a system of ODEs to (1.6) and by using standard arguments common in ODE theory. In Section 3, a more refined stability criterion is formulated; this result characterizes the *local stability behaviour* of the ILM method. Finally, in Section 4, a large number of experiments are presented in order to test the practical value of local stability criteria.

2. Finitely decomposable kernels

If the kernel $k(t,s,y)$ is finitely decomposable, it can be written in the form

$$k(t,s,y) = \sum_{\mu=1}^{m} g_\mu(t) f_\mu(s,y) =: \langle \vec{g}(t), \vec{f}(s,y) \rangle, \tag{2.1}$$

where $\vec{g}$ and $\vec{f}$ are vectors with components g_μ and f_μ, $\mu = 1(1)m$, and where we have introduced the inner product $\langle , \rangle$ in order to simplify the subsequent formulas.

Furthermore, we will assume that the lag term formula is $(\tilde{\rho},\tilde{\sigma})$-*reducible*, that is the quadrature rule used is assumed to correspond to a linear multistep formula $\{\tilde{\rho},\tilde{\sigma}\}$ for ODEs. The weights of such rules satisfy the relations [7,9]

$$\sum_{i=0}^{\tilde{\kappa}} \tilde{a}_i w_{n-i,j} = \begin{cases} 0 & \text{if } j = 0,1,..,n-\tilde{\kappa}-1 \\ \tilde{b}_{n-j} & \text{if } j = n-\tilde{\kappa},..,n \end{cases}, \quad n \geq \tilde{\kappa}. \tag{2.2}$$

where $\{\tilde{a}_i, \tilde{b}_i\}$ define $\{\tilde{\rho},\tilde{\sigma}\}$ and where $w_{n,j} = 0$ for $j > \max\{n, \tilde{\kappa}-1\}$.

Theorem 2.1. Let k be finitely decomposable and let the lag term formula be $(\tilde{\rho},\tilde{\sigma})$-reducible with $\tilde{\rho}(1) = 0$ and $\tilde{\kappa} = \kappa$. Then the ILM method is algebraically equivalent with the recurrence relations

$$\tilde{\rho}(E)\vec{u}_n = h\tilde{\sigma}(E)\vec{f}(t_n,y_n), \quad n \geq 0, \tag{2.3a}$$

$$\theta\rho(E)y_n = h\sigma(E)k(t_n,t_n,y_n) + \sigma(E)\tau(E)g_0(t_n) \tag{2.3b}$$

$$+ \sigma(E) \langle \tau(E)\vec{g}(t_n), \vec{u}_n \rangle, \quad n \geq \kappa,$$

where the starting values $\vec{u}_j$, $j = 0,\ldots,\kappa-1$ satisfy the starting condition

$$g_0(t) + \langle \vec{g}(t), \vec{u}_j \rangle = \tilde{F}_j(t), \quad j = 0,\ldots,\kappa-1. \tag{2.4}$$

Proof. From the $(\tilde{\rho},\tilde{\sigma})$-reducibility of the lag term formula it follows that

$$\tilde{\rho}(E)\tilde{F}_n(t) = h\tilde{\sigma}(E)k(t,t_n,y_n), \quad n \geq 0. \tag{2.5}$$

Furthermore, it follows from (2.1) and (1.4) that

$$\tilde{F}_n(t) = g_0(t) + \langle \vec{g}(t), \vec{u}_n \rangle, \qquad n \geq 0, \tag{2.6}$$

where

$$\vec{u}_n := h \sum_{\ell=0}^{\tilde{n}} w_{n,\ell}\, \vec{f}(t_\ell, y_\ell).$$

From (2.5) and (2.6) it follows that

$$\langle \vec{g}(t), \tilde{\rho}(E)\vec{u}_n - h\tilde{\sigma}(E)\vec{f}(t_n,y_n) \rangle = 0, \qquad n \geq 0,$$

from which (2.3a) is derived.

Relation (2.3b) is obtained on substitution of (2.6) into the ILM formula (1.6). Finally, the starting conditions follow from (2.6). □

2.1 Relation with ODEs

For $\theta = 1$, the recurrence relation (2.3) is recognized as a linear multistep discretization of the system of ODEs

$$\begin{cases} \vec{u}'(t) = \vec{f}(t,y) \\ y'(t) = k(t,t,y(t)) + \frac{1}{h}\,\tau(E)g_0(t) + \frac{1}{h}\langle \tau(E)\vec{g}(t), \vec{u}(t) \rangle \end{cases} \tag{2.7}$$

using different linear multistep methods $\{\tilde{\rho},\tilde{\sigma}\}$ and $\{\rho,\sigma\}$ with integration step h.

In SÖDERLIND [8], such linear multistep methods were called *linear multistep compound* (LMC) methods. The (linear) stability of LMC methods with respect to the test equation

$$\vec{x}'(t) = J\vec{x}, \ J \text{ constant matrix}, \ \vec{x} = [\vec{u},y]^T \tag{2.8}$$

is characterized by the roots of the characteristic equation

$$\det[P(\zeta) - \Sigma(\zeta)hJ] = 0, \tag{2.9}$$

where

$$P(\zeta) := \begin{pmatrix} \tilde{\rho}(\zeta)I_m & 0 \\ 0 & \rho(\zeta) \end{pmatrix}, \Sigma(\zeta) := \begin{pmatrix} \tilde{\sigma}(\zeta)I_m & 0 \\ 0 & \sigma(\zeta) \end{pmatrix},$$

with I_m denoting the m×m unit matrix. If (2.9) is a Schur polynomial then the LMC solution converges to 0 as $t_n \to \infty$. The system (2.7) suggests choosing for J the Jacobian matrix

$$J = \begin{pmatrix} 0 & \frac{\partial \vec{f}}{\partial y}(\bar{t},\bar{y}) \\ h^{-1}(\tau(E)\vec{g}(\bar{t}))^T & \frac{\partial k}{\partial y}(\bar{t},\bar{t},\bar{y}) \end{pmatrix}$$

at some point $(\bar{t},\bar{y})$. The eigenvalues of J are given by m-1 zero-eigenvalues and two eigenvalues satisfying the equation

$$\lambda^2 - \frac{\partial k}{\partial y}(\bar{t},\bar{t},\bar{y})\lambda - h^{-1}\tau(E)\frac{\partial k}{\partial y}(\bar{t},\bar{t},\bar{y}) = 0,$$

where $\tau(E)$ only affects the first argument of $\partial k/\partial y$. It is now easily verified that (2.9) reduces to the equation

$$\rho(\zeta)\tilde{\rho}(\zeta) - h\frac{\partial k}{\partial y}(\bar{t},\bar{t},\bar{y})\sigma(\zeta)\tilde{\rho}(\zeta) - h\tau(E)\frac{\partial k}{\partial y}(\bar{t},\bar{t},\bar{y})\sigma(\zeta)\tilde{\sigma}(\zeta) = 0. \tag{2.10}$$

Notice the resemblance with the characteristic polynomial (1.8).

The equation (2.10) is independent of the decomposition of the kernel. For instance, if k(t,s,y) is of the convolution type $K^*(t-s)y$, then the kernel enters into (2.10) only by the values of $K^*(0)$ and $h^{-1}\tau(E)K^*(0) \approx K_t^*(0)$. Hence, when a stability criterion is based on (2.10), we use only a very limited amount of information on the kernel. In the following section we will derive a stability criterion that takes into account more information on the kernel. Moreover, the first-kind case ($\theta=0$) is included at the same time.

3. A local stability criterion

Let $k(t,s,y)$ be of the linear form $K(t,s)y$ with $K(t,s)$ of separable form: $K(t,s) = \langle\vec{g}(t),\vec{f}(s)\rangle$. Then we can write the recurrence relation (2.3) in the form

$$\sum_{i=0}^{\kappa^*} \mathcal{B}_i(n)\vec{v}_{n-i} = \vec{w}_n, \qquad \kappa^* = \max\{\kappa,\tilde{\kappa}\} \tag{3.1}$$

where

$$\vec{v}_n := [y_n,\vec{u}_n]^T, \quad \vec{w}_n := [\sigma(E)\tau(E)g_0(t_{n-\kappa}),\vec{0}]^T,$$

$$\mathcal{B}_i(n) := \begin{pmatrix} \theta a_i - b_i hK(t_{n-i},t_{n-i}) & -b_i\tau(E)\vec{g}^T(t_{n-i}) \\ -\tilde{b}_i h\vec{f}(t_{n-i}) & \tilde{a}_i I_m \end{pmatrix},$$

with the convention that $a_i = b_i = 0$ for $i > \kappa$ and $\tilde{a}_i = \tilde{b}_i = 0$ for $i > \tilde{\kappa}$.

In analogy to the linear stability analysis used in ODEs we will call the recurrence relation (3.1) *locally stable at* $t_{\bar{n}}$ if the recurrence relation

$$\sum_{i=0}^{\kappa^*} \mathcal{B}_i(\bar{n})\vec{v}_{n-i} = \vec{0}, \quad \bar{n} \text{ fixed} \tag{3.2}$$

is stable, that is if its solutions converge. This leads to the condition

$$\det\left[\sum_{i=0}^{\kappa^*} \mathcal{B}_i(\bar{n})\zeta^{n-i}\right] \text{ is a Schur polynomial.} \tag{3.3}$$

Analogous to the stability analysis in [4] the following theorem can be proved:

Theorem 3.1. The recurrence relation (3.1) is locally stable at $t_{\bar{n}}$ if the polynomial

$$\theta\rho(\zeta)\tilde{\rho}(\zeta) - h\tilde{\rho}(\zeta)\sum_{i=0}^{\kappa} b_i K(t_{\bar{n}-i}, t_{\bar{n}-i})\zeta^{\kappa-i} \tag{3.4}$$
$$- h^2 \sum_{i=0}^{\kappa}\sum_{j=0}^{\tilde{\kappa}} b_i\tilde{b}_j\left(\frac{1}{h}\sum_{\ell=0}^{\kappa} d_\ell K(t_{\bar{n}+\kappa-i-\ell}, t_{n-j}\right)\zeta^{\kappa+\tilde{\kappa}-i-j}$$

is a Schur polynomial. □

In the actual application of this theorem one may consider the approximation

$$\frac{1}{h}\sum_{\ell=0}^{\kappa} d_\ell K(t_{\bar{n}+\kappa-i-\ell}, t_{\bar{n}-j}) \approx K_t(t_{\bar{n}-i}, t_{\bar{n}-j}) \tag{3.5}$$

which slightly simplifies the polynomial (3.4).

In the particular case of convolution kernels where $K(t,s) = K^*(t-s)$, the polynomial (3.4) reduces to

$$\theta\rho(\zeta)\tilde{\rho}(\zeta) - hK^*(0)\tilde{\rho}(\zeta)\sigma(\zeta) - h^2\sum_{i=0}^{\kappa}\sum_{j=0}^{\tilde{\kappa}} b_i\tilde{b}_j K_t^*((j-i)h)\zeta^{\kappa+\tilde{\kappa}-i-j} \tag{3.6}$$

where we have used (3.5). Notice that (3.6) does not depend on n.

We observe that the particular decomposition (2.1) of the kernel does not occur in (3.4). Thus, formally we can apply (3.4) to non-decomposable kernels as well, provided that $K(t,s)$ is also defined for $t < s$.

If $O(h^3)$ terms in (3.6) are neglected, the characteristic polynomial reduces to

$$\theta\rho(\zeta)\tilde{\rho}(\zeta) - hK^*(0)\tilde{\rho}(\zeta)\sigma(\zeta) - h^2K_t^*(0)\tilde{\sigma}(\zeta)\sigma(\zeta). \tag{3.6'}$$

For $\theta = 1$ this polynomial is equivalent to (1.8); for $\theta = 0$ we obtain a polynomial of the form $\tilde{\rho}(\zeta)+h(K_t^*/K^*)(0)\tilde{\sigma}(\zeta)$, indicating that first-kind equations require that $-hK_t^*/K^*$ should lie in the stability region of the LM method $\{\tilde{\rho},\tilde{\sigma}\}$ (we recall that first-kind equations also require that σ is a Schur polynomial, otherwise we have no convergence).

Finally, it should be remarked that the considerations above refer to the stability of the sequence of vectors $\{\vec{v}_n\}$, whereas in actual computation we are only concerned with stability of the first components $\{y_n\}$ of $\{\vec{v}_n\}$. Consequently, these considerations might be conservative in practice.

4. Numerical experiments

In order to test the local stability result of the preceding Section we have integrated a large number of Volterra equations of convolution type. In each experiment we have computed: (i) the number of correct significant digits obtained at the end point T, i.e. the value of

$$sd := -\log\left|\frac{y_N - y(T)}{y(T)}\right| , \quad N := T/h,$$

unless otherwise stated (ii) the value of $\zeta_{max} = \max_j |\zeta_j|$, where ζ_j are the zeros of the polynomial (3.4). ζ_{max} serves as a predictor of stability or instability.

In the tables of results we use the notation AM_p-BD_q indicating that the lag term is based on a p-th order Adams-Moulton formula and the ILM formula is based on a q-th order Backward Differentiation formula.

In all experiments the starting values were derived from the exact solution.

From our experiments we draw the following conclusions

(i) The solutions of all second-kind equations behaved stably if $\zeta_{max} \leq 1$.

(ii) The solutions of all first-kind equations behaved stably if $\zeta_{max} \leq 1$ and if $|K^*(0)|$ is not small.

(iii) $\zeta_{max} > 1$ does not necessarily imply instability this may be explained by observing that $\zeta_{max} > 1$ indicates an unstable behaviour of $\{\vec{v}_n\}$, and not necessarily of $\{y_n\}$.

(iv) The ILM method yields poor results for first-kind equations with $|K^*(0)|$ small.

Table I. $\theta = 1$: Results for second-kind equations obtained at T = 20

Problem		h	AM_4-AM_5 sd	ζ_{max}	AM_4-BD_4 sd	ζ_{max}	BD_4-AM_5 sd	ζ_{max}	BD_4-BD_4 sd	ζ_{max}
1.	$g_0 = \frac{1}{2}t^2e^{-t}$	1/10	2.3	1.0	2.3	1.02	3.4	1.0	2.9	1.0
	$k = \frac{1}{2}(t-s)^2 \exp(-(t-s))y$	1/20	3.3	1.0	3.5	1.01	5.7	1.0	4.0	1.0
	$y = \frac{1}{3}[1-e^{-3/2\ t}(\cos(\frac{1}{2}\sqrt{3}t)+\sqrt{3}\sin(\frac{1}{2}\sqrt{3}t)]$									
2.	$g_0 = 2-2/(t+2)$	1/10	3.4	1.04	3.4	1.05	5.3	.98	5.4	1.05
	$k = -2/(t-s+2)^2.y$	1/20	4.5	1.02	4.5	1.02	6.3	.99	6.3	1.03
	$y = 1$									
3.	$g_0 = 1+t-\cos(t)$	1/10	3.8	1.00	3.8	1.01	4.9	0.99	4.9	1.00
	$k = -\cos(t-s)y$	1/20	5.0	1.00	5.0	1.00	6.5	1.00	6.5	1.00
	$y = t$									
4.	$g_0 = 2t+3$	1/10	3.0	.91	2.9	.90	2.8	.90	3.0	.91
	$k = (-2(t-s)-3)y$	1/20	2.8	.95	3.9	.95	2.7	.95	3.3	.95
	$y = 4e^{-2t}-e^{-t}$									
5.	$g_0 = 1 - \frac{1}{2}\sqrt{2}\ \mathrm{erf}(t)$	1/10	-.8	1.11	-.7	1.09	-.7	1.12	-.6	1.11
	$k = \exp(-(t-s)^2)y$	1/20	-1.0	1.05	-1.0	1.05	-.9	1.05	-.9	1.05
	$y = 1$									
6.	$g_0 = \frac{1}{2}\gamma(1-t^2)\ln(1+t)$	1/10	4.7	1.11	4.7	1.00	5.9	1.56	5.9	1.00
	$+ \frac{3}{4}\gamma t^2$	1/20	5.7	1.03	5.7	1.00	7.0	1.28	7.0	1.00
	$-(\frac{1}{2}\gamma+1)t+1$									
	$k = -\gamma \ln(1+t-s)y$	1/10	-48	2.95	-3.7	1.12	5.8	5.95	-1.3	1.12
	$y = 1-t$	1/20	-23	1.86	-17	1.16	-11	3.98	-19	1.18
	$\gamma = 10, 1000$									
7.	$g_0 = 2t+3-\sin(t)-3\cos(t)$	1/10	4.7	.90	4.7	.90	4.8	.90	4.8	.90
	$k = (-2(t-s)-3)y$	1/20	5.9	.95	5.9	.95	5.9	.95	6.0	.95
	$y = \sin(t)$									
8.	$g_0 = 1$	1/10	2.2	1.05	2.2	1.05	4.0	1.05	4.0	1.05
	$k = e^{-2(t-s)}y$	1/20	3.3	1.03	3.3	1.03	4.9	1.03	5.0	1.03
	$y = 2-e^{-t}$									
9.	$g_0 = 1$	1/10	3.1	.90	3.1	.90	2.9	.90	2.9	.90
	$k = -2e^{t-s}y$	1/20	4.3	.95	4.4	.95	4.1	.95	4.1	.95
	$y = -1+2e^{-t}$									

Table I. (continued) $\theta = 1$: Results obtained at $T = 20$

	Problem	h	AM_4-AM_5 sd	ζ_{max}	AM_4-BD_4 sd	ζ_{max}	BD_4-AM_5 sd	ζ_{max}	BD_4-BD_4 sd	ζ_{max}
10.	$g_0 = \cos(t)$	1/10	2.0	1.00	1.6	1.00	1.3	1.00	1.2	1.00
	$k = -(t-s)\cos(t-s).y$	1/20	3.5	1.00	2.8	1.00	2.4	1.00	2.3	1.00
	$y = \frac{2}{3}\cos(\sqrt{3}t)+1/3$									
11.	$g_0 = t$	1/10	3.5	1.11	3.5	1.11	2.8	1.11	2.8	1.11
	$k = \sin(t-s).y$	1/20	4.5	1.05	4.5	1.05	4.0	1.05	4.0	1.05
	$y = t(1+t^2/6)$									
12.	$g_0 = e^t-2\sin(t)$	1/10	2.6	1.22	2.3	1.22	2.0	1.23	1.9	1.22
	$k = 2\cos(t-s).y$	1/20	3.8	1.11	3.5	1.10	3.2	1.11	3.1	1.11
	$y = e^t(1+t^2)$									
13.	$g_0 = \sinh t$	1/10	3.6	1.00	3.7	.99	3.6	1.00	3.7	1.00
	$k = -\cosh(t-s).y$	1/20	4.8	1.00	4.9	1.00	4.9	1.00	5.0	1.00
	$y = 2\sinh(\sqrt{5}t/2)e^{-\frac{1}{2}t}/\sqrt{5}$									
14.	$g_0 = 1+\frac{1}{2}\sqrt{\gamma}(1-e^{-t^2})$	1/10	2.2	1.00	2.2	1.00	4.8	1.00	4.4	1.00
	$k = -\gamma(t-s)\cdot$	1/20	3.7	1.00	3.7	1.00	5.1	1.00	5.1	1.00
	$.\exp(-(t-s)^2).y$									
	$y = 1$	1/10	-53	1.96	-8	1.14	-6	1.10	-6	1.12
	$\gamma = 10,\ 1000, 1900$	1/20	-30	1.22	-22	1.16	-18	1.14	-25	1.18
	3000, 7500, 12000									
	14000	1/10	-64	2.22	-.6	1.05	2.8	.99	.5	1.03
		1/20	-73	1.57	-24	1.18	-20	1.15	-24	1.18
		1/10	-69	2.35	2.2	.98	-48	1.67	4.3	.95
		1/20	-98	1.82	-21	1.16	-16	1.12	-20	1.15
		1/10	-74	2.52	-49	1.80	-75	2.38	4.3	.79
		1/20	-132	2.21	-5	1.05	5.0	.96	-1	1.03
		1/10	-76	2.57	-57	1.98	-80	2.55	4.3	.72
		1/20	-143	2.35	3.6	.97	-100	1.79	5.1	.95
		1/10	-77	2.58	-59	2.03	-82	2.60	4.3	.70
		1/20	-145	2.39	-34	1.21	-114	1.95	5.1	.92

Table I. (continued) $\theta = 1$: Results obtained at T = 20

Problem	h	AM_4-AM_5 sd	ζ_{max}	AM_4-BD_4 sd	ζ_{max}	BD_4-AM_5 sd	ζ_{max}	BD_4-BD_4 sd	ζ_{max}
15. $g_0 = 1-2\varepsilon^{3/2}/3+t$	1/10	2.7	.99	2.7	.95	7.0	1.23	7.0	.96
$+2(t+\varepsilon)^{3/2}/3$	1/20	3.0	.99	3.0	.97	7.5	1.13	7.5	.97
$k = -(1+\sqrt{t-s+\varepsilon})y$									
$y = 1$	1/10	2.4	1.01	2.4	.95	7.0	1.29	7.0	.95
$\varepsilon = 10^{-2}, 10^{-6}$	1/20	2.5	1.00	2.5	.97	7.4	1.18	7.5	.98

Table II. $\theta = 0$: Results for first-kind equations obtained at T = 20

Problem		h	AM_4-BD_4 sd	ζ_{max}	BD_4-BD_4 sd	ζ_{max}
16. $g_0 = a\cos(t)-\sin(t)-ae^{at}$	a=1	1/10	4.2	1.01	3.9	1.00
$k = (a^2+1)\cos(t-s).y$		1/20	5.5	1.00	5.1	1.00
$y = e^{at}$						
	a=-1*	1/10	3.5	1.01	2.9	1.00
		1/20	4.6	1.00	4.0	1.00
17. $g_0 = -\sinh(at)$	a=1*	1/10	3.6	.90	3.8	.90
$k = a\exp(a(t-s)).y$		1/20	3.5	.95	2.5	.95
$y = e^{-at}$						
	a=-1	1/10	5.4	1.10	3.7	1.11
		1/20	7.2	1.05	4.8	1.05
18. $g_0 = 1-t-e^{-t}$		1/10	3.3	.90	3.5	.90
$k = (1+t-s)y$		1/20	3.4	.95	3.2	.95
$y = te^{-t}$						
19. $g_0 = -a(1-\cos(t))+\frac{1}{2}t\sin(t)$	a=.9	1/10	-21	1.05	-22	1.00
$k = [a-\cos(t-s)]y$		1/20	-20	1.01	-21	1.00
$y = \sin(t)$						
	a=1.1	1/10	4.2	.95	3.3	1.00
		1/20	5.5	.99	4.9	1.00

20.	$g_0 = 1+at-\cos(t)$	a=-.1	1/10	-.2	.40	-.2	.63
	$k = [a-\sin(t-s)]y$		1/20	-.2	.61	-.2	.61
	$y = 1$	a=-.01	1/10	-46	1.73	.5	.50
			1/20	-50	1.34	.5	.57

* In these cases, sd corresponds to absolute error

5. References

[1] Baker, C.T.H. (1977) The numerical treatment of integral equations. (Clarendon, Oxford).

[2] Brunner, H. and Lambert, J.D. (1974) Stability of numerical methods for integro-differential equations. Computing 12, 75-89.

[3] Houwen, P.J. van der and Riele, H.J.J. te (1983) Linear multistep methods for Volterra integral and integro-differential equations. Report NW151/83, Mathematisch Centrum, Amsterdam (submitted for publication in Math. Comp.).

[4] Houwen, P.J. van der and Wolkenfelt, P.H.M. (1980) On the stability of multistep formulas for Volterra integral equations of the second kind. Computing 24, 341-347.

[5] Linz, P. (1967) The numerical solution of Volterra integral equations by finite difference methods. MRC Tech. Summ. Report #825, Math. Research Center, Madison, U.S.A.

[6] Linz, P. (1969) Linear multistep methods for Volterra integro-differential equations. JACM 16, 295-301.

[7] Matthijs, J. (1976) A-stable linear multistep methods for Volterra integro-differential equations. Numer. Math. 27, 85-94.

[8] Söderlind, G. (1979) Some stability properties of linear multistep compound discretizations of partitioned differential systems. Report TRITA-NA-7910, The Royal Institute of Technology, Stockholm.

[9] Wolkenfelt, P.H.M. (1982) The construction of reducible quadrature rules for Volterra integral and integro-differential equations. IMA J. Numer. Anal. 2, 131-152.

Professor Dr. P.J. van der Houwen, Department of Numerical Mathematics, Centre for Mathematics and Computer Science, Kruislaan 413, 1098 SJ Amsterdam, The Netherlands.

International Series of
Numerical Mathematics, Vol. 73

THE DESIGN OF ACOUSTIC TORPEDOS

D. Kershaw

University of Lancaster

1. Introduction

A problem in the designing of a torpedo is that of finding the pressure distribution about it when it is moving steadily in a direction parallel to its axis of symmetry. In the case of an acoustic torpedo (one which is guided by the noise emitted by the target) this is especially important since low pressures tend to cause cavitation thus producing noise which may interfere with the homing mechanism. An acoustic torpedo has a flat nose to accommodate this mechanism and since the main part of the body is a circular cylinder it is necessary to connect these two surfaces in such a way that the minimum pressure is as high as possible. By Bernoulli's equation this is equivalent to the requirement that if u is the speed of flow of the water on the surface of the torpedo then u^2 should be as small as possible. This paper will be concerned with the primary problem of finding the speed of the flow.

2. Boundary value problem

A torpedo is a body of revolution, and we shall assume that it moves steadily in the direction of its axis of symmetry in an inviscid, incompressible fluid without rotation. As usual we take the body to be fixed and impose a uniform unit flow at infinity which moves parallel to the x-axis (the axis of symmetry).

The problem can then be formulated as follows:

Find Φ which satisfies the axisymmetric potential equation

$$\frac{\partial^2\Phi}{\partial x^2} + \frac{\partial^2\Phi}{\partial r^2} + \frac{1}{r}\frac{\partial\Phi}{\partial r} = 0 \tag{2.1}$$

outside the torpedo T, and such that there is no flow through its surface, ie, if n denotes the external normal derivative then

$$\frac{\partial\Phi}{\partial n} = 0 \quad \text{on} \quad T, \tag{2.2}$$

and such that the free stream velocity is unity,

$$\frac{\partial\Phi}{\partial x} = 1 \quad \text{at} \quad \infty. \tag{2.3}$$

When Φ has been found the speed of flow on the body is given by

$$\frac{\partial\Phi}{\partial s} = u(s) \text{ say,} \tag{2.4}$$

where s is denotes arc length measured along the generating curve of the torpedo.

The solution of the problem in this form will clearly be wasteful since it necessitates finding Φ at all points outside the body in order to find Φ_s on it. For this reason it seems more sensible to try to find an equation directly for u. This leads naturally to a formulation in terms of an integral equation.

Two such equations are known to me but as far as I am aware they have not appeared in the available literature. A third but more general equation for the flow around an arbitrary body was given in [3], a numerical study of this should prove to be both interesting and valuable.

The equation which is used in this paper was first found by F. VANDREY and published in 1951 as an internal report of the Admiralty Research Laboratory [7]. The derivation was based on the idea of replacing the body by a system of vortex rings and depended heavily on hydrodynamic techniques. We shall present here an alternative approach which depends only on Green's third theorem.

As we shall see VANDREY'S equation is a Fredholm integral equation of the second kind with a weakly singular (logarithmic) kernel which is satisfied by the speed of flow u.

In the same year L. LANDWEBER gave in an internal report [6] of the David Taylor Model Basin a Fredholm integral of the first kind which is also satisfied by the speed of flow. This has a particularly simple form, it is given together with a sketch of his proof in the appendix. I am grateful to Professor LANDWEBER for giving me his permission to do this.

3. VANDREY'S integral equation

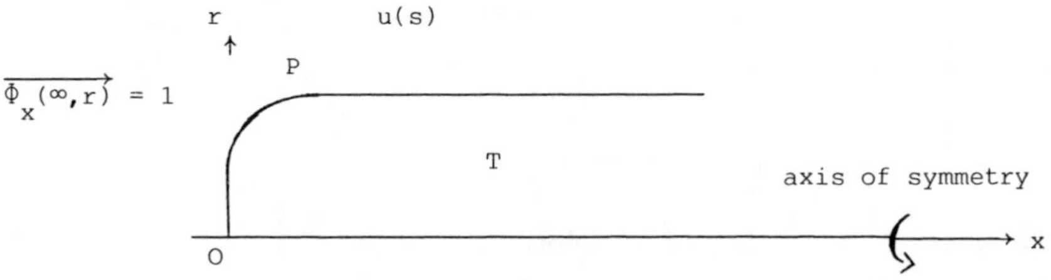

Let $\Phi \equiv \Phi(x,y,z)$ satisfy Laplace's equation outside the torpedo, and let the free stream velocity be unity,

$$\frac{\partial \Phi}{\partial x} = 1 \quad \text{at } \infty. \tag{3.1}$$

Then $\Phi(x,y,z)-x$ will satisfy Green's third identity which will be written as

$$\Phi(P)-x(P) = \frac{1}{2\pi} \iint_{\partial T} \left\{ \frac{1}{R} \frac{\partial}{\partial \nu_Q} [\Phi(Q)-x(Q)] - [\Phi(Q)-x(Q)] \frac{\partial}{\partial \nu_Q} \frac{1}{R} \right\} d\sigma_Q \tag{3.2}$$

where $P \in \partial T$, the surface of the torpedo, ν_Q denotes the direction of the normal at Q directed into the torpedo, $d\sigma_Q$ is an element of area and

$$R = \mathrm{dist}(P,Q) = \sqrt{(x-\xi)^2+(y-\eta)^2+(z-\zeta)^2}.$$

Since x is harmonic inside T also we can apply Green's third theorem to it to give

$$-\chi(P) = \frac{1}{2\pi} \iint_{\partial T} \{ \frac{1}{R} \frac{\partial}{\partial \nu_Q} \chi(Q) - \chi(Q) \frac{\partial}{\partial \nu_Q} \frac{1}{R} \} \, d\sigma_Q. \tag{3.3}$$

The use of this together with the Neumann condition $\frac{\partial \Phi}{\partial \nu_Q} = 0$ on ∂T in (3.2) will give

$$\Phi(P) - 2\chi(P) = \frac{1}{2\pi} \iint_{\partial T} \Phi(Q) \frac{\partial}{\partial \nu_Q} \frac{1}{R} \, d\sigma_Q. \tag{3.4}$$

This equation is satisfied for any body in a steady uniform unit flow. We now take cylindrical polar coordinates and write

$$P \equiv (x, r\cos\theta, r\sin Q), \quad Q \equiv (\xi, \rho\cos\phi, \rho\sin\phi),$$

denote by s and σ the corresponding distances of P and Q from O measured along ∂T. Let L be the total length of ∂T.

Clearly $d\sigma_Q = \rho \, d\phi \, d\sigma$

and (3.4) becomes (with a slight abuse of notation)

$$\Phi(x,r) = 2x + \frac{1}{2\pi} \int_0^L \Phi(\xi,\rho) \frac{\partial}{\partial \nu_Q} [\phi_1(x,r;\xi,\rho)] \, \rho \, d\sigma \tag{3.5}$$

where

$$\phi_1(x,r;\xi,\rho) = \int_0^{2\pi} \frac{1}{\sqrt{(x-\xi)^2 + r^2 - 2\rho r\cos\phi + \rho^2}} \, d\phi. \tag{3.6}$$

It can be shown that ϕ_1 satisfies the axisymmetric potential equation (2.1) in (x,r) and in (ξ,ρ).

Now the axisymmetric potential equation (2.1) can be written

$$\frac{\partial}{\partial x} \left(r \frac{\partial \Phi}{\partial x} \right) + \frac{\partial}{\partial r} \left(r \frac{\partial \Phi}{\partial r} \right) = 0 \tag{3.7}$$

and so there exists Ψ, the corresponding Stokes' stream function, which satisfies the Beltrami equations:

$$\frac{\partial \Psi}{\partial r} = r \frac{\partial \Phi}{\partial x}, \quad \frac{\partial \Psi}{\partial x} = -r \frac{\partial \Phi}{\partial r}. \tag{3.8}$$

This pair of equations provides an analogue of the Cauchy-Riemann equations of two dimensional potential theory and we write them more conveniently for the present problem as

$$r\,\frac{\partial\Phi}{\partial s} = -\,\frac{\partial\Psi}{\partial n}\,,\quad r\,\frac{\partial\Phi}{\partial n} = \frac{\partial\Psi}{\partial s} \tag{3.9}$$

where n denotes differentiation in the direction of the <u>inward</u> normal.

The (Stokes') stream function satisfies

$$\frac{\partial^2\Psi}{\partial x^2} + \frac{\partial^2\Psi}{\partial r^2} - \frac{1}{r}\frac{\partial\Psi}{\partial r} = 0. \tag{3.10}$$

We now think of ϕ_1 as being a function of ξ and ρ, then there will be a corresponding stream function $\psi_1(x,r;\,\xi,\rho)$ which is given by

$$\psi_1(x,r;\xi,\rho) = \int_0^{2\pi} \frac{[\rho(\xi-x)(\rho-r\cos\phi)]}{r^2-2\rho r\cos\phi+\rho^2}\,\frac{d\phi}{\sqrt{(x-\xi)^2+r^2-2\rho r\cos\phi+\rho^2}}\,. \tag{3.11}$$

Thus we can write (3.5) as

$$\Phi(x,r) = 2x + \frac{1}{2\pi}\int_0^L \Phi(\xi,\rho)\,\frac{\partial}{\partial\sigma}\,\psi_1(x,r;\,\xi,\rho)\,d\sigma. \tag{3.12}$$

Integrate by parts and use the fact that ψ_1 vanishes for $\sigma=0$, L (i.e. when $\rho=0$) to give

$$\Phi(x,r)=2x - \frac{1}{2\pi}\int_0^L \psi_1(x,r;\xi,\rho)\,\frac{\partial\Phi}{\partial\sigma}\,d\sigma,$$

now take the derivative of this equation with respect to s then, with

$$\frac{\partial\Phi}{\partial s} = u(s),\quad \frac{\partial\Phi}{\partial\sigma} = u(\sigma),$$

we have

$$u(s) = 2x'(s) - \frac{1}{2\pi}\int_0^L u(\sigma)\,\frac{\partial}{\partial s}[\psi_1(x,r;\,\xi,\rho)]\,d\sigma, \tag{3.13}$$

where the prime denotes differentiation with respect to arc length.

It remains now to simplify $\frac{\partial}{\partial s}\,\psi_1(x,r;\,\xi,\rho)$. After a great deal of calculation we arrive at Vandrey's equation:

$$u(s) = 2x'(s) - \frac{1}{\pi}\int_0^L N(s,\sigma)u(\sigma)d\sigma,\quad 0\leqq s\leqq L, \tag{3.14}$$

where

$$N(s,\sigma) = \frac{1}{\sqrt{(x-\xi)^2+(r+\rho)^2}}\{\frac{[x'r-r'(x-\xi)]}{r}[K(k)-E(k)]$$

$$- 2\rho\frac{[x'(r-\rho)-r'(x-\xi)]}{(x-\xi)^2+(r-\rho)^2} E(k)\} , \qquad (3.15)$$

K and E are the complete elliptic integrals of the first and second kinds with argument k given by

$$k^2 = \frac{4r\rho}{(x-\xi)^2+(r+\rho)^2} . \qquad (3.16)$$

4. Analysis of Vandrey's equation

As is well known K has a logarithmic singularity at k=1, which for N occurs when $\sigma=s$, and so we shall write

$$N(s,\sigma) = P(s,\sigma) \log|\sigma-s| + Q(s,\sigma). \qquad (4.1)$$

It is not difficult to verify that P is continuous, but that Q(s,s) suffers step discontinuities at discontinuities of curvature of the generating curve. For the calculation of P and Q we used approximations given by W.J. CODY in [2]. These use the complementary modulus $k'^2 = 1-k^2$ which is fortunately more useful for our purposes. CODY gives approximations in the form:

$$\left.\begin{array}{l} K(k) \sim A(k')-\log(k'^2)B(k') \\ \text{and} \\ E(k) \sim C(k')-\log(k'^2)D(k') \end{array}\right\} \qquad (4.2)$$

where A,B,C and D are polynomials.

With the aid of these we can write

$$P(s,\sigma) = - \frac{2}{P\bar{Q}}\{ L(s,\sigma)[B(k')-D(k')]-M(s,\sigma).D(k') \}, \qquad (4.3)$$

$$Q(s,\sigma) = \frac{1}{P\bar{Q}} \{L(s,\sigma)\Big[[A(k')-C(k')]+[B(k')-D(k')]\log\frac{(\sigma-s)^2}{k'^2}\Big] \qquad (4.4)$$

$$-M(s,\sigma) \Big[[C(k')+D(k')\log \frac{(\sigma-s)^2}{k'^2}]\Big] \},$$

where $\overline{PQ} = \sqrt{(x-\xi)^2 + (r+\rho)^2}$,

$$L(s,\sigma) = \frac{[x'r-r'(x-\xi)]}{r} \tag{4.5}$$

$$M(s,\sigma) = 2\rho \frac{[x'(r-\rho)-r'(x-\xi)]}{(x-\xi)^2 + (r+\rho)^2} . \tag{4.6}$$

It is not difficult to show that

$$P(s,s) = -\frac{x'}{2r} , \; Q(s,s) = -\frac{1}{2}(x''r'-x'r'') + \frac{x'}{2r}[-1+\log 8r]. \tag{4.7}$$

5. Numerical method

The complicated nature of the kernel seems to preclude all methods except those of Nyström type. A type of weighted quadrature was proposed to the author by G.F. MILLER of the National Physical Laboratory and was used successfully. A description will be found in [4]. Since then K. ATKINSON has given an analysis of similar methods [1].

We give here a new method for which no theory exists, indeed the method exists only in an *ad hoc* sense. For simplicity we present it first for the numerical solution of

$$f(x) = g(x) + \frac{1}{\pi}\int_0^1 f(t) \log|t-x| dt, \tag{5.1}$$

a type of integral equation which arises in surface wave theory.

Let $x_1, x_2, \ldots, x_n$ be distinct points and let

$$P_n(x) = (x-x_1)(x-x_2)\ldots(x-x_n). \tag{5.2}$$

Then, with the aid of Lagrange's interpolation formula, we can write

$$f(x) = \sum_{j=1}^{n} \frac{1}{P_n'(x_j)} \frac{P_n(x)}{(x-x_j)} f(x_j) + \frac{P_n(x)}{n!} f^{(n)}(\xi).$$

Hence, from (5.1) with $x=x_i$,

$$f(x_i)=g(x_i) + \sum_{j=1}^{n} H_{ij} f(x_j) + \frac{1}{\pi}\int \frac{P_n(t)}{n!} f^{(n)}(\xi)\log|t-x_i| dt$$

$$i = 1,2,\ldots,n \tag{5.3}$$

where $$H_{ij} = \frac{1}{P_n'(x_j)} \int_0^1 \frac{P_n(t)}{t-x_j} \log|t-x_i|\, dt, \quad 1 \leq i,j \leq n. \tag{5.4}$$

If we set the remainder terms in (5.3) to zero we get the following system of equations:

$$f_i = g_i + \sum_{j=1}^{n} H_{ij} f_j, \quad i = 1,2,\ldots,n. \tag{5.5}$$

When f is a polynomial of degree n-1 then the equation (5.1) can be solved exactly and $f(x_i) = f_i$, $i = 1,2,\ldots,n$ for any choice of quadrature points. On the other hand if f is of degree n then the remainders are multiples of

$$\int_0^1 P_n(t) \log|t-x_i|dt, \quad i = 1,2,\ldots,n, \tag{5.6}$$

and if we can find $x_1,x_2,\ldots,x_n$ to satisfy (5.6) then these can be taken as quadrature points which will give one extra degree of precision to the quadrature formulae. At first sight this may seem a small increase, but no more can be expected since we are requiring that n remainders should be zero, indeed P_n has to be orthogonal to the n weight functions $\log|t-x_i|$, $i=1,2,\ldots,n$. A simpler version of this problem has been analysed in [5]. We remark here that (5.6) is a set of n nonlinear equations to be solved for $x_1,x_2,\ldots,x_n$.

No theory has been found which will assure us of the existence of these points in this particular case. However in a private communication A. Pinkus has shown that the equations

$$\int_a^b K(x_i,t)\, P_n(t)dt = 0, \; i = 1,2,\ldots,n \tag{5.7}$$

have a solution if the kernel function K is strictly totally positive, a property which is not possessed by the logarithmic kernel.

The existence of solutions of (5.6) therefore depends on numerical computation and these have been found for n=1,2,...,13. The following remarkable but empirical facts have been found for these values of n.

1. Solutions exist, are real distinct and lie within (0,1),
2. the zeros of P_n separate the zeros of P_{n+1},
3. the quadrature weights $\{H_{ij}\}$ are all of the same sign.

If the range of integration is not (0,1) then adjustments have to be made as follows: Suppose the equation is

$$F(x) = G(x) + \int_a^b F(t)\log|t-x|dt, \qquad (5.8)$$

set

$$x = a+(b-a)x', \quad t = a+(b-a)t'$$

to give

$$F(a+(b-a)x')=G(a+(b-a)x')+(b-a)\int_0^1 F(a+(b-a)t')[$$

$$\log|t'-x'| + \log|b-a|]dt'. \qquad (5.9)$$

In order to use the values tabulated for (0,1) the corresponding quadrature weights with the same quadrature points but with constant weight function were tabulated. For n=1,2,...13 it was found that these also have the same sign. A table for n=5 will be found in appendix 2.

Comment

There is one particular kernel for which it is possible to give a complete solution to the problem of existence namely

$$K(x,t) = \begin{cases} (1-x)(1+t) & -1 \; t \; x \; 1 \\ (1-t)(1+x) & -1 \; x \; t \; 1 \end{cases},$$

for in this case it is easy to show that

$$\int_{-1}^{1} K(x,t)C_n^{(3/2)}(t)dt = (n+1)(n+2)(1-x^2)C_n^{(3/2)}(x),$$

where $C_n^{(3/2)}$ is an nth Gegenbauer polynomial.

The positivity of the corresponding weights has been observed in special cases but not proved in general.

6. Numerical Solution of Vandrey's equation

The equation is written as

$$u(s) = 2x'(s) - \frac{1}{\pi}\int_0^L [P(s,\sigma)\log|s-\sigma| + Q(s,\sigma)]u(\sigma)d\sigma, \tag{6.1}$$

and the generating curve was subdivided into major intervals of varying length. Since it is expected (and found) that the speed of flow along the horizontal part of the torpedo quickly becomes almost constant larger intervals were taken there than around the nose where the kernel and speed of flow changes rapidly. Thus we have

$$u(s)=2x'(s)- \frac{1}{\pi}\sum_{r=0}^{N-1}\int_{s_r}^{s_{r+1}} [P(s,\sigma)\log|s-\sigma| + Q(s,\sigma)]u(\sigma)d\sigma \tag{6.2}$$

and then in each of the intervals (s_r, s_{r+1}) the quadrature points were taken. When s is given appropriate values the result will be a set of linear equations to solve for the approximations to the solution at the quadrature points.

The exact solution when the 'torpedo' is the sphere generated by

$$x(s) = 1-\cos s, \; y(s) = \sin s$$

is given by

$$u(s) = \frac{3}{2}\sin s \tag{6.3}$$

which provides a useful test case.

For the acoustic torpedo as shown in the figure

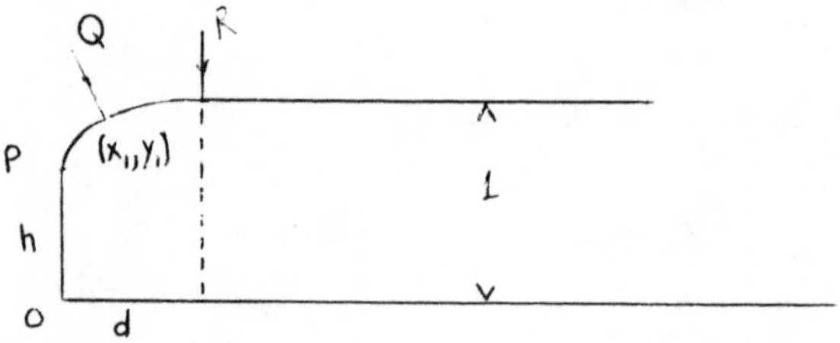

the following mathematical description was used. (The profile was parameterized with respect to t instead of s since this avoids the rectification of the curves joining P to R.)

OP : $0 \leq t \leq h$, $x(t) = 0$, $y(t) = t$,

PQ : $h \leq t \leq h+x_1^{\frac{1}{2}}$, $x(t) = (t-h)^2$, $y(t)=h+x^{\frac{1}{2}}\,[a_1+a_2x+a_3x^2]$

QR : $h+x_1^{\frac{1}{2}} \leq t \leq d+h+x_1^{\frac{1}{2}}-x_1$

$$x(t) = t-h-x_1^{\frac{1}{2}}+x_1,\quad y(t) = 1-\frac{(1-y_1)}{(d-x_1)}\,(d-x)^3$$

R onwards : $d+h+x_1^{\frac{1}{2}}-x_1 \leq t$

$$x(t)=t-h-x_1^{\frac{1}{2}}+x_1,\quad y(t) = 1.$$

For a given point $Q(x_1,y_1)$ the parameters a_1,a_2,a_3 are chosen so that x,y $\frac{dx}{dt}$ and $\frac{dy}{dt}$ were continuous at P, Q and R.

Thus the profile is dependent only on the point (x_1,y_1), and the aim is to choose this point so that $\max|u(s)|$ is a minimum. This was done by a simple search method. However it must be reported that if P and R are joined by the quadrant of the appropriate ellipse then this gave the best result of all. It would be interesting to find if this was indeed the optimum shape.

Appendix 1

Landweber's integral equation

The following appear in [6] and is reproduced here with the kind permission of Professor L. LANDWEBER of the University of Iowa.

It will be convenient to change the notation slightly in this section, this is indicated in the diagram

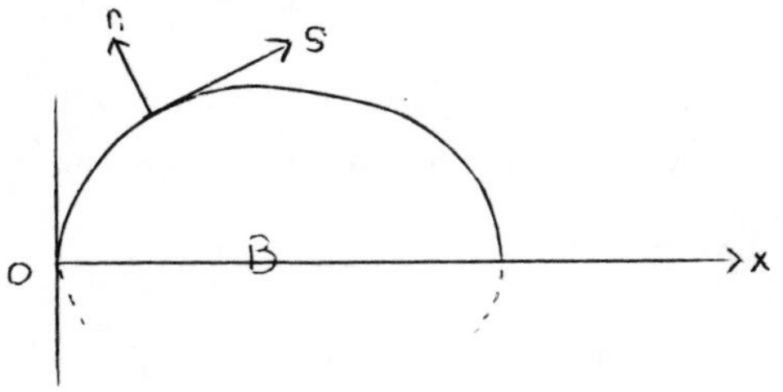

Denote as before arc length measured along the generating curve by s and let u(s) be the (tangential) speed of flow. Then with L being the total length of the generating curve, Landweber's equation is

$$\int_0^L \frac{u(s)\ y^2(s)}{[(x(s)-t)^2+y^2(s)]^{3/2}}\ ds = 2 \text{ for } x(0)<t<x(L). \tag{A1.1}$$

We give now a sketch of the proof.

Green's second identity is

$$\iint_{\partial B} \phi_1 \frac{\partial \phi_2}{\partial n} \cdot dS = \iint_{\partial B} \phi_2 \frac{\partial \phi_2}{\partial n} \cdot dS \tag{A1.2}$$

where ϕ_1, ϕ_2 satisfy Laplace's equation outside B and vanish at ∞.

Let the free stream velocity be unity and set

$$\phi_1 = \Phi - x$$

where Φ is the harmonic function of section 3, then $\phi_1(\infty) = 0$, and so

$$\iint_{\partial B} [\Phi - x] \frac{\partial}{\partial n} \phi_2 \quad dS = \iint_{\partial B} \phi_2 \frac{\partial}{\partial n} [\Phi - x] dS. \tag{A1.3}$$

Impose the Neumann condition on Φ and the requirement that the problem has axial symmetry, i.e.

$$\frac{\partial \Phi}{\partial n} = 0 \text{ on } \partial B, \text{ and } dS = 2\pi y ds \tag{A1.4}$$

to replace (A1.3) by

$$\int_0^L \Phi \frac{\partial}{\partial n} \phi_2 \quad y\ ds = \int_0^L \left[x \frac{\partial \phi_2}{\partial n} - \phi_2 \frac{\partial x}{\partial n} \right] y\ ds. \tag{A1.5}$$

Since ϕ_2 is (now) an axisymmetric potential function there will correspond to it a Stokes' stream function ψ_2 which satisfies

$$y \frac{\partial \phi_2}{\partial n} = \frac{\partial \psi_2}{\partial s} \ . \tag{A1.6}$$

Hence

$$\int_0^L \Phi \frac{\partial \phi_2}{\partial n} y \, ds = \int_0^L \Phi \frac{\partial \psi_2}{\partial s} ds$$

$$= \Big[\Phi\psi_2\Big]_0^L - \int_0^L \psi_2 \; u(s) ds$$

where $u(s) = \dfrac{\partial \Phi}{\partial s}$.

When this is used in (A1.5) the result will be

$$\int_0^L u \, \psi_2 \, ds = \Big[\Phi\psi_2\Big]_0^L - \int_0^L \left[x \frac{\partial \psi_2}{\partial s} - \phi_2 \, y \frac{\partial x}{\partial n}\right] ds \; . \tag{A1.7}$$

Since $\dfrac{\partial x}{\partial n} = - \dfrac{\partial y}{\partial s}$ the right hand side of this can be written

$$\Big[\Phi\psi_2\Big]_0^L - \int_0^L \left[x \frac{\partial \psi_2}{\partial s} + \phi_2 \, y \frac{\partial y}{\partial s}\right] ds \; ,$$

which, after an integration by parts of the first term under the integral sign, becomes

$$\Big[(\Phi - x) \, \psi_2\Big]_0^L + \int_0^L \left[\psi_2 \frac{dx}{ds} - y\phi_2 \frac{dy}{ds}\right] ds. \tag{A1.8}$$

But

$$\frac{\partial}{\partial x} [-y\phi_2] = - y \frac{\partial \phi_2}{\partial x}$$

and

$$\frac{\partial}{\partial y} [\psi_2] = \frac{\partial \psi_2}{\partial y} = - y \frac{\partial \phi_2}{\partial x}$$

from the Beltrami equation, consequently

$$\psi_2 \frac{dx}{ds} - y \, \phi_2 \frac{dy}{ds} \tag{A1.9}$$

is an exact differential, and so there exists a function Ω so that

$$\psi_2 \frac{dx}{ds} - y \, \phi_2 \frac{dy}{ds} = \frac{d\Omega}{ds} \; . \tag{A1.10}$$

Hence (A1.7) can be written

$$\int_0^L u\psi_2 \, ds = \Big[(\Phi-x)\psi_2 + \Omega\Big]_0^L . \tag{A1.11}$$

Landweber chooses

$$\Omega(x,y) = \frac{(x-t)}{[(x-t)^2+y^2]^{\frac{1}{2}}} , \ \min(x) < t < \max(x). \tag{A1.12}$$

It is not difficult to verify that Ω is a solution of the stream function equation (3.10).

With this choice of Ω we have

$$\psi_2(x,y) = \frac{y^2}{[(x-t)^2+y^2]^{3/2}} , \ \Phi_2(x,y) = \frac{(x-t)}{[(x-t)^2+y^2]^{3/2}} . \tag{A1.13}$$

Since $\psi_2(x,y) = 0$ when $y = 0$, and $\Omega(0,0) = -1$, $\Omega(x(L),0) = 1$ we see that (A1.12) becomes Landweber's equation:

$$\int_0^L \frac{u(s)y^2(s)}{[(x(s)-t)^2+y^2(s)]^{3/2}} ds = 2. \tag{A1.14}$$

Appendix 2

Points and weights for n = 5

x_i	H_i
0.05388 13676	0.13235 00799
0.24358 71433	0.23310 54203
0.5	0.26908 89996
0.75641 28567	0.23310 54203
0.94611 86324	0.13235 00799

$-H_{ij}$ $(= -H_{6-i,6-j})$ for $1 \leq i \leq 3$, $1 \leq j \leq 5$

0.49251 75929	0.40808 06340	0.20970 71664	0.08499 28001
0.01449 099363			
0.22793 39028	0.74534 88271	0.38203 13900	0.15264 13351
0.04224 145790			
0.10443 72739	0.33438 08637	0.81551 09053	etc.

Then

$$\int_0^1 p(t) \log|t-x_i|dt = \sum_{j=1}^{5} H_{ij} p(x_j), \quad i = 1,2,\ldots,5$$

when p is any polynomial of degree 5,

and

$$\int_0^1 q(t)dt = \sum_{j=1}^{5} H_j q(x_j)$$

when q is any polynomial of degree 4.

References

1. Atkinson, K.E. (1976) A survey of numerical methods for the solution of Fredholm equations of the second kind. SIAM.

2. Cody, W.J. (1965) Chebyshev approximations for the complete elliptic integrals K and E. Maths of Comp. 19 pp 105-112.

3. Grodtkjaer, E. (1973) A direct integral equation method for the potential flow about arbitrary bodies. International J. for Numerical Methods in Engineering 6 pp 253-264.

4. Kershaw, D. (1961) A numerical solution of an integral equation satisfied by the velocity distribution around a body of revolution in axial flow. Aero. Research Council. R & M 3308.

5. Kershaw, D. (1970) A note on orthogonal polynomials. Proc. Edin. Maths Soc. 17 (Series II) pp 83-93.

6. Landweber, L. (1951) The axially symmetric potential flow about elongated bodies of revolution. David Taylor Model Basin. Report 761, NS 715-084.

7. Vandrey, F. (1951) A direct iteration method for the calculation of the velocity distribution of bodies of revolution and symmetric profiles. Admiralty Research Laboratory Report R1/G/HY/12/2.

Department of Mathematics,
University of Lancaster,
Lancaster LA1 4YL,
Lancashire,
England.

International Series of
Numerical Mathematics, Vol. 73

ON THE CONDITION NUMBER OF BOUNDARY INTEGRAL EQUATIONS IN ACOUSTIC SCATTERING USING COMBINED DOUBLE- AND SINGLE-LAYER POTENTIALS

Rainer Kress

Institut für Numerische
und Angewandte Mathematik
Universität Göttingen, Lotzestr. 16-18
D-3400 Göttingen, Germany

The non-uniqueness problems arising in boundary integral equations for the exterior boundary-value problems for the Helmholtz equation, that is, in time-harmonic acoustic scattering, can be resolved by seeking the solutions in the form of a combined double- and single-layer potential. We present an outline of an analysis of the appropriate choice of the coupling parameter in order to minimize the condition number of the integral equations.

In order to describe our results we first need to give the formulation of the exterior boundary-value problems of acoustic scattering. For the sake of brevity we confine ourselves to Dirichlet boundary conditions, that is, to scattering at acoustically soft obstacles. Let $D \subset \mathbb{R}^3$ be a bounded domain with a sufficiently smooth connected boundary surface ∂D. By ν we denote the unit normal to ∂D directed into the exterior $\mathbb{R}^3 \setminus D$. Consider the exterior Dirichlet problem for the Helmholtz equation

$$(1) \qquad \Delta u + k^2 u = 0 \quad \text{in } \mathbb{R}^3 \setminus \bar{D}$$

with boundary condition

$$(2) \qquad u = f \quad \text{on } \partial D$$

subject to the Sommerfeld radiation condition

$$(3) \qquad \frac{\partial u}{\partial r} - iku = o\left(\frac{1}{r}\right), \quad r = |x| \to \infty,$$

uniformly in all directions $x/|x|$. Here the wave number k is a given positive number and f is a given function on ∂D.

The classical way to reduce this boundary-value problem to boundary integral equations is to seek the solution in the form of an acoustic double- or single-layer potential in terms of the free-space fundamental solution

$$(4) \qquad \Phi(x,y) := \frac{e^{ik|x-y|}}{4\pi|x-y|}, \quad x \neq y,$$

to the Helmholtz equation in $\mathbb{R}^3$. The double-layer potential

$$(5) \qquad u(x) = \int_{\partial D} \psi(y) \frac{\partial \Phi(x,y)}{\partial \nu(y)} ds(y), \quad x \in \mathbb{R}^3 \setminus \bar{D},$$

solves the exterior Dirichlet problem provided the density ψ solves the integral equation of the second kind

$$(6) \qquad \psi(x) + 2 \int_{\partial D} \psi(y) \frac{\partial \Phi(x,y)}{\partial \nu(y)} ds(y) = 2f(x), \quad x \in \partial D.$$

The single-layer potential

$$(7) \qquad u(x) = \int_{\partial D} \psi(y)\Phi(x,y)ds(y), \quad x \in \mathbb{R}^3 \setminus \bar{D},$$

solves the exterior Dirichlet problem provided the density ψ solves the integral equation of the first kind

$$(8) \qquad 2 \int_{\partial D} \psi(y)\Phi(x,y)ds(y) = 2f(x), \ x \in \partial D.$$

These integral equations can be discussed either in the Banach space $C(\partial D)$ leading to classical solutions to the boundary-value problem or in the Hilbert spaces $H^s(\partial D)$ leading to weak solutions. For the classical treatment we refer to the recent monograph by Colton and Kress [3] on integral equation methods in scattering theory. A fairly complete discussion of the integral equations in the Sobolev spaces $H^s(\partial D)$ is contained in the habilitation thesis by Kirsch [5]. A major advantage of Kirsch's approach is the reduction of the mapping properties of the single- and double-layer potential operators in the spaces $H^s(\partial D)$ to the classical mapping properties of these operators in the Hölder spaces $C^{m,\alpha}(\partial D)$ by employing a functional analytic result due to Lax and thus avoiding to rely on the concept of pseudo-differential operators.

In either setting the homogeneous form of the integral equation (6) has non-trivial solutions if and only if the homogeneous interior Neumann problem for the Helmholtz equation in D has non-trivial solutions, with other words, if and only if k^2 is an eigenvalue of the interior Neumann problem. The homogeneous form of the integral equation (8) has non-trivial solutions if and only if the homogeneous interior Dirichlet problem in D has non-trivial solutions, that is, if and only if k^2 is an interior Dirichlet eigenvalue. Note that for each of the interior problems there exists a countable set of positive eigenvalues accumulating only at infinity.

Therefore, when the integral equations (6) or (8) are used to obtain approximate solutions to the exterior Dirichlet problem the system of linear equations derived by discretizing the integral equations will become ill-conditioned for wave numbers in the neighbourhood of the corresponding interior eigenvalues and for a general domain D we do not know beforehand where these eigenvalues are. Hence, for numerical purposes the integral equations (6) and (8) are unsatisfactory and it is necessary to develop integral equations which are uniquely solvable for all positive wave numbers.

To achieve uniquely solvable integral equations Leis [16], Brakhage and Werner [1], and Panich [18] independently suggested to seek the solution in the form

$$(9) \qquad u(x) = \int_{\partial D} \psi(y)\left\{\frac{\partial\Phi(x,y)}{\partial\nu(y)} - i\eta\Phi(x,y)\right\}ds(y),\ x \in \mathbb{R}^3\setminus\bar{D},$$

with a positive constant η. This combined double- and single-layer potential solves the exterior Dirichlet problem provided the density solves the integral equation

$$(10) \qquad \psi(x) + 2\int_{\partial D} \psi(y)\left\{\frac{\partial\Phi(x,y)}{\partial\nu(y)} - i\eta\Phi(x,y)\right\}ds(y) = 2f(x), x \in \partial D,$$

and this integral equation is uniquely solvable for all positive wave numbers k.

This approach can be extended to the exterior Neumann problem and there is also a variant of the integral equation (10) due to Burton and Miller [2] based on Green's representation theorem for radiating solutions of the Helmholtz equation (for details see [3]).

Numerical implementations of the integral equations based on this combined potential approach have been given by various authors, mostly for the special choice of the coupling parameter $\eta = 1$. Since from a numerical point of view the integral equation (10) has been introduced to overcome the bad condition of the classical integral equations (6) and (8) in the neighbourhood of the interior eigenvalues a reasonable criterium for the choice of the parameter η is to optimize the condition of equation (10). Rewrite (10) in the operator form

$$(11) \qquad A\psi = 2f$$

with an obvious meaning of the operator A. Then the condition number of A is given by

$$(12) \qquad \text{cond}\,(A) = \|A\|\,\|A^{-1}\|$$

and for numerical purposes it is desirable to have cond (A) as close to one as possible. Provided the condition number is small, then small perturbations of the operator A and the right-hand side f will lead to small changes in the solution ψ of (11). Since we may consider any numerical approximation method for solving the integral equation (11) as a perturbation of the original equation we therefore can expect good error estimates if the condition number of A is small.

In three papers by Kress and Spassov [13, 14, 15] the condition number of the operator $A : H^s(\partial D) \to H^s(\partial D)$ is investigated for the special case of a sphere ∂D (and a circle ∂D with the obvious modifications of the fundamental solution (4) in $\mathbb{R}^2$). The analysis uses the fact that the condition number in a Hilbert space is given by

$$(13) \qquad \text{cond}\,(A) = \left(\frac{\lambda_{max}}{\lambda_{min}}\right)^{1/2}$$

where λ_{max} and λ_{min} denote the largest and smallest spectral values of A^*A. In the case of a sphere these spectral values can be expressed in terms of spherical Bessel and Hankel functions. The main result can be summarized by the statement that the condition number of the integral equation (10) is close to minimal for the choice

$$(14) \qquad \eta = k.$$

Despite the fact that it seems to be difficult to carry out a similar analysis for non-spherical domains the special result (14) may serve as a guide for the choice of the parameter η also for arbitrary domains. As pointed out by Kleinman [6] there is also some heuristic argument for the choice $\eta = k$. In this case the kernel of the integral equation (10) becomes

$$(15) \qquad \frac{\partial\Phi(x,y)}{\partial\nu(y)} - ik\Phi(x,y)$$

which by the radiation condition (3) for the fundamental solution is caused to be kind of concentrated around the diagonal $x = y$. The result (14) also coincides with an observation made by Meyer et al [17]. Their numerical experiments for various geometries and various wave numbers indicate that from the three choices $\eta = 0$, $\eta = 1$ and $\eta = k$ the latter gives the most accurate results.

The analysis in [14] also includes a discussion of the condition number for boundary integral equations in electromagnetic scattering, that is, for exterior boundary-value problems for the time-harmonic Maxwell equations. Here, the analog to the combined double- and single-layer acoustic potential is the electromagnetic field generated by a combined magnetic- and electric-dipole distribution. The integral equations arising from this approach have been investigated by Knauff and Kress [8, 9, 10, 11, 12] (see also [3]).

In closing we want to mention that in an other method to attain uniquely solvable integral equations Jones [4] has proposed to modify the fundamental solution (4) by adding a series of outgoing spherical waves. An analysis of how to choose the intensities of these outgoing waves in order to minimize condition numbers has been carried out by Kleinman and Kress [7].

References

[1] Brakhage, H., Werner, P. (1965) Über das Dirichletsche Außenraumproblem für die Helmholtzsche Schwingungsgleichung. Arch. Math. 16, 325-329.

[2] Burton, A.J., Miller, G.F. (1971) The application of integral equation methods to the numerical solution of some exterior boundary-value problems. Proc. Royal Soc. London A 323, 201-220.

[3] Colton, D., Kress, R. (1983) Integral equation methods in scattering theory. Wiley-Interscience.

[4] Jones, D.S. (1974) Integral equations for the exterior acoustic problem. Q.J. Mech. Appl. Math. 27, 129-142.

[5] Kirsch, A. (1984) Generalized boundary-value and control problems for the Helmholtz equation. Habilitationsschrift, Göttingen.

[6] Kleinman, R.E. (1983) Private communication.

[7] Kleinman, R.E., Kress, R. (1983) On the condition number of integral equations in acoustics using modified fundamental solutions. IMA Jour. Appl. Math. 31, 79-90.

[8] Knauff, W. (1981) Ein numerisches Verfahren zur Lösung eines Außenraumproblems für die vektorielle Helmholtzgleichung. NAM-Bericht Nr. 28, Göttingen.

[9] Knauff, W., Kress, R. (1979) On the exterior boundary-value problem for the time-harmonic Maxwell equations. J. Math. Anal. Appl. 72, 215-235.

[10] Knauff, W., Kress, R. (1980) A modified integral equation method for the electric boundary-value problem for the vector Helmholtz equation. ISNM 53, 157-170.

[11] Kress, R. (1980) On the existence of a solution to a singular integral equation in electromagnetic reflection. J. Math. Anal. Appl. 77, 555-566.

[12] Kress, R. (1980) On boundary integral equation methods in stationary electromagnetic reflection. Springer-Verlag Lecture Notes in Mathematics, Vol. 846, 210-226.

[13] Kress, R. (1984) On the condition number of boundary integral operators in scattering theory. Strathclyde Seminars in Classical Scattering, Nantwich, Shiva.

[14] Kress, R. (1984) Minimizing the condition number of boundary integral operators in acoustic and electromagnetic scattering. Q.J. Mech. Appl. Math. (to appear).

[15] Kress, R., Spassov, W.T. (1983) On the condition number of boundary integral operators for the exterior Dirichlet problem for the Helmholtz equation. Numer. Math. 42, 77-95.

[16] Leis, R. (1965) Zur Dirichletschen Randwertaufgabe des Außenraums der Schwingungsgleichung. Math. Zeit. 90, 205-211.

[17] Meyer, W.L., Bell, W.A., Stallybrass, M.P., Zinn, B.T. (1979) Prediction of the sound field radiated from axisymmetric surfaces. J. Acoustic Soc. America 65, 631-638.

[18] Panich, O.I. (1965) On the question of the solvability of the exterior boundary-value problem for the wave equation and Maxwell's equations. Russian Math. Surveys 20, 221-226.

International Series of
Numerical Mathematics, Vol. 73

NUMERICAL SOLUTION OF SINGULAR INTEGRAL EQUATIONS AND AN APPLICATION TO THE THEORY OF JET-FLAPPED WINGS

Frieder Kuhnert and Rolf Haftmann

Technische Hochschule Karl-Marx-Stadt, Sektion Mathematik, GDR

The numerical solution of singular integral equations by means of Gauß type quadrature formulas is considered. The direct quadrature method is applied to a special integral equation arising from airfoil theory. Finally computational results are given.

1980 Mathematics Subject Classification:
Primary 65R20; secondary 65D32, 76B05

The flow around a wing can be improved by a trailing jet (see, e.g. [23],[24]). By this means it is possible to increase the lift of the wing essentially. For the jet-flapped wing the ground interference is a question of engineering interest ([22],[21]). Under rigorous simplifications RUMPEL [22] has given the following Cauchy type singular integral

---

A more detailed German version of some results presented here has been published as ref. [7] (MR 84b:65129).

equation for the vorticity distribution $\gamma(x)$ ($0 < x < 1$: wing; $1 < x$: jet) simulating the effect of the wing and of the jet:

$$(W\gamma)(x) = \int_0^\infty \frac{\gamma(y)}{y-x}\,dy - \int_0^\infty \gamma(y)\,\frac{y-x}{(y-x)^2+b^2}\,dy = \overset{\circ}{r}(x) \qquad (1)$$

The constant b is the doubled distance between the jet exit and the ground.

W is proved in [6] to be a bounded, but not normal solvable operator in all spaces $L_p(0, \infty)$ $(1 < p < \infty)$. Equation (1) is not solvable for each right-hand side. The image space of W, however, is dense in L_p. If a solution of (1) exists it is unique. In the case $1 < p < 2$ equation (1) is solvable for $\overset{\circ}{r}(x)$ if $x\overset{\circ}{r}(x)$ is an element of L_p too.

The leading edge of the wing and the jet exit at the trailing edge induce high overspeeds of the flow. Hence $\gamma(x)$ is tending to infinity for $x \to 0$ and $x \to 1$ whereas it is continuous at all other points x. The right-hand side $\overset{\circ}{r}(x)$ is bounded and continuous with an only exception at the point $x = 1$ where it has a finite jump. It is useful to treat the singularity at $x = 1$ before solving (1) numerically. For this the function

$$s(x) = \frac{1}{\pi^2}\left(\ln\left|\frac{\sqrt{x}+1}{\sqrt{x}-1}\right| - \frac{2}{\sqrt{x}} - \frac{2}{3\sqrt{x}\,(x+1)} - \frac{16}{15\sqrt{x}\,(x+1)^2}\right) \qquad (2)$$

can be used. This function yields

$$(Ws)(x) = \begin{cases} 1 & 0 < x < 1 \\ 0 & 1 < x \end{cases} + \hat{r}(x)$$

with an everywhere bounded and Lipschitz continuous function $\hat{r}(x)$. The behaviour of $s(x)$ is as $x^{-1/2}$ for $x \to 0$, as $\ln(|x-1|)$ for $x \to 1$, and as $x^{-7/2}$ for $x \to \infty$. Since W is a linear operator, it is possible to substitute $\overset{\circ}{r}(x)$ in (1) by a continuous right-hand side $r(x)$. The solution of (1) for $r(x)$ will not have a singularity.

In a greater distance from the trailing edge an effect of the jet will not be measurable. Thus, $\gamma(x)$, $\overset{\circ}{r}(x)$ and $r(x)$ vanish there. Through the consideration of the problem along the infinite half-axis the domain of the influence of the jet must not be given in advance. On the other hand, however, this kind of consideration implies important mathematical difficulties of W already mentioned above. Hence it is suitable to substitute the upper limit of integration ∞ by a larger finite number G. On the interval (0,G) the operator of the second integral in (1) will be a compact one contrary to the situation on (0, ∞).

The solution of the equation with the right-hand side r(x) is tending to ∞ for $x \longrightarrow 0$ whereas it is tending to 0 for $x \longrightarrow G$. Thus, it is of the form $\sqrt{(G-x)/x}\ g(x)$ with a Hölder continuous function g(x). Hence the equation

$$\int_0^G g(y)\sqrt{\frac{G-y}{y}}\frac{dy}{y-x} - \int_0^G g(y)\ \frac{y-x}{(y-x)^2+b^2}\sqrt{\frac{G-y}{y}}\ dy = r(x) \qquad (3)$$

is to be solved.

The numerical treatment of singular integral equations of the type

$$\int_a^b g(y)\ \frac{p(y)}{y-x}\ dy + \int_a^b g(y)\ k(x,y)\ p(y)\ dy = r(x) \qquad (4)$$

is considered in a great number of papers. A very simple method for practical computation can be obtained by restriction of (4) to appropriate collocation points and approximation of the integrals in (4) by quadrature formulas. It is very convenient and useful to apply Gauß type quadrature formulas to both the integrals in (4). Let $P_n(x)$ denote the polynomials orthogonal with respect to the weight function p(x). Further let $Q_n(x)$ denote the functions

$$Q_n(x) = -\int_a^b P_n(y)\ \frac{p(y)}{y-x}\ dy\ . \qquad (5)$$

The Gauß formula with respect to p(x)

$$\int_a^b g(y)\ p(y)\ dy \approx \sum_{i=1}^{N} A_i^{(N)}\ g(y_i^{(N)}) \qquad (6)$$

is exact whenever g(x) is a polynomial of degree $\leq$ 2N-1. It can be shown that the quadrature formulas

$$\int_a^b g(y)\,\frac{p(y)}{y-x}\,dy \approx \sum_{i=1}^{N} \frac{A_i^{(N)}\, g(y_i^{(N)})}{y_i^{(N)} - x}\left(1 - \frac{Q_N(x)}{Q_N(y_i^{(N)})}\right) \qquad (7)$$

and

$$\int_a^b g(y)\,\frac{p(y)}{y-x}\,dy \approx \sum_{i=1}^{N} \frac{A_i^{(N)}\, g(y_i^{(N)})}{y_i^{(N)} - x} - g(x)\,\frac{Q_N(x)}{P_N(x)} \qquad (8)$$

have the degree of exactness N-1 and 2N, respectively. These formulas are often associated with the names of Elliott and Hunter, respectively. It should be mentioned, however, that they have been given earlier by Kornejchuk and Sanikidze (for references, see [9] and [11]). Formula (7) can be obtained from (8) by approximating g(x) by Lagrange interpolation ([14], [27]). In the zeros $x_k^{(N)}$ of $Q_N(x)$ both formula (7) and formula (8) are of the simple form

$$\int_a^b g(y)\,\frac{p(y)}{y-x}\,dy \approx \sum_{i=1}^{N} \frac{A_i^{(N)}\, g(y_i^{(N)})}{y_i^{(N)} - x_k^{(N)}} \qquad (9)$$

This formula has the structure of Gauß formula (6), and it's degree of exactness is 2N. References concerning the remainder and the convergence of (7), (8), and (9) are given in [11], for newer results see [14] and [27]. The convergence of (8) has been recently the matter of o controversy between THEOCARIS and IOAKIMIDIS ([14],[27],[15]). A survey of Gauß type quadrature formulas for singular integrals can be found in [3].

Using formulas (9) and (6) at the points $x_k^{(N)}$ (4) can be approximated by the system of equations

$$\sum_{i=1}^{N} A_i^{(N)}\, g(y_i^{(N)}) \left[\frac{1}{y_i^{(N)} - x_k^{(N)}} + k(x_k^{(N)}, y_i^{(N)})\right] = r(x_k^{(N)}). \qquad (10)$$

In the case of the weight function $p(x) = \sqrt{(b-x)/(x-a)}$ occuring in (3) we have $P_N(x) = P_N^{(1/2,-1/2)}(x)$ and $Q_N(x) = P_N^{(-1/2,1/2)}(x)$ as Jacobi polynomials related to the interval (a,b). Thus, $A_i^{(N)}$, $y_i^{(N)}$, and $x_k^{(N)}$ can be given in a simple form, and the number of collocation points is equal to N.

The method (10) has been used by many authors, for

references, see, e.g. [10]. Convergence results for this method have been missed during a long time. The second author of the present paper investigated this question in [6] (see also [10]): Let p(x) be one of the special weight functions $1/\sqrt{(b-x)(x-a)}$, $\sqrt{(b-x)/(x-a)}$, and $\sqrt{(x-a)/(b-x)}$, further (4) is provided to possess a unique solution, then for continuous k(x,y) and Riemann integrable r(x) the system (10) possesses a unique solution too and the interpolation $\hat{g}(x)$ over this solution converges to g(x) in the norm of the space L_2 with the weight function p(x). Further, if both for k(x,y) and r(x) the derivatives of order m ($m \geq 0$) exist and are Hölder continuous with exponent η the estimate

$$\| g(x) - \hat{g}(x) \|_{L_2(p(x))} \leqq C_1 N^{-m-\eta} \tag{11}$$

has been demonstrated. Further, in [6], [10] uniform convergence results are given. In the case $m+\eta \geqq 1/2$ the estimates

$$\| g(x) - \hat{g}(x) \|_{\infty} \leqq C_2 N^{1/2-m-\eta} \tag{12}$$

and

$$\| \sqrt{b-x}\, (g(x)-\hat{g}(x)) \|_{\infty} \leqq C_2 N^{1/2-m-\eta}, \| \sqrt{x-a}\, (g(x)-\hat{g}(x)) \|_{\infty} \leqq C_2 N^{1/2-m-\eta}$$

have been proved for the three weight functions mentioned above, respectively. At last, in the case $m+\eta \geqq 3/2$ for $\sqrt{(b-x)/(x-a)}$ and $\sqrt{(x-a)/(b-x)}$

$$\| g(x) - \hat{g}(x) \|_{\infty} \leqq C_3 N^{3/2-m-\eta} \tag{13}$$

holds.

Independently the existence of a unique solution of (10) in the case $p(x) = 1/\sqrt{(b-x)(x-a)}$ has been proved by GERASOULIS [4] whereas uniform convergence of $\hat{g}(x)$ for this weight function has been demonstrated by IOAKIMIDIS and THEOCARIS [16] provided both k(x,y) and r(x) are at least twice continuously differentiable functions. The estimate (12), however, is better than that of [16], since the result of [16] for $m \geqq 1$, $\eta = 1$ can be given as

$$\| g(x) - \hat{g}(x) \|_{\infty} \leqq C_4 N^{1-m-\eta}.$$

Later the equivalence of the method (10) to the classical "indirect" method of previous regularization of (4) to an equivalent Fredholm integral equation has been reportet in [17] and [13] (comp. the Einleitung of [18]). Following this idea convergence proofs have been given in [26] and [5].

Further, a great number of questions of the theory of polynomial approximation methods for Cauchy type singular integral equations of the first and of the second kind with variable coefficients have been answered in a uniform and general way by JUNGHANNS and SILBERMANN [20] (comp. also [18], [19]). In the special case mentioned above the L_2-convergence estimates of [20] and [18] and the uniform convergence estimates of [19] and [18] have been reportet already in [6]. They are given in the present paper as formulas (11), (12), and (13). Meanwhile uniform convergence results for singular integral equations of the first and of the second kind with variable coefficients have been improved by ELLIOTT [2] (comp. also [1]) using the technique of previous regularization. From the results of [2] instead of (12) the estimate

$$\| g(x) - \hat{g}(x) \|_{\infty} \leq C_5 \; N^{-m-\eta} \ln^2 N$$

can be given for $m+\eta > 0$. For the weight functions $\sqrt{(b-x)/(x-a)}$ and $\sqrt{(x-a)/(b-x)}$, however, the results of [2] are not applicable.

Numerical test results for the method (10) in application to the equation (1) reduced to (3) have been reportet in detail in [6]. It must be taken into consideration that the solution of (3) does not vanish for arguments greater than a certain G as it is clear from the treatment of the singularity at the point x=1 with the function (2). Thus, for the test of the method functions $\gamma_n(x) = 1/(\sqrt{x}(x+1)^n)$ (n = 1,2,3,4) and $\gamma_5(x) = \exp(-x)/\sqrt{x}$ were given. Then method (10) for equation (3) was applied to the right-hand sides $r_n(x) = (W\gamma_n)(x)$ (b = 10). It should be mentioned that the restriction of $\gamma_n(x)$ to the interval (0,G) cannot be the exact solution $\sqrt{(G-x)/x}\, g(x)$ of (3) as it is clear from $\gamma_n(G) = 0$. Nevertheless good test results have been achieved.

Table I gives some results for the right-hand side

$r_1(x)$ obtained from the solution of (10) by Lagrange interpolation formula (for other interpolation formulas, comp. [13]).

Table I. Numerical solutions for the right-hand side $r_1(x)$

x	$\gamma_1(x)$ exact	G=30 N=30	G=50 N=90	G=100 N= 90	G=200 N= 90	G=400 N=150	G=600 N=150	G=1000 N=200
0.1	2.8748	2.8480	2.8613	2.8697	2.8729	2.8741	2.8744	2.8746
0.2	1.8634	1.8442	1.8538	1.8597	1.8620	1.8629	1.8631	1.8633
0.8	0.6211	0.6110	0.6160	0.6192	0.6204	0.6209	0.6210	0.6211
2.0	0.2357	0.2285	0.2321	0.2343	0.2352	0.2355	0.2356	0.2356
10.0	0.0287	0.0234	0.0261	0.0277	0.0284	0.0286	0.0287	0.0287
50.0	0.0028	------	------	0.0018	0.0024	0.0026	0.0027	0.0027

Table I demonstrates the improvement of the results with increasing upper limit of integration G.

In the physical problem the vorticity integral along the wing $\Gamma = \int_0^1 \gamma(y)\,dy$ is of special interest. Therefore approximate values for the integrals $\Gamma_n = \int_0^1 \gamma_n(y)\,dy$ have been calculated from the solutions of (10). A comparison of exact and approximate values of Γ_n is given in tables II and III.

Table II. Approximate values for Γ_n. Number of equations N=30

given function	Γ_n exakt	approximate values G = 15	G = 30	G = 50	G = 100
$\gamma_1(x)$	1.570796	1.528481	1.553403	1.562022	1.567697
$\gamma_2(x)$	1.285398	1.283066	1.284908	1.285116	1.286220
$\gamma_3(x)$	1.089049	1.088917	1.089085	1.088626	1.090558
$\gamma_4(x)$	0.949207	0.949200	0.949329	0.948380	0.951285
$\gamma_5(x)$	1.493648	1.493648	1.493647	1.493648	1.493650

Table III. Approximate values for Γ_1=1.570796, given function $\gamma_1(x)$

N	G = 50	G = 100	G = 150	G = 200	G = 600	G = 1000
30	1.562022	1.567697	1.571457	1.573813		
45	1.562055	1.567463	1.568799	1.569559		
60	1.562054	1.567474	1.568939	1.569531		
75	1.562055	1.567474	1.568935	1.569572		
90	1.562054	1.567474	1.568935	1.569568		
150					1.570551	
200						1.570681

From table II we can see that the approximation is as better as the solution decreases faster for $x \longrightarrow \infty$. On the other hand, for faster decreasing functions the approximation for greater G, for which the 30 quadrature nodes are distributed on a longer interval, can be worse than those for lower G.

A report on numerical results for right-hand sides of (1) resulting from physical considerations is given in [6] and [8].

A further ability for the numerical solution of singular integral equations on the half-axis is given by the use of quadrature formulas of Laguerre type related to the weight function $p(x) = x^{\alpha} \exp(-x)$ ([12]). Since from the influence of the function (2) exponential decrease of the function to be found numerically cannot be expected, this idea has not been used in [6] . Further, the collocation points associated with the Laguerre formula would have been calculated numerically too. Results of such computations are reportet in [12] only for $N \leqq 10$. The same problem occurs if the influence of the singularity at the point $x = 1$ is taken into consideration with the help of a weight function with a singularity $\ln|x-1|$ ([25]) instead of the method described above. For the problem of numerical computation of quadrature and collocation points, see also [18].

References

[1] Elliott, D. (1982) The classical collocation method for singular integral equations. SIAM J. Numer. Anal. 19, 4, 816-832

[2] Elliott, D. (1984) Rates of convergence for the method of classical collocation for solving singular integral equations, SIAM J. Numer. Anal. 21, 1, 136-148

[3] Gautschi, W. (1981) A survey of Gauss-Christoffel quadrature formulae. In: E. B. Christoffel. The influence of his work on mathematics and the physical sciences, ed. by P. L. Butzer and F. Fehér (Birkhäuser, Basel), 72-147

[4] Gerasoulis, A. (1981) On the existence of approximate solutions for singular integral equations of Cauchy type discretized by Gauss-Chebyshev quadrature formulae. BIT 21, 3, 377-380

[5] Gerasoulis, A. (1982) Singular integral equations - the convergence of the Nyström interpolant of the Gauss-Chebyshev method. BIT 22, 2, 200-210

[6] Haftmann, R. (1979) Numerische Behandlung einer singulären Integralgleichung aus der Strömungsmechanik, Diss., Techn. Hochsch. Karl-Marx-Stadt, Fak. Math. Nat.

[7] Haftmann, R. (1980) Quadraturformeln vom Gaußtyp für singuläre Integrale und ihre Anwendung zur Lösung singulärer Integralgleichungen. Techn. Hochsch. Karl-Marx-Stadt, Sektion Mathematik, Wissenschaftliche Informationen 17

[8] Haftmann, R. (1980) Numerische Berechnungen zur Tragflügelumströmung mit Hinterkantenausblasung und Bodeninterferenz. Wiss. Z. d. Techn. Hochsch. Karl-Marx-Stadt 22, 4, 321-326

[9] Haftmann, R. (1981) Quadraturformeln vom Gaußtyp für singuläre Integrale, Beitr. Numer. Math. 9, 63-71

[10] Haftmann, R. (1981) Über die Quadraturformelmethode zur Lösung singulärer Integralgleichungen. Beitr. Numer. Math. 10, 47-56

[11] Haftmann, R. (1984) Gauss type quadrature formulas for singular integrals. Computational Mathematics (Semester February 20 -May 30, 1980). Banach Center Publications, Warsaw, 13, 665-669

[12] Ioakimidis, N. I. (1981) Application of the Gauss- and Radau-Laguerre quadrature rules to the numerical solution of Cauchy type singular integral equations of the first kind. Computers & Structures 14, 1-2, 63-70

[13] Ioakimidis, N. I. (1981) On the natural interpolation formula for Cauchy type singular integral equations of the first kind. Computing 26, 1, 73-77

[14] Ioakimidis, N. I. (1982) Further convergence results for two quadrature rules for Cauchy principal value integrals. Aplikace mat. 27, 6, 457-466

[15] Ioakimidis, N. I. (1983) Some comments on the paper: "Modified quadrature rules for the numerical evaluation of certain Cauchy principal values"[Rev. Roum. Sci. Techn. Sér. Méc. Appl. 26 (1981)5, 725-730] by P. S. Theocaris and J. G. Kazantzakis. Rev. Roum. Sci. Techn. Sér. Méc. Appl. 28, 1, 89-97, with authors' reply.

[16] Ioakimidis, N. I. and Theocaris, P. S. (1980) On convergence of two direct methods for solution of Cauchy type singular integral equations of the first kind. BIT 20, 1, 83-87

[17] Ioakimidis, N. I. and Theocaris, P. S. (1980) A comparison between the direct and the classical numerical methods for the solution of Cauchy type singular integral equations. SIAM J. Numer. Anal. 17, 1, 115-118

[18] Junghanns, P. (1984) Polynomiale Näherungsverfahren für singuläre Integralgleichungen auf beschränkten Intervallen. Diss. B, Techn. Hochsch. Karl-Marx-Stadt, Fak. Math. Nat.

[19] Junghanns, P. (1984) Uniform convergence of approximate methods for Cauchy-type singular integral equations over (-1, 1). Wiss. Z. d. Techn. Hochsch. Karl-Marx-Stadt 26, 2, 251-256

[20] Junghanns, P. und Silbermann, B. (1981) Zur Theorie der Näherungsverfahren für singuläre Integralgleichungen auf Intervallen. Math. Nachr. 103, 199-244

[21] Löhr, R. (1976) Der Strahlklappenflügel in Bodennähe unter besonderer Berücksichtigung großer Anstell- und Strahlklappenwinkel, Z. f. Flugwiss. 24, 4, 187-196

[22] Rumpel, H. (1969) Über eine Methode der Strömungsbeeinflussung. Wiss. Z. d. Techn. Hochsch. Karl-Marx-Stadt 11, 5, 677-684

[23] Spence, D. A. (1956) The lift coefficient of a thin, jet-flapped wing. Proc. Roy. Soc. London 238, 46-68

[24] Spence, D. A. (1984) Some new results for the integro-differential equation of jet-flap theory. IMA J. Appl. Math. 32, 1-3, 289-309

[25] Theocaris, P. S., Chrysakis, A. C., and Ioakimidis, N. I. (1979) Cauchy-type integrals and integral equations with logarithmic singularities. J. Eng. Math. 13, 1, 63-74

[26] Tsamasphyros, G. and Theocaris, P. S. (1981) Equivalence and convergence of direct and indirect methods for the numerical solution of singular integral equations. Computing 27, 1, 71-80

[27] Tsamasphyros, G. and Theocaris, P. S. (1983) On the convergence of some quadrature rules for Cauchy principal-value and finite-part integrals. Computing 31, 2, 105-114

Prof. Dr. rer. nat. habil. Frieder Kuhnert, Technische Hochschule Karl-Marx-Stadt, Sektion Mathematik, DDR-9010 Karl-Marx-Stadt, Postschließfach 964

International Series of
Numerical Mathematics, Vol. 73

TIKHONOV-PHILLIPS REGULARIZATION OF THE RADON TRANSFORM

Alfred K. Louis

Fachbereich Mathematik, Universität Kaiserslautern

With the help of the singular value decomposition of the Radon transform the Tikhonov-Phillips regularization with suitable Sobolev norm is analytically computed. This allows for studying the influence of the regularization norm. Even more important is the effect of the regularization parameter which can now be studied explicitly, and optimally selected dependent on data noise and additional information on the searched-for function.

1. Introduction

The Radon transform serves as a model for describing the physical background in many technical applications. Examples are electron microscopy, non-destructive testing, radio astronomy. Most spectacular is its application in medical imaging. Here the data are interpreted as the Radon transform of the searched-for density distribution in x-ray computerized

This paper is in final form and no version of it will be submitted for publication elsewhere.

tomography, nuclear magnetic resonance zeugmatography, in simple models of ultrasound tomography, and generalizations of the Radon transform are needed in positron emission tomography and in single particle emission computerized tomography.

This integral transform has an unbounded inverse in an L_2-setting. Hence we face an ill-posed problem in these for our applications natural function spaces. For standard applications of the Radon transform its inversion formula, based on a result of RADON [15] is implemented. But in nonstandard applications, which arise in future scanners, say limited angle tomography for example, and in emission computerized tomography, where the attenuated Radon transform has to be used, these elegant techniques are not available. Also if additional information can be used one has to rely on other regularization methods for the inversion.

Here we study the application of the Tikhonov-Phillips regularization where we have to come to two decisions. First we have to select a regularization norm. This depends on the smoothness of the function to be determined, for a discussion of this problem see NATTERER [14]. The crucial part is then the selection of the regularization parameter which has to be dependent on the above chosen norm and on the noise level in the data. Although asymptotic results are known, in general applications one has to rely on trial and error. Here with the help of the singular value decomposition we can explicitly determine the Tikhonov-Phillips regularization and then study the influence of this regularization parameter, and hence get enough information how to select it.

In Chapter 2 we introduce the Radon transform and its singular value decomposition between weighted L_2-spaces. In the next chapter we discuss the nonuniqueness problem of the Radon transform for finitely many directions and estimate the worst case error caused by this indeterminacy under the assumption that some Sobolev norm of these functions is bounded. Finally in Chapter 4 we explicitly construct the Tikhonov-Phillips regularization and study the influence of the above mentioned parameters.

2. The Radon Transform

Let f be a real-valued function in $\mathbb{R}^N$ with compact support, say

$$\text{supp } f \subset \Omega = V(0,1) \subset \mathbb{R}^N$$

where V(a,r) denotes the ball around a with radius r. Its Radon transform is a real-valued function on the unit cylinder $Z = \mathbb{R} \times S^{N-1}$ in $\mathbb{R}^{N+1}$ where S^{N-1} denotes the unit sphere in $\mathbb{R}^N$. It is defined as

$$\mathcal{R}f(s,\omega) = \int_{\mathbb{R}^N} f(x)\,\delta(s-x\cdot\omega)\,dx \tag{2.1}$$

where δ denotes the Dirac measure.

An important tool for studying the Radon transform is its relation to the Fourier transform which is defined as

$$\hat{\psi}(\xi) = (2\pi)^{-M/2} \int_{\mathbb{R}^M} \psi(x) e^{-ix\xi} dx \tag{2.2}$$

for a function on $\mathbb{R}^M$. The aforementioned relation is known as the projection theorem, see e.g. LUDWIG [11], stating that

$$\hat{f}(\sigma\cdot\omega) = (2\pi)^{(1-N)/2} (\mathcal{R}f)^{\wedge}(\sigma,\omega)\,, \quad \sigma \in \mathbb{R}\,, \quad \omega \in S^{N-1} \tag{2.3}$$

where $(\mathcal{R}f)^{\wedge}$ denotes the one-dimensional Fourier transform of $\mathcal{R}f$ with respect to the first variable.

The following study is based on the singular value decomposition of the integral operator $\mathcal{R}$ as mapping between weighted L_2-spaces, see LOUIS [8]. To this end we introduce some special functions.

With $P_n^{(\alpha,\beta)}$ we denote the Jacobi polynomial of degree n and with

C_n^ν the Gegenbauer polynomial of degree n. Let $Y_{\ell k}$, $k = 1,\dots,M(N,\ell)$, denote an orthonormal basis of the spherical harmonics of degree ℓ. Finally let

$$W_\nu(x) = (1-|x|^2)^{\nu-N/2} \tag{2.4}$$

be a weight on the unit ball in $\mathbb{R}^N$ and

$$w_\nu(s) = (1-s^2)^{\nu-1/2} \tag{2.5}$$

be the corresponding weight on the unit interval.

<u>Theorem 2.1</u>. Let

$$V_{m\ell k}^\nu(x) = W_\nu(x)\,|x|^\ell P_{(m-\ell)/2}^{(\nu-N/2,\,\ell+N/2-1)}(2|x|^2-1)\,Y_{\ell k}(x/|x|), \tag{2.6}$$

$$v_{m\ell k}^\nu(s,\omega) = d_{m\ell} w_\nu(s)\; C_m^\nu(s)\,Y_{\ell k}(\omega) \tag{2.7}$$

$$\sigma_{m\ell k}^2 = \sigma_{m\ell}^2 = \pi^{N-1}2^{2\nu}\,\frac{\Gamma(\frac{m+\ell}{2}+\nu)\,\Gamma(\frac{m-\ell}{2}+\nu-\frac{N}{2}+1)\,\Gamma(m+1)}{\Gamma(\frac{m+\ell+N}{2})\,\Gamma(\frac{m-\ell}{2}+1)\,\Gamma(m+2\nu)} \tag{2.8}$$

where

$$d_{m\ell} = \pi^{N/2-1}2^{2\nu-1}\,\frac{\Gamma(\frac{m-\ell}{2}+\nu-\frac{N}{2}+1)\,\Gamma(m+1)\,\Gamma(\nu)}{\Gamma(\frac{m-\ell}{2}+1)\,\Gamma(m+2\nu)} \tag{2.9}$$

Then $(V_{m\ell k}^\nu, v_{m\ell k}^\nu, \sigma_{m\ell k})$, $m \geq 0$, $0 \leq \ell \leq m$ with $m+\ell$ even, $k=1,\dots,M(N,\ell)$, forms a complete singular system for the Radon transform as mapping between $L_2(\Omega, W_\nu^{-1})$ and $L_2(Z, w_\nu^{-1})$.

For a proof see LOUIS [8], the special case N=2 and ν=1 is treated in CORMACK [2] and MARR [12].

Later on we make use of the Fourier transform of the singular functions given above.

Corollary 2.2. Let $V^{\nu}_{m\ell k}$ be as in (2.6). Then

$$\hat{V}^{\nu}_{m\ell k}(\xi) = c_{m\ell}|\xi|^{-\nu}J_{m+\nu}(|\xi|)Y_{\ell k}(\xi/|\xi|) \tag{2.10}$$

with

$$c_{m\ell} = (-i)^{\ell}(-1)^{(m-\ell)/2}2^{\nu-N/2}\frac{\Gamma(\frac{m-\ell}{2}+\nu-\frac{N}{2}+1)}{\Gamma(\frac{m-\ell}{2}+1)} \tag{2.11}$$

3. Nonuniqueness and worst case error

In all applications only a finite number of measurements can be supplied. In the following we use the somewhat idealized assumption that complete projections are given for p+1 fixed directions forming the set

$$A = \{\omega_0,\ldots,\omega_p\}, \qquad \omega_i \in S^{N-1}, \tag{3.1}$$

i.e., $\mathcal{R}f(\cdot,\omega)$ is given for $\omega \in A$. The discrete case with respect to the first variable is then handled via Shannon's sampling theorem, see e.g. [6]. Even for complete projections it was shown by SMITH-SOLMON-WAGNER [16] that the Radon transform for finitely many directions has a non-trivial null space. This nullspace, defined as

$$\mathcal{N}_A = \{f \in L_2(\Omega) \; : \; \mathcal{R}f(s,\omega) = 0 \quad \text{a.a.} \quad s \in \mathbb{R}, \omega \in A\}, \tag{3.2}$$

can be characterized with the help of the singular value decomposition given in the last chapter, see [8]. Due to the complicated structure of algebraic varieties on spheres for $N \geq 3$ we make the following assumption.

(V) Let p and A be such that

i) there is an n with $p = \dim \mathcal{P}_{n-1}$,

ii) there is no nontrivial $q \in \mathcal{P}_{n-1}$ with $q(\rho) = 0$ for all $\omega \in A$.

Here $P_n = \text{span}\,\{Y_{\ell k} : 0 \leq \ell \leq n,\ \ell+n \text{ even},\ k=1,\dots,M(N,\ell)\}$. Condition ii) demands the directions to be in general position and i) guarantees that the number of directions needed is minimal. Those conditions have always to be met for minimizing the number of measurements for a fixed resolution in the reconstructed image. For practical applications the directions ω should be selected such that the condition number of the matrix with entries $Y_{\ell k}(\omega)$, $\omega \in A$, is minimal for all sets A fulfilling (V).

We now can characterize the functions in the null space, the so-called ghosts. For the sake of simplicity we give their Fourier transform.

Theorem 3.1. Let A be such that (V) is fulfilled and let $f \in N_A$. Then

$$\hat{f}(\sigma\cdot\omega) = \sigma^{-N/2} \sum_{m=n}^{\infty} i^n J_{m+N/2}(\sigma) q_m(\omega) \tag{3.3}$$

where $q_m \in P_m$ and $q_m(\omega) = 0$ for all $\omega \in A$.
Here J_ν denotes the Bessel function of order ν.

For a proof see [8].

The functions in the null space show a very special behaviour concerning their frequency distribution.
Let

$$\mu_n(c) = \sup\{\|\hat{f}\|^2_{L_2(V(0,c))} / \|f\|^2_{L_2(\mathbb{R}^N)} : f \in N_A\},$$

then $\mu_n(c_n)$ tends to 0 for $c_n < n$ and $\mu_n(c_n)$ tends to 1 for $c_n > n$. This was first shown by LOGAN [7] for N=2 and with the help of Theorem 3.1 in LOUIS [9]. This means that most power of the spectrum of the ghosts is concentrated outside the ball around 0 with radius n, where n is related to the number of directions by $p = \dim P_{n-1}$.

Now we use additional information for treating the ill-posed problem of recovering f from its Radon transform. We suppose that f is in some Sobolev space H^α with norm

$$\|f\|^2_{H^\alpha} = \int (1+|\xi|^2)^\alpha |\hat{f}(\xi)|^2 d\xi \tag{3.4}$$

Theorem 3.2. Let the worst case error

$$r(n,\alpha) = \sup\{\|f\|_{L_2(\mathbb{R}^N)} : f \in N_A \text{ and } \|f\|_{H^\alpha} \leq 1\}. \tag{3.5}$$

Then for $\alpha \geq 0$ we have

$$r(n,\alpha) \geq c(\alpha) n^{-\alpha}. \tag{3.6}$$

Proof: We select a suitable function $f \in N_A$, namely

$$\hat{f}(\sigma \cdot \omega) = (-i)^n q_n(\omega) \sigma^{-(N/2+\alpha)} J_{n+N/2+\alpha}(\sigma) \tag{3.7}$$

with $q_n \in P_n$, $q_n \not\equiv 0$ and $q_n(\omega) = 0$ for all $\omega \in A$. This is possible because the degree of freedom in the selection of q_n is equal to $\dim P_n$ and this is larger than the number p of conditions given above.

According to the projection theorem (2.3) and Formula 7.321 in [3] the Radon transform of f given in (3.7) is

$$Rf(s,\omega) = \begin{cases} c(n,\alpha)(1-s^2)^{(N-1)/2+\alpha} C_n^{N/2+\alpha}(s) q_n(\omega) & \text{for } |s| \leq 1 \\ 0 & \text{for } |s| > 1 \end{cases}$$

with some constant $c(n,\alpha)$. This function is in the range of the Radon transform and it is obviously in the null space N_A. Its L_2 norm can be computed to

$$\|f\|^2_{L_2} = Q_n I_{2\alpha}$$

where $Q_n = \int_{S^{N-1}} q_n^2(\omega) d\omega$ and $I_{2\alpha}$ is the Weber-Schafheitlin integral, see Formula 6.574.2 in [3],

$$I_{2\alpha} = \int_0^\infty \sigma^{-(1+2\alpha)} J^2_{n+N/2+\alpha}(\sigma)d\sigma$$

$$= \frac{\Gamma(1+2\alpha)}{[\Gamma(1+\alpha)]^2} 2^{-(1+2\alpha)} \frac{\Gamma(n+N/2)}{\Gamma(n+N/2+1+2\alpha)} \qquad (3.8)$$

For the computation of the H^α-norm we use

$$\sigma^{2\alpha} \leq (1+\sigma^2)^\alpha \leq 2^{\alpha-1}(1+\sigma^{2\alpha}), \quad \alpha \geq 0$$

and get

$$Q_n I_o \leq \|f\|^2_{H^\alpha} \leq 2^{\alpha-1} Q_n (I_o + I_{2\alpha}) \leq 2^\alpha Q_n I_o$$

$$= 2^\alpha Q_n (2n+N)^{-1}.$$

We normalize q_n such that the H^α-norm is bounded by 1 to get

$$\|f\|^2_{L_2} = c(\alpha) 2^{-2\alpha} \frac{\Gamma(n+N/2+1)}{\Gamma(n+N/2+1+2\alpha)} .$$

With the asymptotic formula 6.1.39 in [1] for the gamma function follows the result.

Remark: This is for N=2 the result of NATTERER [13] who also considers the case of noisy data. The knowledge of the series expansion for the ghosts in Theorem 3.1 leads to a direct proof.

For motivating the Tikhonov-Phillips regularization we use the following result from LOUIS-NATTERER [10].

Theorem 3.3. Let the data error be bounded by ε; i.e.,

$$\|Rf - g\|_{L_2} \leq \varepsilon$$

and let f be in H^α with norm bounded by ρ.

Then there exists a reconstruction f^* with

$$\|f-f^*\|_{L_2} \leq c(N)\,\varepsilon^{2\alpha/(N-1+2\alpha)}\rho^{(N-1)/(N-1+2\alpha)}.$$

4. Tikhonov-Phillips Regularization

Now we assume that the data g are possibly erreneous and hence we compute the minimum norm solution regularized by a semi-norm on H^α. This means that we consider the functional

$$J_\omega(f) = \|\mathcal{R}f-g\|^2_{L_2(Z,w_\nu^{-1})} + \omega|f|^2_{H^\alpha} \tag{4.1}$$

where

$$|f|^2_{H^\alpha} = \int_{\mathbb{R}^N} |\xi|^{2\alpha}|f(\xi)|^2 d\xi. \tag{4.2}$$

The regularized solution f_ω is then defined as

$$J_\omega(f_\omega) \leq J_\omega(f) \qquad \text{for all } f \in H^\alpha. \tag{4.3}$$

The most critical part is then the determination of the regularization parameter ω. The following study exhibits its influence on f_ω.

Let Σ^* be the sum over all $m \geq 0$, $0 \leq \ell \leq m$ with $m+\ell$ even and $k=1,\ldots,M(N,\ell)$. Then we can represent the function f as

$$f = \Sigma^* f_{m\ell k}V^\nu_{m\ell k}$$

and hence we have with $d_{m\ell}$ from (2.9)

$$\mathcal{R}f = \Sigma^* d_{m\ell}f_{m\ell k}v^\nu_{m\ell k}.$$

Denoting with $h_{m\nu} = \int_{-1}^{1} w_\nu(s)(C_m^\nu(s))^2 ds$ we get

$$\| Rf-g\|^2_{L_2(Z,w_\nu^{-1})} = \Sigma^* h_{m\nu}(d_{m\ell}f_{m\ell k}-g_{m\ell k})^2 + \tilde{g}$$

where $\tilde{g}$ is the L_2-norm of the projection g onto (range $R)^\perp$. The H^α-seminorm of f is with $c_{m\ell}$ from (2.11)

$$|f|^2_{H^\alpha} = \sum_{m,m'} \sum_{\ell,\ell'} \sum_{k,k'} f_{m\ell k} f_{m'\ell' k'} \int_{S^{N-1}} Y_{\ell k}(\omega) Y_{\ell' k'}(\omega) d\omega$$

$$\cdot\ c_{m\ell} c_{m'\ell'} \int_0^\infty \sigma^{N-1+2\alpha-2\nu} J_{m+\nu}(\sigma) J_{m'+\nu}(\sigma) d\sigma .$$

Because of the orthonormality of the spherical harmonics the integral over the sphere is $\delta_{\ell\ell'}\ \delta_{kk'}$. Orthogonality with respect to σ is fulfilled if the exponent of σ is equal to -1; i.e.,

$$\nu = \alpha + \frac{N}{2} \tag{4.4}$$

see [1], Formula 11.4.6, m and m' must have the same parity because of the first integral. Thus we get

$$|f|^2_{H^\alpha} = \Sigma^* f^2_{m\ell k} c^2_{m\ell} \frac{1}{2(m+\nu)} .$$

Hence $J_\omega(f)$ is minimized by

$$f_\omega = \Sigma^* f^\omega_{m\ell k} V^\nu_{m\ell k} \tag{4.5}$$

where

$$f^\omega_{m\ell k} = \frac{g_{m\ell k}}{d_{m\ell}} \frac{1}{1+\omega\gamma_m}$$

with

$$\gamma_m = \frac{c^2_{m\ell}}{2(m+\nu)h_{m\nu} d^2_{m\ell}} = 2^{-N}\pi^{N-1} \frac{\Gamma(m+N+2\alpha)}{\Gamma(m+1)} \tag{4.6}$$

Using asymptotic formulas for the Γ-function we find

$$\gamma_m = O(m^{N-1+2\alpha}).$$

This means that the expansion coefficients are regularized by a non-stationary Butterworth filter, see e.g. HAMMING [4].

Choosing ω such that $\omega\gamma_m$ is small for $m \leqq \mu$ means that the $f_{m\ell k}$ with $m \leqq \mu$ are reliably recovered whereas the expansion coefficients with $m > \mu$ are attenuated. If we put $g_{m\ell k} = d_{m\ell} f_{m\ell k} + \varepsilon_{m\ell k}$; i.e., exact data plus data error we notice that in general

$$\frac{\varepsilon_{m\ell k}}{d_{m\ell}} \to \infty \quad \text{for } m \to \infty$$

because we cannot assume the $\varepsilon_{m\ell k}$ to behave like the Radon transform of a function. In contrast to this

$$\frac{\varepsilon_{m\ell k}}{d_{m\ell}} \frac{1}{1+\omega\gamma_m} \to 0$$

if the $\varepsilon_{m\ell k}$ do not grow to fast.

We also notice the influence of the chosen semi-norm: the larger α the faster grows γ_m which means that more expansion coefficients are filtered and this results in smoother pictures, as expected.

Finally we can give the following error estimate.

<u>Theorem 4.1</u>. Let f_ω be defined as in (4.5) and $g = \mathcal{R}f + \varepsilon$. Then

$$f - f_\omega = \Sigma^* \left(f_{m\ell k} \frac{\omega\gamma_m}{1+\omega\gamma_m} - \frac{\varepsilon_{m\ell k}}{d_{m\ell}} \frac{1}{1+\omega\gamma_m} \right) V^\nu_{m\ell k} \,. \tag{4.7}$$

The first term in (4.7) is the filter error, the second the data error. Again it becomes obvious that a small ω provides a small filter error but the data error may explode. On the other hand, if the data errors are large we have to select a large ω thus resulting in a large filter error.

References

[1] Abramowitz, M., Stegem, I.A. (eds.) (1965) Handbook of mathematical functions (Dover, New York).

[2] Cormack, A.M. (1964) Representation of functions by its line integrals, with some radiological applications II. J. Appl. Phys. 35, 2908-2913.

[3] Gradstheyn, I.S., Ryzhik, I.M. (1980) Table of integrals, series and products, 3rd edn. (Academic Press, New York).

[4] Hamming, R.W. (1977) Digital Filters (Prentice Hall, Englewood Cliffs, N.J.).

[5] Herman, G.T. (1980) Image reconstruction from projections: the fundamentals of computerized tomography (Academic Press, New York).

[6] Jerry, A.J. (1977) The Shannon sampling theorem - its various extensions and applications: a tutorial review. Proc. IEEE 65, 1565-1596.

[7] Logan, B.F. (1975) The uncertainty principle in reconstructing functions from projections. Duke Math. J. 42, 661-706.

[8] Louis, A.K. (1984) Orthogonal function series expansions and the null space of the Radon transform. SIAM J. Math. Anal. 15, 621-633.

[9] Louis, A.K. (1984) Nonuniqueness in inverse Radon problem: the frequency distribution of the ghosts. Math. Z. 185, 429-440.

[10] Louis, A.K., Natterer, F. (1983) Mathematical problems of computerized tomography. Proc. IEEE 71, 379-389.

[11] Ludwig, D. (1966) The Radon transform on Euclidean spaces. Comm. Pure Appl. Math. 19, 49-81.

[12] Marr, R.B. (1974) On the reconstruction of a function on a circular domain from sampling of its line integrals. J. Math. Anal. Appl. 19, 357-374.

[13] Natterer, F. (1980) A Sobolev space analysis of picture reconstruction. SIAM J. Appl. Math. 39, 402-411.

[14] Natterer, F. (1983) On the order of regularization methods. In: Hämmerlin, G., Hoffmann, K.-H. (eds.) Improperly posed problems and their numerical treatment. (Birkhäuser, Basel, Boston, Stuttgart), 189-203.

[15] Radon, J. (1917) Über die Bestimmung von Funktionen durch ihre Integralwerte längs gewisser Mannigfaltigkeiten. Ber. Verh. Sächs. Akad. Wiss. Leipzig 69, 262-277.

[16] Smith, K.T., Solmon, D.C., Wagner, S.L. (1977) Practical and mathematical aspects of reconstructing objects from radiographs. Bul. AMS 83, 1227-1270.

Prof. Dr. Alfred K. Louis, Fachbereich Mathematik, Universität Kaiserslautern, D - 6750 Kaiserslautern, Germany (FRG).

International Series of
Numerical Mathematics, Vol. 73

NUMERICAL SOLUTION OF A FIRST KIND FREDHOLM INTEGRAL EQUATION ARISING IN ELECTRON-ATOM SCATTERING

Herman J.J. te Riele and René W. Wagenaar

Centre for Mathematics and Computer Science, Amsterdam and
Philips Data Systems, Apeldoorn, The Netherlands

The regularization method of Phillips and Tihonov is applied to a first kind Fredholm integral equation arising in the field of electron-atom scattering.

{This paper is in final form and no version of it will be submitted for publication elsewhere}

1. Introduction

Collision processes, taking place between (sub)atomic particles, are generally expressed in terms of scattering amplitudes. These functions, when squared, represent the probabilities of obtaining specific outcomes in a scattering event as to the momentum and energy transfer between colliding partners. The amplitudes themselves are functions of the projectile's incoming and outgoing momentum vector.

Titchmarsh [9] has shown that a function, which is analytic and bounded in its complex continuated variable, can be written in the form of an integral expression. Applying this theorem to the scattering amplitude for forward elastic scattering of electrons on noble gas atoms yields the so-called dispersion relation [3]

$$\text{(1.1)} \qquad \operatorname{Re} f(E) = f_B - g_B(E) + \pi^{-1} P \int_0^\infty \frac{\operatorname{Im} f(E')}{E'-E}\, dE' \;.$$

Here, E is the projectile electron's impact energy and P the principal value integral. Since electrons are indistinguishable, the amplitude consists of a direct and an exchange part; the latter accounts for the interchange of the projectile electron and one of the atomic electrons. The subscript B denotes the first Born approximations to these two parts respectively. The real and imaginary parts are related to the differential and total cross sections respectively, which are both in principle measurable quantities.

It remains, however, to prove the analytical behaviour of the amplitude for this relation to be valid. Recent investigations [1,2] have shown that (1.1) has to be modified: an extra term, the "discrepancy function" $\Delta(E)$, is added to the right-hand side due to a cut along the part of the negative real energy axis, where the exchange amplitude appeared to be non-analytic.

$$(1.2) \qquad \Delta(E) = \pi^{-1} \int_a^\infty \frac{\rho(E')}{E + E'}\, dE' , \qquad c \le E \le d,$$

where $\rho(E')$ is the discontinuity of the non-Born part of the exchange amplitude across this cut. Sofar, direct computation of $\rho(E')$ has not been possible yet, not even for the simplest system of electron-atomic hydrogen scattering [2]. On the other hand, a recent experimental study [10] has addressed the magnitude of $\Delta(E)$ at various impact energies, where helium was used as target.

By inverting (1.2), it is hoped then to gain more insight into the behaviour of $\rho(E')$, in particular with respect to the possible existence of isolated singularities.

The discrepancy function $\Delta(E)$ is measured in a set of 23 non-equidistant points E_i, $i = 1,2,\ldots,23$, in the interval $[1,300]$, with a relative error which varies between 1 and 5%. For $E > 500$, $\Delta(E)$ may be assumed to vanish.

With respect to the unknown function $\rho(E')$ in (1.2), we may assume that it tends to zero, as $E' \to \infty$, at least as fast as $(E')^{-\frac{1}{2}}$. Under this assumption we replace the infinite upperbound in (1.2) by a finite number b. The neglected part $\int_b^\infty$ can then be estimated as follows:

$$(1.3) \qquad \left|\frac{1}{\pi} \int_b^\infty (E+E')^{-1} \rho(E')dE'\right| < \frac{1}{\pi} \int_b^\infty (E+E')^{-1}(E')^{-\frac{1}{2}}dE' < \frac{1}{\pi}\int_b^\infty (E')^{-3/2}dE'.$$

The last term equals $2\pi^{-1}b^{-\frac{1}{2}}$. Hence, by taking b large enough, the neglected part can be made small, compared with the error in $\Delta(E)$ (cf. section 4).

Equation (1.2) is a special case of a Fredholm integral equation of the first kind:

$$(1.2') \qquad \Delta(E) = \int_a^b K(E,E')\rho(E')dE', \qquad c \le E \le d.$$

This type of integral equation arises in the mathematical analysis of problems from many branches of physics, chemistry and biology [5]. Also various classical mathematical problems, like the problem of harmonic continuation, numerical inversion of the Laplace transform, the backwards heat equation and numerical differentiation, can be formulated in terms of equations of the form (1.2').

First kind Fredholm equations belong to the class of ill-posed problems [4]. In particular, this means that (i) there may be no solution, (ii) a solution may not be unique and (iii) if we perturb the given function Δ with a small amount, the solution of the perturbed problem (if it exists) may differ from the original solution with a very large amount. Therefore, great care must be exercised when we solve (1.2) numerically, in particular, in view of the inexact data function Δ.

In this paper we present the results of experiments with the well-known regularization method of Phillips and Tihonov [6,8] for numerically solving (1.2'). The results show that it is possible to obtain satisfactory results with the regularization method at least in a qualitative sense, for problems (1.2') with highly inexact data.

2. The regularization method of Phillips and Tihonov

The regularization method of Phillips and Tihonov essentially amounts to the replacement of (1.2') by the well-posed problem

Minimize the quadratic functional $\Phi_\alpha(\rho)$, defined by

$$(2.1) \qquad \Phi_\alpha(\rho) := \| K\rho - \Delta \|^2 + \alpha \| L\rho \|^2$$

over all functions in the compact set $\{\rho : \| K\rho - \Delta\| \le \varepsilon\}$.

Here, $K : F \to G$ is a linear operator defined by $(K\rho)(E) := \int_a^b K(E,E')\rho(E')dE'$, where F and G are certain linear spaces and $\| \cdot \|$ is some norm in F and G.

L is a linear operator ($L : F \to F$) and α is a fixed positive number, to be chosen a priori. For later use, we write: $L\rho = a_0(\rho-\hat{\rho}) + a_1 d\rho/dE + a_2 d^2\rho/dE^2$, where $a_i = 0$ or 1 and $\hat{\rho} = \hat{\rho}(E)$ is an a priori known approximation to ρ. The number ε in (2.1) reflects the presence of error in the data function Δ; if Δ were known exactly, we would look for ρ such that $K\rho = \Delta$; since, however, Δ is known only approximately, we (have to) content ourselves with finding ρ such that $\| K\rho - \Delta \| \leq \varepsilon$.

Under certain, mild conditions (which we assume to be fulfilled), (2.1) has a unique solution, which we denote by ρ_α.

The proper choice of α and L in (2.1) is of crucial importance. Unfortunately, no general rule for choosing α and L is known. The following heuristics may be helpful. As is well-known, the presence of α in (2.1) provides a balance between, on one hand, minimization of $\| K\rho - \Delta \|$, i.e., solving $K\rho = \Delta$ ($\alpha=0$) and, on the other hand, minimization of the "penalty" term $\| L\rho \|$ (α large). Therefore, it seems reasonable to choose α in such a way that the solution ρ_α of (2.1) satisfies $\| K\rho_\alpha - \Delta \| \approx \varepsilon$, where ε is the (average) error in Δ. Another possibility is to let α be approximately equal to ε^2. This choice is motivated by the fact that, under certain conditions, the solution ρ_α of (2.1) tends to the solution of $K\rho = \Delta$ (if it exists) if $\varepsilon \to 0$ and if α satisfies $C_1\varepsilon^2 < \alpha < C_2\varepsilon^2$, $C_1, C_2 > 0$.

3. Numerical solution of (2.1)

In [7], a subroutine for numerically solving first kind Fredholm integral equations (1.2') via the minimization problem (2.1) of Phillips and Tihonov has been described and documented. In this subroutine, a linear system of equations is solved which results from discretization of the continuous problem (2.1). Here, we only give the linear system and for its derivation we refer to [7].

Suppose that $\Delta(E)$ is given in N points $E=E_i$, $i=1,2,\ldots,N$ ($c \leq E_1 < \ldots < E_N \leq d$) with $\Delta(E_i) =: \Delta_i$; moreover, let the integration interval $[a,b]$ be subdivided by the N+1 points $E'=E'_j$, $j=0,1,\ldots,N$ ($a=E'_0 < E'_1 < \ldots < E'_N=b$). The points E_i and E'_j need not be equidistant. Discretization of (2.1) (where the integrals over $[E'_j, E'_{j+1}]$ are approximated by using the mid-point rule) leads to the following linear system:

$$(3.1)\qquad \{K^TK + \alpha(a_0H_0 + a_1H_1 + a_2H_2)\}\,\vec{\rho} = K^T\vec{\Delta} + \alpha a_0\vec{\hat{\rho}}\ .$$

Here, $K=(K_{ij})$, where $K_{ij}=(E'_j-E'_{j-1})K(E_i,\bar{E}'_j)$, $\bar{E}'_j=\frac{1}{2}(E'_{j-1}+E'_j)$;

$\vec{\rho}=(\rho_1,\rho_2,\ldots,\rho_N)^T$, $\rho_j\approx\rho(\bar{E}'_j)$ is an approximation of ρ in the mid-point $\bar{E}'_j$;

$\vec{\Delta}=(\Delta_1,\Delta_2,\ldots,\Delta_N)^T$;

$\vec{\hat{\rho}}=(\hat{\rho}_1,\hat{\rho}_2,\ldots,\hat{\rho}_N)^T$, $\hat{\rho}_j$ is an approximation of ρ_j to be given a priori, if $a_0=1$;

H_0 is the N×N identity matrix,

$$H_1=\begin{bmatrix} 1 & -1 & & & & \\ -1 & 2 & -1 & & & \\ & -1 & 2 & -1 & & \\ & & \ddots & \ddots & \ddots & \\ & & & -1 & 2 & -1 \\ & & & & -1 & 2 \end{bmatrix}_{N\times N} \qquad H_2=\begin{bmatrix} 1 & -2 & 1 & & & & \\ -2 & 5 & -4 & 1 & & & \\ 1 & -4 & 6 & -4 & 1 & & \\ & \ddots & \ddots & \ddots & \ddots & \ddots & \\ & & 1 & -4 & 6 & -4 & 1 \\ & & & 1 & -4 & 5 & -2 \\ & & & & 1 & -2 & 1 \end{bmatrix}_{N\times N}.$$

4. Numerical experiments

4.1 A problem with known solution

As a test, we first solved the equation

$$(4.1)\qquad \int_1^3 (E + E')^{-1}\rho(E')dE' = E^{-1}\ln\left(\frac{1+E/a}{1+E/b}\right), \qquad 1 \le E \le 2,$$

which has a known solution $\rho(E') = (E')^{-1}$. In table I we list the minimum number of correct digits obtained with N=8 data points, for $\alpha=10^{-i}$, i=0,1,..., 9, for $L\rho=\rho$, $L\rho=d\rho/dE$ and $L\rho=d^2\rho/dE^2$, respectively. We also list in table I the corresponding results obtained in case the data points Δ_j were perturbed with 1% random error (i.e., the exact values Δ_j were multiplied by the factor $1 + 0.01\times(2\times\gamma_j-1)$, where γ_j is a random number taken from the interval [0,1)).

In the case of exact data, the best results were obtained for α in the range $(10^{-8} - 10^{-4})$, whereas in the case of inexact data the best results were obtained for much larger values of α $(10^{-4} - 10^{-3})$.

Table I. The regularization method of Phillips and Tihonov applied to (4.1)
First entry :minimum number of correct digits in $\overline{E}'_j$, j=0,1,...,7;
second entry: $\| K\vec{\rho}-\vec{\Delta} \|$, $\| \cdot \|$ is the Euclidean vector norm; a(-b) means: $a \cdot 10^{-b}$.

	α	$L\rho = \rho$		$L\rho = d\rho/dE$		$L\rho = d^2\rho/dE^2$	
Data exact	1	0.1	7(-1)	0.2	5(-3)	0.6	3(-5)
	1(-1)	0.5	2(-1)	0.2	5(-3)	0.6	3(-5)
	1(-2)	0.7	3(-2)	0.2	5(-3)	0.6	3(-5)
	1(-3)	0.7	4(-3)	0.5	3(-3)	0.6	3(-5)
	1(-4)	1.1	1(-3)	1.0	7(-4)	0.6	3(-5)
	1(-5)	1.4	2(-4)	0.9	9(-5)	0.6	3(-5)
	1(-6)	1.2	3(-5)	0.9	3(-5)	0.7	3(-5)
	1(-7)	1.4	1(-5)	1.0	2(-5)	1.4	1(-5)
	1(-8)	1.3	5(-6)	1.0	7(-6)	0.8	2(-6)
	1(-9)	1.1	8(-7)	0.7	1(-6)	0.8	4(-7)
Data inexact	1	0.1	7(-1)	0.2	9(-3)	0.8	3(-3)
(random error,	1(-1)	0.5	2(-1)	0.2	9(-3)	0.8	3(-3)
maximum 1%)	1(-2)	0.7	3(-2)	0.2	9(-3)	0.8	3(-3)
	1(-3)	0.8	8(-3)	0.7	7(-3)	0.8	3(-3)
	1(-4)	0.8	5(-3)	0.5	5(-3)	0.8	3(-3)
	1(-5)	0.3	4(-3)	0.5	5(-3)	0.8	3(-3)
	1(-6)	0.2	4(-3)	0.1	4(-3)	0.5	3(-3)
	1(-7)	-0.2	4(-3)	-1.0	4(-3)	-0.1	3(-3)
	1(-8)	-0.6	4(-3)	-1.6	2(-3)	-0.3	3(-3)
	1(-9)	-0.7	4(-3)	-1.7	2(-3)	-0.1	3(-3)

Other experiments with a problem with known solution and inexact data (maximum 3% random error) show a similar pattern of results [7].

4.2 Numerical solution of problem (1.2)

In view of (1.3), we replaced the infinite upperbound in (1.2) by $b = 2\times10^6$, which adds an error to Δ whose absolute value is less than 0.0005. This is small compared with the measuring errors in the physical data $\Delta(E_i)$. These data values are given in table II (set I). The lowerbound of integration in (1.2) was given to be a=24.5. In order to work with an interval for E which has about the same length as the integration interval for E' ($[24.5,2\times10^6]$), we added 11 points E_i with value $\Delta(E_i)=0$ (see table II). This gave a total of N=34 data points. The points E'_j were chosen such that their distribution was similar to that of the points E_i:

$$E'_0 = 24.5,\ E'_{33} = 10^6,\ E'_{34} = 2\times10^6,$$

$$E'_j = E'_0 + \frac{E_{j+1}-E_1}{E_{34}-E_1} \times (E'_{33} - E'_0),\ j = 1,2,\dots,32. \tag{4.2}$$

With these provisions (1.2) was solved with the regularization method of Phillips and Tihonov for $\alpha = 10^{-4}$, and $L\rho = d^2\rho/dE^2$.

Table II. Data values $\Delta(E_i)$
(unmentioned values in the data sets II, III and IV are equal to the corresponding values in data set I)

		$\Delta(E_i)=\Delta_i$			
i	E_i	I(lump in E=26)	II(lump smoothed out)	III(lump in E=20)	IV(lump in 30)
1	1.5	0.60	.	.	.
2	2.5	0.55	.	.	.
3	3.1	0.52	.	.	.
4	5.1	0.49	.	.	.
5	7.1	0.47	.	.	.
6	9.1	0.45	.	.	.
7	11.2	0.42	.	.	.
8	13.1	0.40	.	.	.
9	15.1	0.39	.	0.38	.
10	17.1	0.37	.	0.38	.
11	20.0	0.35	0.35	0.39 ←	.
12	22.0	0.35	0.34	0.37	0.34
13	24.5	0.33	0.33	0.35	0.33
14	26.0	0.36 ←	0.32	0.33	0.32
15	28.0	0.34	0.31	0.31	0.31
16	30.0	0.33	0.30	0.30	0.33 ←
17	35.0	0.29	0.28	0.28	0.31
18	40.0	0.25	.	.	0.25
19	50.0	0.17	.	.	0.19
20	70.0	0.13	.	.	0.14
21	100	0.11	.	.	.
22	200	0.06	.	.	.
23	300	0.02	.	.	.

In the data sets I, II, III and IV, 11 zero values $\Delta_{24},\ldots,\Delta_{34}$ were added, viz., for E=500, 1000, 2500, 5000, 10000, 25000, 50000, 100000, 250000, 500000 and 1000000.

Figure I gives a graph of the numerical solution ρ_α, obtained by drawing a smooth curve through the computed values ρ_i. Figure II shows the corresponding graph obtained with the data set II given in table II. This data set was obtained from data set I by smoothing out the small lump around E=26. Data sets III and IV were obtained from data set I by moving the lump from E=26 to E=20 and to E=30, respectively. The resulting graphs are shown in figures III and IV. The curves in figures I, III and IV, although quantitatively different, show one common qualitative feature: there is one (relative) maximum. As the lump in the data is shifted towards greater values of E, this maximum decreases and moves slowly to greater values of E'. Figure II shows that this maximum in ρ_α has a one-to-one relationship with the lump in the data Δ. A final experiment with data set I was carried out as follows: the starting point E_0' of integration in (1.2) was changed from $E_0'=24.5$ to $E_0'=20$

Figures I and II Numerical solutions ρ_α obtained with data sets I and II, resp.

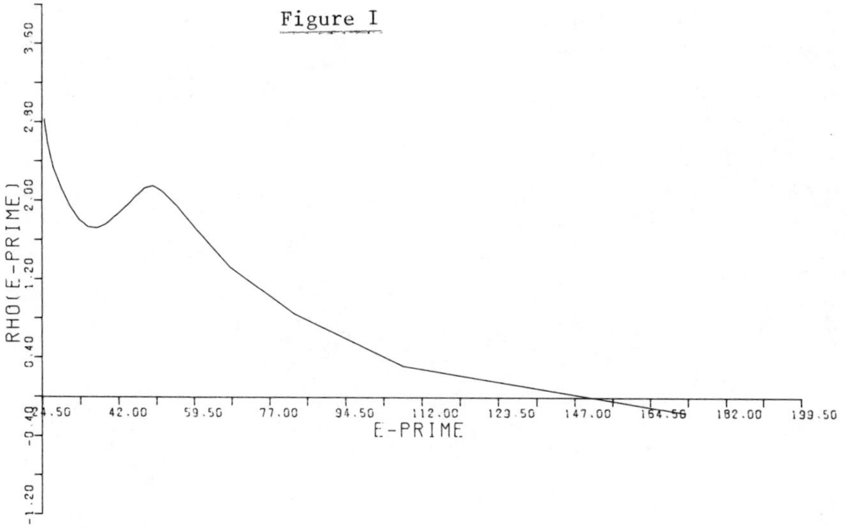

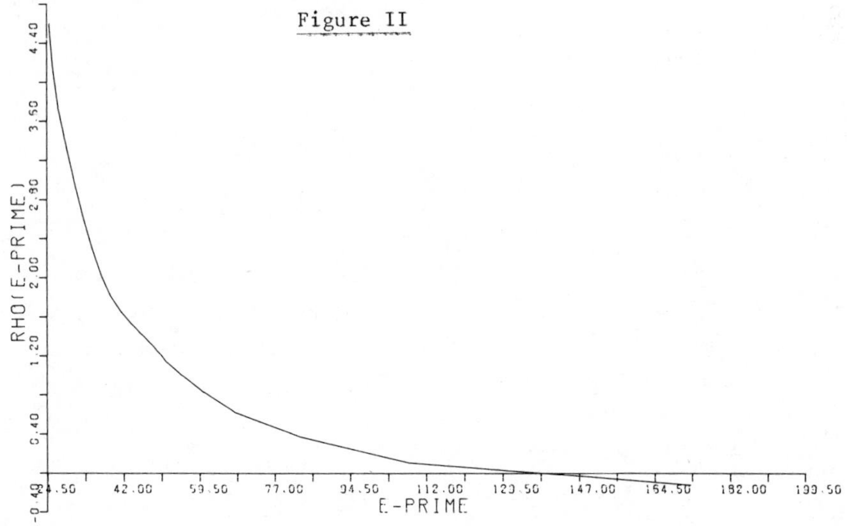

Figures III - IV Numerical solutions ρ_α obtained with data sets III - IV, resp.

Figure III

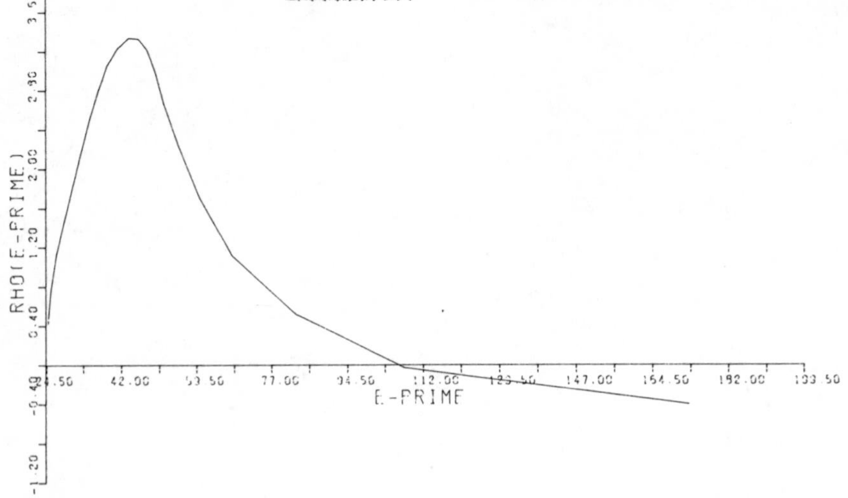

Figure IV

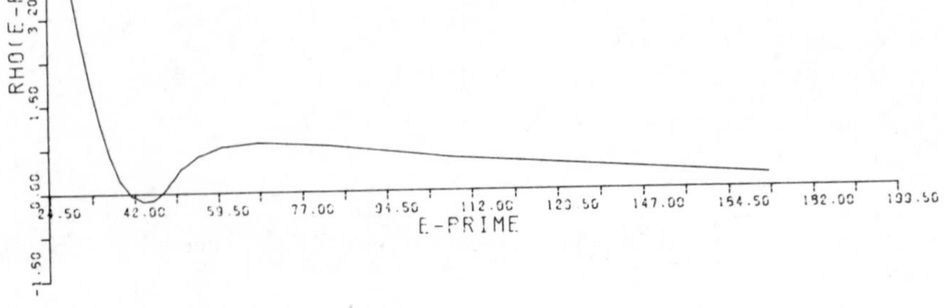

and to $E_0'=15$, respectively. The points E_j', $j=1,2,\ldots,32$ were recomputed according to (4.2), and the system (3.1) was solved. In both cases, the resulting curves showed the same qualitative behaviour as the curve in figure I. Moreover, the following common quantitative feature was observed: the location of the relative maximum in ρ_α was approximately the same for the three experiments, viz., $E' \approx 48$.

The experiments described above were also carried out for several other values of α in the range $(10^{-5} - 10^{-3})$ and the results were very similar to the results obtained for $\alpha=10^{-4}$. In our experiments with problems with a known solution and inexact data (cf. section 4.1 and [7]), we used the same kernel $(E+E')^{-1}$ as in (1.2) and we obtained the best results also for α in the range $(10^{-5} - 10^{-3})$. Therefore, we may conclude that the numerical solution obtained for the physical problem (2.1) in figure I is reliable, at least in a qualitative sense, and that this is the best result that can be obtained, given the errors in the data function Δ, and given the mathematical model (1.2) of the physical problem.

5. References

[1] Combes, J.M. and A. Tip(1983) CNRS preprint.
[2] Dumbrajs, O. and M. Martinis(1982) J. Phys. B: Atomic and Molecular Physics 15, 961.
[3] Gerjuoy, E. and N.A. Krall(1962) Physical Review 127, 2105.
[4] Lavrentiev, M.M.(1967) Some improperly posed problems of mathematical physics, Springer Tracts in natural philosophy, vol. 11(Springer, Berlin).
[5] Nedelkov, I.P.(1972) Improper problems in computational physics, Comp. Phys. Comm. 4, 157-164.
[6] Phillips, D.L.(1962) A technique for the numerical solution of certain integral equations of the first kind, J.ACM 9, 84-97.
[7] te Riele, H.J.J.(1984) A program for solving first kind Fredholm integral equations by means of regularization, preprint, submitted for publication.
[8] Tihonov, A.N. and V.Y. Arsenin(1977) Solution of ill-posed problems (V.H. Winter and Sons, Washington D.C.).
[9] Titchmarsh, E.C.(1948) Introduction to the theory of Fourier integrals (The Clarendon Press, Oxford).
[10] Wagenaar, R.W.(1984) Small angle elastic scattering of electrons by noble gas atoms, Doctor's Thesis (Amsterdam).

Dr. ir. Herman J.J. te Riele, Centre for Mathematics and Computer Science, Kruislaan 413, 1098 SJ Amsterdam, The Netherlands

Dr. René W. Wagenaar, Philips Data Systems, Postbus 245, 7300 AE Apeldoorn, The Netherlands

International Series of
Numerical Mathematics, Vol. 73

APPROXIMATE SOLUTION OF ILL-POSED EQUATIONS: ARBITRARILY SLOW CONVERGENCE VS. SUPERCONVERGENCE

Eberhard Schock
Fachbereich Mathematik, Universität Kaiserslautern

The aim of this note is to discuss the convergence properties of various methods for the approximate solution of ill-posed equations. If an operator T between Banach spaces has a non-closed range, then there exists no linear uniformly convergent approximation method, but at most pointwise approximation methods for the approximate solution of an equation

(1) $$Tx = y.$$

These methods in general converge arbitrarily slow, i.e. there may exist some y for which the approximations have a good convergence rate, but in general for each order of convergence there are right hand sides y with a worse convergence rate. This phenomenon is not restricted to ill-posed equations. Recently I have shown [12] that many common approximation schemes for integral equations of the second kind show arbitrarily slow convergence, too.

On the other hand for such y for which the approximations show a bad convergence their values of some functionals show a good rate of convergence. This effect is called superconvergence.

This paper is in final form and no version of it will be submitted for publication elsewhere.

Systematically this was first considered by G.A. CHANDLER [2] for integral equations of the second kind, C.W. GROETSCH [6] noticed this phenomenon for equations of the first kind.

1. Definitions

Let X,Y be infinite dimensional Banach spaces $T: X \to Y$ a continuous linear operator. Let M be a method for the approximate solution of

$$Tx = y$$

which assigns to each $y \in \text{Range } T$ or equivalently for each $x = T^{-1}y$ and each real $\alpha > 0$ an $x_\alpha^M \in X$. Let $R_\alpha^M : X \to X$ be the remainder

$$R_\alpha^M x = x - x_\alpha^M.$$

Then the approximation method is said to be *converging*, if for all $x \in X$ hold $\lim R_\alpha^M x = 0$, and a converging method is said to be *arbitrarily slow converging*, if for each monotone increasing positive function $\omega : \mathbb{R}^+ \to \mathbb{R}^+$ with $\omega(0) = 0$ there is an $x \in X$ such that $(x - x_\alpha^M)$ converges worse than $\omega(\alpha)$, i.e.

$$\limsup_{\alpha \to 0} \frac{\|x - x_\alpha^M\|}{\omega(\alpha)} = \infty.$$

Otherwise the method M is said to be *uniformly converging*. The following essentially known lemma [12] clarifies the notion of arbitrarily slow convergence for linear approximation methods.

Lemma 1

Let X, Y be Banach spaces and M a convergent approximation method for the equation (1), such that all remainders R_α^M are continuous linear operators. Then

(a) $\sup \|R_\alpha^M\| < \infty$.

(b) *M is arbitrarily slow converging, if and only if*

$$\limsup_{\alpha \to 0} \|R_\alpha^M\| > 0.$$

(c) *If M is arbitrarily slow converging, then for each positive monotone increasing function $\omega : \mathbb{R}^+ \to \mathbb{R}^+$ with $\omega(0) = 0$ the set*

$$M(\omega) = \{x \in X : \|R^M x\| = O(\omega(\alpha))\}$$

is of first category in X.

Proof

The first statement is the principle of uniform boundedness.

If ω is a monotone increasing function with $\omega(0) = 0$, then $\limsup \|R_\alpha^M\| > 0$ implies $\limsup \omega(\alpha)^{-1} \|R_\alpha^M\| = \infty$. By a consequence of the principle of uniform boundedness there is a dense set of $x \in X$ such that

$$\lim \omega(\alpha)^{-1} \|R_\alpha^M x\| = \infty$$

and that the set of $x \in X$ such that

$$\lim \omega(\alpha)^{-1} \|R_\alpha^M x\| = 0$$

is of first category in X (see e.g. J. WLOKA [16]).

On the other hand, if $\limsup \|R_\alpha^M\| = 0$, then for

$$\omega(\alpha) = \max_{\beta \leq \alpha} \|R_\beta^M\|$$

we have

$$\|x - x_\alpha^M\| \leq \omega(\alpha) \cdot \|x\|$$

and M converges uniformly. □

Most of the common linear approximation methods for ill-posed equations are restricted to the Hilbert space setting. (A special result on an arbitrarily slow convergent approximation method for ill-posed equations in Banach spaces I have given in [10].) Thus let X and Y be Hilbert spaces. We recall that if $T : X \to Y$ is a bounded linear operator, then the closed operator $T^+ : D(T^+) \to X$ which associates with each $y \in D(T^+) = R(T) \oplus R(T)^\perp$ the element T^+y which is the minimal norm least square solution of the equation (1), is called the (Moore-Penrose) generalized inverse of T. A.B. BAKUSHINSKII [1] and C.W. GROETSCH [3] have shown that the family $\{g_\alpha(T^*T)T^*, \alpha > 0\}$ of operators converges pointwise to T^+ on $D(T^+)$, where $\{g_\alpha, \alpha > 0\}$ is a family of continuous real functions on the interval $\sigma = [0, \|T\|^2]$, which satisfies

(2) $$\sup_{\alpha>0, \lambda\in\sigma} |\lambda g_\alpha(\lambda)| < \infty.$$

(3) For each $\lambda > 0$ hold $\lim_{\alpha\to 0} 1 - \lambda g_\alpha(\lambda) = 0$.

Then for each $y \in D(T^+)$

$$x_\alpha^g = g_\alpha(T^*T)T^*y$$

is an approximation of $x = T^+y$ with

$$\lim_{\alpha\to 0} x_\alpha^g = x.$$

Let $R_\alpha^g : X \to X$ be the remainder

$$R_\alpha^g x = x - x_\alpha^g.$$

In the sequel let $E[d\lambda]$ be the spectral measure, $\sigma(T^*T)$ the spectrum of T^*T, and $Q : Y \to \overline{\text{Range } T}$ the ortho-projection onto $\overline{\text{Range } T}$. If Range T is not closed, the O is a cluster point of $\sigma(T^*T)\setminus\{0\}$.

2. Convergence Rates

The examples in the next section will show that the common approximation methods converge arbitrarily slow, if Range T is not closed. With additional assumptions on y it is possible to obtain convergence rates. The following theorem improves results of C.W. GROETSCH [5]. The difference is the replacement of the capital-O-condition by the little-o-condition.

Theorem 2

Let $Qy \in \text{Range}\, T(T^*T)^\nu$ (or equivalently $x = T^+y \in \text{Range}(T^*T)^\nu$) for some positive ν and let $\{g_\alpha, \alpha > 0\}$ be a family of continuous real functions on σ satisfying (2) and (3). Let $\omega : \mathbb{R}^+ \to \mathbb{R}^+$ be a monotone real function with $\lim \omega(\alpha) = 0$ such that

(4) *for each compact subset κ of $(0, \|T\|^2)$*

$$\lim_{\alpha\to 0} \frac{\lambda^\nu}{\omega(\alpha)^\nu} |1-\lambda g_\alpha(\lambda)| = 0 \text{ uniformly for } \lambda \in \kappa.$$

(5) $$\gamma = \sup_{\substack{\lambda>0\\ \alpha>0}} \frac{\lambda^\nu}{\omega(\alpha)^\nu} |1-\lambda g_\alpha(\lambda)| < \infty$$

then

$$x - x_\alpha^g = o(\omega(\alpha)^\nu).$$

Proof

Let $x = T^+y = (T^*T)^\nu z \in \text{Range}(T^*T)^\nu$ for some $z \in X$. Then

$$x - x_\alpha^g = (I - g_\alpha(T^*T)T^*T)(T^*T)^\nu z.$$

By (5) the set of operators

$$\int_{\sigma} \frac{\lambda^{\nu}}{\omega(\alpha)^{\nu}} (1-\lambda g_{\alpha}(\lambda))E[d\lambda] \quad , \qquad \alpha > 0$$

is uniformly bounded. Let P_{κ} be the spectral projection of κ

$$P_{\kappa} = \int_{\kappa} E[d\lambda].$$

The set of all $P_{\kappa}z$, $z \in X$, κ an arbitrary compact subset of $(0, \|T\|^2)$ is dense in X. Thus

$$\lim_{\alpha\to 0} \int_{0}^{\|T\|^2} \frac{\lambda^{\nu}}{\omega(\alpha)^{\nu}} (1-\lambda g_{\alpha}(\lambda))E[d\lambda]P_{\kappa}z =$$

$$\lim_{\alpha\to 0} \int_{\kappa} \frac{\lambda^{\nu}}{\omega(\alpha)^{\nu}} (1-\lambda g_{\alpha}(\lambda))E[d\lambda]z = 0$$

implies by the principle of uniform boundedness for all $z \in X$, $x = (T^*T)^{\nu}z$

$$\lim \omega(\alpha)^{-\nu} \int_{\sigma} (1-\lambda g_{\alpha}(\lambda))E[d\lambda]x = 0$$

or equivalently

$$x-x_{\alpha}^{g} = o(\omega(\alpha)^{\nu}).$$

If only (5) is fulfilled, then we have an order

$$x-x_{\alpha}^{g} = O(\omega(\alpha)^{\nu}).$$ □

The next theorem shows that this result is in a certain sense optimal.

Theorem 3

Let $T : X \to Y$ be a compact operator and $\{g_{\alpha}, \alpha > 0\}$ a family of functions satisfying (2)-(5) and

(6) $$\exists_{\gamma > 0} \forall_{\lambda} \exists_{\alpha} \frac{\lambda^{\nu}}{\omega(\alpha)^{\nu}} (1-\lambda g_{\alpha}(\lambda)) \geq \gamma.$$

Let for all $x \in U_{\nu} = (T^*T)^{\nu}U$, U the unit ball in X, uniformly

$$x-x_{\alpha} = o(\omega(\alpha)^{\nu}),$$

then T has finite rank.

Proof

$$x-x_{\alpha} = \int \lambda^{\nu}(1-\lambda g_{\alpha}(\lambda))E[d\lambda]u$$

with an appropriate $u \in U$. The condition of uniform convergence implies

$$\sup_{x\in U_\nu} \frac{\|x-x_\alpha\|}{\omega(\alpha)^\nu} = \sup_{u\in U} \|\int \frac{\lambda^\nu}{\omega(\alpha)^\nu} (1-\lambda g_\alpha(\lambda))E[d\lambda]u\|$$

$$\geq \sup_{u_k\in U} \frac{\lambda_k^\nu}{\omega(\alpha)^\nu} (1-\lambda_k g_\alpha(\lambda_k)) \geq \gamma$$

where u_k is a unit eigenvector of T*T with the corresponding eigenvalue λ_k. If there is an infinite number of non-zero eigenvalues then by (6) there is an infinite number of α_k with $\lim_{k\to\infty} \alpha_k = 0$, and $\|x-x_\alpha^g\| \geq \gamma\omega(\alpha)^\nu$, but this is a contradiction to the convergence. □

Remark

We show by an example that condition (6) is necessary:

Let

$$g_\alpha(\lambda) = \frac{1}{\lambda+\alpha},\ \omega(\alpha)^\nu = \alpha^{\nu-\varepsilon},\ 0 < \varepsilon < \nu.$$

Then

$$\frac{\lambda^\nu}{\omega(\alpha)^\nu} (1-\lambda g_\alpha(\lambda)) = \frac{\alpha^\varepsilon \cdot (\frac{\lambda}{\alpha})^\nu}{\frac{\lambda}{\alpha}+1} \leq \frac{1}{2}\alpha^\varepsilon \to 0$$

and

$$\sup_{x\in U_\nu} \frac{\|x-x_\alpha\|}{\alpha^\nu} \leq \frac{1}{2}\alpha^\varepsilon,$$

this is uniform convergence for $x \in U_\nu$. □

3. Superconvergence

The theorems 2 and 3 imply, that for $x \in \mathrm{Range}(T^*T)^\nu$ a convergence rate

$$\lim \omega(\alpha)^{-\nu} \|x-x_\alpha^g\| = 0$$

is optimal, but that this convergence is not uniformly in x, except in the trivial cases. In contrast to this, if $u^* \in X$ is a certain linear functional, the values $(x-x_\alpha^g, u^*)$ may have a better rate of convergence. This phenomenon is called *superconvergence*.

Theorem 4

Let $Qy \in \mathrm{Range}\ T(T^*T)^\rho$, $w \in \mathrm{Range}(T^*T)^\mu$ for some positive reals

ρ,μ and $g_\alpha,\alpha>0$ and ω functions satisfying (2)-(5) with $\nu=\rho+\mu$. Then

$$(x-x_\alpha^g,w) = o(\omega(\alpha)^{\rho+\mu}).$$

Proof

Analogue to the proof of theorem 2 we have

$$(x-x_\alpha^g,w) = (I-g_\alpha(T^*T)(T^*T)^\rho z,(T^*T)^\mu v)$$

for some properly chosen $z,v\in X$ and

$$(x-x_\alpha^g,w) = (\int_\sigma \frac{\lambda^{\rho+\mu}}{\omega(\alpha)^{\rho+\mu}}(1-\lambda g_\alpha(\lambda))E[d\lambda]z,v).$$

Then the proof follows the lines of theorem 2. □

4. Examples

In this section we will consider some specific choices for the functions g_α and we will find functions ω which determine rates of convergence.

The approximations given by *Showalter's integral formula* [13] have the form

$$x_\alpha = \int_0^{1/\alpha} \exp(-\xi T^*T)T^*y\, d\xi.$$

That is

$$g_\alpha(\lambda) = \frac{1}{\lambda}(1-e^{-\lambda/\alpha}).$$

If Range T is closed, then for each function ω with $0<\omega(\alpha)\le\gamma\cdot e^{-\mu/\alpha}$, $\gamma>0$, $\mu<\min\{\lambda>0 : \lambda\in\sigma(T^*T)\}$

$$\omega(\alpha)^{-1}|1-g_\alpha(\lambda)\lambda| \le \gamma\cdot e^{\mu/\alpha}e^{-\lambda/\alpha} = \gamma\cdot e^{\frac{\mu-\lambda}{\alpha}}$$

is bounded for all $\alpha>0$, $\mu\le\lambda<\infty$, therefore in this case

$$x-x_\alpha^g = O(e^{-\mu/\alpha}).$$

If Range T is not closed and $\omega:\mathbb{R}^+\to\mathbb{R}^+$ is an arbitrary monotone function with $\omega(0)=0$, then

$$\sup_{\substack{\alpha>0\\ \lambda>0}} \omega(\alpha)^{-1}|1-\lambda g_\alpha(\lambda)| = \infty$$

thus the convergence is arbitrarily slow.

If $\omega(\alpha)=\alpha$, then

$$\frac{\lambda^\nu}{\alpha^\nu}(1-\lambda g_\alpha(\lambda)) = (\frac{\lambda}{\alpha})^\nu e^{-\frac{\lambda}{\alpha}}$$

is uniformly bounded and

$$\lim_{\alpha\to 0} \left(\frac{\lambda}{\alpha}\right)^{\nu} e^{-\frac{\lambda}{\alpha}} = 0$$

uniformly for each λ in each compact subset of $(0, \|T\|^2)$, therefore the convergence rate is

$$x - x_\alpha^g = o(\alpha^\rho) \qquad \text{for} \quad x \in \text{Range}(T^*T)^\rho$$

resp.

$$(x - x_\alpha^g, w) = o(\alpha^{\rho+\mu})$$

for $x \in \text{Range}(T^*T)^\rho$, $w \in \text{Range}(T^*T)^\mu$, $\nu = \rho+\mu$.

The *iterated Tikhonov regularization* is given by the formulas

$$(T^*T+\alpha I)x_\alpha^{(j)} = T^*y+\alpha x_\alpha^{(j-1)}, \quad x_\alpha^{(0)} = 0, \quad j=1,2,\ldots,n,$$

therefore

$$g_\alpha(\lambda) = \frac{1}{\lambda}\left(1 - \left(\frac{\alpha}{\lambda+\alpha}\right)^n\right)$$

and

$$R_\alpha^g x = x - x_\alpha^{(n)} = \int_\sigma \left(\frac{\alpha}{\lambda+\alpha}\right)^n E[d\lambda]x.$$

Since

$$\|R_\alpha^g\| = \sup_{\lambda\in\sigma} \left(\frac{\alpha}{\lambda+\alpha}\right)^n = 1$$

if Range T is not closed, the convergence in general is arbitrarily slow. The conditions (4) and (5) are satisfied with $\omega(\alpha) = \alpha$, and $\nu < n$, thus

$$\|x - x_\alpha^{(n)}\| = o(\alpha^\rho), \quad (x - x_\alpha^{(n)}, w) = o(\alpha^{\rho+\mu})$$

for $x \in \text{Range}(T^*T)^\rho$, $w \in \text{Range}(T^*T)^\mu$, $\rho+\mu < n$ and

$$\|x - x_\alpha^{(n)}\| = O(\alpha^\rho), \quad |(x - x_\alpha, w)| = O(\alpha^{\rho+\mu}),$$

if $\rho \geq n$ resp. $\rho+\mu \geq n$.

This improves a result of J.T. KING and D. CHILLINGWORTH [8], see also [9] and [11].

The approximations via *Landweber iteration* are given by

$$x_{n+1} = x_n + \beta T^*(y - Tx_n), \quad x_0 = 0, \quad 0 < \beta < \|T\|^{-2}.$$

We write $\tilde{g}_n(\lambda) = g_{1/\alpha}(\lambda)$ for $\alpha = \frac{1}{n}$. Then

$$\tilde{g}_n(\lambda) = \frac{1}{\lambda}(1-(1-\beta\lambda)^n).$$

Since

$$(\frac{\lambda}{\alpha})^{\nu}(1-\beta\lambda)^{n} = \tau^{\nu}(1-\frac{\beta\tau}{n})^{n} \leq \tau^{\nu}e^{-\beta\tau}$$

is bounded for all $\nu > 0$, $\tau > 0$ and converges uniformly on compact subsets of $(0, \|T\|^2)$, we obtain a rate of convergence of

$$\|x-x_n\| = o(\alpha^{\rho}) \quad \text{or} \quad (x-x_n, w) = o(\alpha^{\rho+\mu})$$

for $x \in \text{Range}(T^*T)^{\rho}$, $w \in \text{Range}(T^*T)^{\mu}$, otherwise the convergence is arbitrarily slow, since

$$\sup_{\lambda\in\sigma} (1-\beta\lambda)^{n} = 1$$

if Range T is not closed.

Further examples can be found in [4] and [16].

References

[1] A.B. Bakushinskii, A General Method of Constructing Regularization Algorithms for a Linear Ill-Posed Equation in Hilbert Space, USSR Comp. Math. Phys. 7(3), 1967, 279-287.

[2] G.A. Chandler, Superconvergence for Second Kind Integral Equations, in R.S. Anderssen et al. Eds. The Application and Numerical Solution of Integral Equations. Noordhoff, Leyden 1980.

[3] C.W. Groetsch, Generalized Inverses of Linear Operators: Representation and Approximation, Dekker, New York 1977.

[4] C.W. Groetsch, On a Class of Regularization Methods, Boll. U.M.I. (5) 17-B (1980) 1411-1419.

[5] C.W. Groetsch, On Rates of Convergence for Approximations to the Generalized Inverse, Numer. Funct. Anal. and Optimiz. 1(2), 195-201 (1979).

[6] C.W. Groetsch, On a Regularization-Ritz Method for Fredholm Equations of the First Kind, J. Integral Equations 4 (1982) 173-182.

[7] C.W. Groetsch, The Theory of Tikhonov Regularization for Fredholm Equations of the First Kind, Pitman Boston 1984.

[8] J.T. King, D. Chillingworth, Approximation of Generalized Inverses by Iterated Regularization, Num. Functional Analysis and Optimization 1(5) (1979) 499-513.

[9] E. Schock, On the Asymptotic Order of Accuracy of Tikhonov Regularization, J. Optimiz. Theory and Appl. (to appear)

[10] E. Schock, On the Approximate Solution of Ill-Posed Equations in Banach Spaces, Proc. Conference on Functional Analysis, Vorlesungen Fachbereich Mathematik, Essen 10 (1983) 351-362.

[11] E. Schock, Regularization of Ill-Posed Equations with Self-adjoint Operators, in: German-Italian Symposium on the Applications of Mathematics in Technology (Proceedings) Eds: V. Boffi, H. Neunzert, Teubner Verlag Stuttgart 1984.

[12] E. Schock, Arbitrarily Slow Convergence, Uniform Convergence and Superconvergence of Galerkin-Like Methods, IMA J. Num. Analysis (submitted).

[13] D. Showalter, Representation and Computation of the Pseudoinverse, Proc. AMS 18 (1967) 584-586.

[14] D. Showalter and A. Ben-Israel, Representation and Computation of the Generalized Inverse of a Bounded Linear Operator between Two Hilbert Spaces, Accad. Naz. dei Lincei 48 (1970) 194-194.

[15] G. Vainikko, Solution Methods for Linear Incorrectly Posed Problems in Hilbert Spaces (Russian), Tartu State University, Tartu, Estonian SSR, 1982.

[16] J. Wloka, Funktionalanalysis und Anwendungen, de Gruyter, Berlin 1970.

Prof. Dr. Eberhard Schock
Fachbereich Mathematik
Universität Kaiserslautern
Erwin-Schrödinger-Straße
D - 6750 Kaiserslautern

International Series of
Numerical Mathematics, Vol. 73

A UNIFIED ANALYSIS OF DISCRETIZATION METHODS FOR VOLTERRA-TYPE EQUATIONS*

Jennifer A Scott (née Dixon)
University of Oxford, England

1. Introduction

Consider the nonlinear equation

$$\Phi(y) = 0, \quad \Phi: X \to Y. \tag{1.1}$$

To obtain a numerical approximation y^h to y (1.1) is replaced by a discretization

$$\Phi^h(y^h) = 0, \quad \Phi^h: X^h \to Y^h, \tag{1.2}$$

where h belongs to a non-empty set $J \subset \mathbb{R}^+$ with inf J=0. The replacement is to be such that as $h \to 0$ the more accurate are the approximations y^h to the solution y of (1.1).

There are essentially two ways to effect a comparison between $y \in X$ and $y^h \in X^h$.

(i) Define a sequence of prolongation operators $p^h: X^h \to X$; the sequence $\{p^h y^h\}_{h \in J}$ p-converges to y in X if $||p^h y^h - y||_X \to 0$ as $h \to 0$.

(ii) Define a sequence of restriction operators $r^h: X \to X^h$; the sequence $\{y^h\}_{h \in J}$ r-converges to y if $||r^h y - y^h||_{X^h} \to 0$ as $h \to 0$.

The aim of this paper is to simplify and unify convergence analysis by setting up a general framework which will allow the consideration of both approaches to convergence for an extensive class of discretization methods for Volterra-type equations.

---

* This paper is based on two more detailed papers which have been submitted for publication elsewhere.

2. The analytic fundamental form

To illustrate the approach to be adopted let $X=C(\Omega)$, $\Omega:=[0,T]$, $||x||_X = ||x||_\infty$; the extension to more general spaces will be discussed in section 4.

Definition 2.1 Equation (1.1) will be said to have an analytic fundamental form (i.e. to be of Volterra-type) if it is expressible in the form

$$y = g + H(y) \tag{2.1}$$

where $H : C(\Omega)\to C(\Omega)$ is a nonlinear Volterra operator satisfying

$$|H(y) - H(z)| \le K|y-z|, \text{ for all } y,z\in C(\Omega), \tag{2.2}$$

where $(K|y|)(t) = \int_0^t k(t,s)\ |y(s)|ds,\ t\in\Omega,$

and the Volterra kernel $k(t,s)$ satisfies

(CI) $k(t,s)$ is non-negative on the triangle, $0\le s\le t\le T$

(CII) for each $t\in\Omega$ $k(t,s)$ is integrable as a function of s

(CIII) there exists $\mu\in\mathbb{N}$ such that the μth iterated kernel $k^{(\mu)}(t,s)$ of $k(t,s)$ is continuous in t,s.

Theorem 2.1 (DIXON AND MCKEE (1984a)) The analytic fundamental form possesses a unique solution $y\in C(\Omega)$.

For example consider Abel's equation of the second kind

$$y(t) = g(t) + \int_0^t G(t,s,y(s))(t-s)^{-\alpha}ds,\ t\in\Omega, \tag{2.3}$$

where $0<\alpha<1$.

This is of the form (2.1) with $k(t,s) = L(t-s)^{-\alpha}$, where L is the Lipschitz constant for $G(t,s,y)$ with respect to y. This kernel satisfies CI - CIII provided $\mu\ge\rho+1$ where $\rho\in\mathbb{N}$ is uniquely chosen such that $\rho-1/\rho<\alpha \le \rho/\rho+1$.

3. The discrete fundamental form

As $h\to 0$ it is anticipated that the discretization will in some sense tend to the underlying operator equation and that therefore any analysis for the original problem (1.1) will have a parallel in the approximating problem (1.2). Following this view a discrete version of the space $C(\Omega)$ is introduced.

Definition 3.1 Let T, $h_0 > 0$ be given, $T/h_0 = n_0$, a positive integer. Define $J:=\{h: h = T/n, n\in\mathbb{N}, n\geq n_0\}$. Given a positive integer m, independent of h, let $N = n-\delta+1$, $\delta = \min(2,m)$ and set $\Omega_m^h = \{0,1,\ldots,Nm\}$.
Let

$$X^h = C(\Omega_m^h):=\{x^h: x^h=(x_0,x_1,\ldots,x_N)^T,\ x_i=(x_{i\sigma})^T\in\mathbb{R}^m,\ 0\leq i\leq N\}$$

with norm $||x^h||_{X^h} = ||x^h||_\infty := \max_{0\leq i\leq N} |x_i|_m$, $|x_i|_m := \max_{1\leq\sigma\leq m} |x_{i\sigma}|$.

Definition 3.2 Let h,N be defined as above. The discrete function k_{ij} defined on the integers i,j, $0\leq j,i\leq N$, is a discrete Volterra kernel if $k_{ij} = 0$ for $j>i$. The discrete iterated kernels $k_{ij}^{(n)}$ $(n=1,2,\ldots)$ of k_{ij} are defined to be

$$k_{ij}^{(1)} = k_{ij},\quad k_{ij}^{(n)} = h\sum_{\ell=j}^{i} k_{i\ell}\, k_{\ell j}^{(n-1)},\quad n\geq 2. \tag{3.1}$$

Provided $0\leq hk_{ii}<1$ for each i, $0\leq i\leq N$, and all $h\in J$ sufficiently small, it will be convenient to introduce the discrete Volterra kernel $\overline{k}_{ij}$ defined by

$$\overline{k}_{ij} = \begin{cases} k_{ij}/(1-hk_{ii}), & j<i \\ 0, & j\geq i. \end{cases} \tag{3.2}$$

Definition 3.3 The discretization (1.2) will be said to have a discrete fundamental form if it is expressible in the form

$$y^h = g^h + H^h(y^h) \tag{3.3}$$

where $H^h : C(\Omega_m^h)\to C(\Omega_m^h)$ is a discrete Volterra operator satisfying

$$|H^h(y^h)-H^h(z^h)|_m \leq K^h|y^h-z^h|_m, \text{ for all } y^h,z^h\in C(\Omega_m^h), \tag{3.4}$$

where $$(K^h|y^h|_m)_i = h\sum_{j=0}^{i} k_{ij}|y_j|_m,\quad 0\leq i\leq N,$$

with $0\leq hk_{ii}<1$, $0\leq i\leq N$, $h\in J$ sufficiently small. The discrete Volterra kernel $\overline{k}_{ij}$ defined by (3.2) is required to satisfy

(DI) $\bar{k}_{ij} \geq 0$ for $0 \leq j < i \leq N$

(DII) for each i, $0 \leq i \leq N$, $h \sum_{j=0}^{i-1} \bar{k}_{ij}$ is bounded independently of h

(DIII) there exists $\mu \in \mathbb{N}$ such that the μth discrete iterated kernel $\bar{k}_{ij}^{(\mu)}$ of $\bar{k}_{ij}$ is bounded in i,j, independently of h.

Theorem 3.1 (DIXON AND MCKEE (1984b)) For all $h \in J$ sufficiently small the discrete fundamental form possesses a unique solution $y^h \in C(\Omega_m^h)$.

To illustrate the discrete fundamental form consider the following product integration method for equation (2.3):

$$y_i = g(t_i) + h \sum_{j=0}^{i} W_{ij}\, G(t_i, t_j, y_j), \quad 1 \leq i \leq N, \tag{3.5}$$

where y_i denotes an approximation to $y(t_i)$ with $t_i = ih$, $0 \leq i \leq N$, $Nh = T$, $y(0)=g(0)$ and the weights W_{ij} are given by

$$W_{io} = h^{-2} \int_0^{t_1} (t_i - s)^{-\alpha}(t_1 - s)ds, \quad 1 \leq i \leq N,$$

$$W_{ij} = h^{-2}\Big\{\int_{t_j}^{t_{j+1}} (t_i - s)^{-\alpha}(t_{j+1} - s)ds + \int_{t_{j-1}}^{t_j} (t_i - s)^{-\alpha}(s - t_{j-1})ds\Big\}, \quad 1 \leq j \leq i-1, \; 2 \leq i \leq N,$$

$$W_{ii} = h^{-2} \int_{t_{i-1}}^{t_i} (t_i - s)^{-\alpha}(s - t_{i-1})ds, \quad 1 \leq i \leq N.$$

It can be shown that for some M, independent of h,

$0 < W_{ij} \leq M(h(i-j))^{-\alpha}$, $0 \leq j \leq i \leq N$ $(0^{-\alpha} \equiv 1)$.

The discretization (3.5) may then be written in the form (3.3) with m=1 and $k_{ij} = LM(h(i-j))^{-\alpha}$. It can be shown (see SCOTT) that the related discrete kernel $\bar{k}_{ij} = M'(h(i-j))^{-\alpha}$, $M' = LM/(1-h^{1-\alpha}LM)$, satisfies DI - DIII provided $\mu \geq \rho+1$ where again $\rho-1/\rho < \alpha \leq \rho/\rho+1$. Hence the product integration method (3.5) is expressible in discrete fundamental form.

Throughout the rest of this paper symbols C,M, with or without subscripts or superscripts, will be assumed to be positive constants bounded independently of h, unless otherwise stated.

4. p- and r- convergence results

For $h \in J$ let $p^h : X^h \to X$ and $r^h : X \to X^h$ denote respectively linear prolongation and restriction operators. Prolongation and restriction operators have been widely used in the error analysis of collocation schemes for Fredholm equations (NOBLE). Further, they have been applied extensively by the French school in connection with elliptic systems (CÉA and AUBIN). In this paper prolongation and restriction operators will reduce the problem of comparing y and y^h to that of considering the effect of perturbations in the fundamental forms using the following continuous and discrete generalized Gronwall inequalities given by DIXON AND MCKEE (1984c).

<u>Lemma 4.1</u> For any $\phi \in C(\Omega)$ if $x \in C(\Omega)$ satisfies

$$x(t) \leq \phi(t) + \int_0^t k(t,s)x(s)ds, \quad t \in \Omega,$$

where k(t,s) satisfies CI - CIII, then

$$x(t) \leq y(t), \quad t \in \Omega,$$

where $y \in C(\Omega)$ is the unique solution of the integral equation

$$y(t) = \phi(t) + \int_0^t k(t,s)y(s)ds, \quad t \in \Omega.$$

Moreover, if $x \geq 0$ and $\phi \geq 0$ then for some constant C independent of ϕ

$$||x||_\infty \leq C \, ||\phi||_\infty. \tag{4.1}$$

<u>Lemma 4.2</u> For any sequence $\{\phi_i\}_{i=0}^N$ of real numbers if the sequence $\{x_i\}_{i=0}^N$ of real numbers satisfies

$$x_i \leq \phi_i + h \sum_{j=0}^{i-1} \bar{k}_{ij} \, x_j, \quad 0 \leq i \leq N,$$

where $\bar{k}_{ij}$ satisfies DI - DIII, then

$$x_i \leq y_i, \quad 0 \leq i \leq N,$$

where $\{y_i\}_{i=0}^N$ is the unique solution of the discrete equation

$$y_i = \phi_i + h \sum_{j=0}^{i-1} \overline{k}_{ij}\, y_j, \quad 0 \le i \le N.$$

Moreover, if $x_i \ge 0$ and $\phi_i \ge 0$, $0 \le i \le N$, then for some constant C independent of h and ϕ_i, $0 \le i \le N$,

$$\max_i (x_i) \le C \max_i (\phi_i). \tag{4.2}$$

To introduce p- and r- consistency of a discretization assume

$$y = g + H(y),\ H: X \to X, \tag{4.3}$$

$$y^h = g^h + H^h(y^h),\ H^h: X^h \to X^h. \tag{4.4}$$

Definition 4.1 The discrete operators H^h, $h \varepsilon J$ sufficiently small, are said to be p- consistent of order $s > 0$ to H if for all $x^h \varepsilon X^h$ with $||x^h||_{X^h} < M$

$$||p^h H^h(x^h) - H(p^h x^h)||_X \le Ch^s + O(h^{s+1}). \tag{4.5}$$

Definition 4.2 The discrete operators H^h, $h \varepsilon J$ sufficiently small, are r-consistent of order $s > 0$ if for all $x \varepsilon X$ sufficiently smooth

$$||r^h H(x) - H^h(r^h x)||_{X^h} \le C' h^s + O(h^{s+1}). \tag{4.6}$$

Again take $X = C(\Omega)$ and $X^h = C(\Omega_m^h)$.

Theorem 4.1 Let the solution y of (1.1) satisfy the analytic fundamental form 2.1 with CI - CIII satisfied and let the approximation y^h be defined by a discretization expressible in the form (4.4). Let H^h be p- consistent of order s. If $p^h g^h$ p- converges to g with order s then for h sufficiently small

$$||p^h y^h - y||_\infty \le Ch^s + O(h^{s+1}). \tag{4.7}$$

Proof The prolonged approximation $p^h y^h$ satisfies the perturbed analytic fundamental form

$$p^h y^h = g + H(p^h y^h) + \theta$$

where $\theta = (p^h H^h(y^h) - H(p^h y^h)) + (p^h g^h - g) \ \varepsilon\ C(\Omega)$.

Subtracting (2.1) and using (2.2)

$$|(p^h y^h - y)(t)| \leq \int_0^t k(t,s)|(p^h y^h - y)(s)|ds + |\theta(t)|, \; t\epsilon\Omega.$$

Invoking lemma 4.1 and using (4.1) the required result follows.

Similarly, r-convergence of y^h to y may be proved using the generalized discrete Gronwall inequality (lemma 4.2).

Theorem 4.2 Assume equation (1.1) for y may be written in the form (4.3), and let the approximation y^h satisfy the discrete fundamental form (3.3) with DI - DIII satisfied. Let H^h be r- consistent of order s. If g^h r- converges to g with order s then for h sufficiently small

$$||r^h y - y^h||_\infty \leq C' h^s + O(h^{s+1}). \tag{4.8}$$

The above convergence results can be extended to more general spaces X, X^h using the following Gronwall inequality for abstract operators.

Lemma 4.3 Let X be a partially ordered Banach space with X^+ closed. For $\phi \in X$ if $x \in X$ satisfies the inequality

$$x \leq \phi + Kx$$

where $K \in L(X)$ is a positive operator with K^n a contraction mapping for some $n \in \mathbb{N}$, then

$$x \leq y$$

where $y \in X$ is the unique solution of the operator equation

$$y = \phi + Ky.$$

Moreover, if X is a Banach lattice and $x\epsilon X^+$ and $\phi\epsilon X^+$ then for some constant C independent of ϕ

$$||x||_X \leq C||\phi||_X.$$

Further details are given in DIXON AND MCKEE (1984a) and SCOTT.

5. Two-sided error bounds

The error bounds (4.7) and (4.8) imply p- and r-convergence respectively of order at least s. To deduce the exact order of convergence it is necessary to derive two-sided error bounds of the form

$$C_L\xi(h) \leq ||p^h y^h - y||_\infty \leq C_U\xi(h), \qquad (5.1)$$

$$C_L'\xi(h) \leq ||r^h y - y^h||_\infty \leq C_U'\xi(h) \qquad (5.2)$$

where $\xi(h) = h^s + O(h^{s+1})$ and C_L, C_L', C_U, C_U' are non-zero constants.

The following concepts of optimal consistency will permit two-sided error bounds to be derived.

<u>Definition 5.1</u> Assume equation (1.1) for y may be written in the form (4.3), and let y^h be the solution of the discretization (1.2). The discretization is optimally p-consistent of order s>0 if for all hεJ sufficiently small there exists C>0 such that

$$||\theta||_X := ||p^h y^h - g - H(p^h y^h)||_X = Ch^s + O(h^{s+1}). \qquad (5.3)$$

<u>Definition 5.2</u> Let y be the solution of (1.1) and let y^h be the solution of the discretization (1.2) which is expressible in the form (4.4). The discretization is said to be optimally r- consistent of order s>0 if for all hεJ sufficiently small there exists C'>0 such that

$$||\theta^h||_{X^h} := ||r^h y - g^h - H^h(r^h y)||_{X^h} = C'h^s + O(h^{s+1}). \qquad (5.4)$$

Two-sided error bounds are presented for $X = C(\Omega)$, $X^h = C(\Omega_m^h)$.

<u>Theorem 5.1</u> Assume the solution y of (1.1) satisfies the analytic fundamental form 2.1 with CI - CIII satisfied, and let y^h be defined by a discretization which is optimally p- consistent of order s. Then for all hεJ sufficiently small there exists a two-sided bound of the form (5.1) for $p^h y^h - y$.

<u>Proof</u> The upper bound follows using lemma 4.1 and definition 5.1.

To obtain the lower bound, from (2.1) and (5.3)

$$\theta = p^h y^h - y - (H(p^h y^h) - H(y)).$$

Using (2.2), for all $t \in \Omega$,

$$|\theta(t)| \leq (1+||K||)\ ||p^h y^h - y||_\infty.$$

Taking the supremum yields the required bound.

Theorem 5.2 Let y be the solution of (1.1) and assume y^h is defined by the discretization (1.2) which is expressible in discrete fundamental form (3.3) with DI - DIII satisfied. If the discretization is optimally r- consistent of order s then for all $h \in J$ sufficiently small there exists a two-sided bound of the form (5.2) for $r^h y - y^h$.

Verifying optimal consistency may be difficult in practice or may require additional continuity conditions. Without these conditions it may only be possible to show, for example, that for some $C \geq 0$

$$||\theta^h||_\infty \leq Ch^s + O(h^{s+1}).$$

In this case the upper bound in (5.2) (with $C_U' \geq 0$) may be used to deduce r- convergence of order at least s.

To illustrate this consider the product integration method (3.5). Defining $(r^h y(t))_i = y(t_i)$, $0 \leq i \leq N$, and using definition 5.2

$$||\theta^h||_\infty = ||\int_0^{t_i} G(t_i,s,y(s))(t_i-s)^{-\alpha} ds - h \sum_{j=0}^{i} W_{ij} G(t_i,t_j,y(t_j))||_\infty.$$

If y is assumed smooth on Ω it can be shown that

$$||\theta^h||_\infty = Ch^2 + O(h^3),$$

that is, the method is optimally r- consistent of order 2 and theorem 5.2 implies r- convergence of order exactly 2. In most practical examples, however, the solution y of (2.4) possesses discontinuous derivatives at the origin and in this case

$$||\theta^h||_\infty \leq Ch^{1-\alpha} + O(h),$$

and the upper bound at (5.2) implies r- convergence of order at least $1-\alpha$.

6. An application

The general convergence results will be illustrated using a class of block quadrature methods for the first kind Volterra integral equation

$$\int_0^t G(t,s)y(s)ds = f(t),\ f(0) = 0,\ t\varepsilon\Omega, \tag{6.1}$$

where $G(t,t) \neq 0$ on Ω and f,G are assumed smooth.

<u>Definition 6.1</u> Consider the class of block quadrature methods which are expressible in the form

$$h\psi^h y^h = f^h \tag{6.2}$$

where $f^h = (h\tilde{y}_0, h\tilde{y}_1, \ldots, h\tilde{y}_{q-1}, f_q, \ldots, f_N)^T \varepsilon\ C(\Omega_m^h)$ with $\tilde{y}_i = (\tilde{y}_{i\sigma})^T \varepsilon\ \mathbb{R}^m$, $0\leq i\leq q-1$, $f_i = (f(t_{i\sigma}))^T \varepsilon\ \mathbb{R}^m$, $q\leq i\leq N$, and

$$(h\psi^h y^h)_{i\sigma} = \begin{cases} \tilde{y}_{i\sigma}, & 1\leq\sigma\leq m,\ 0\leq i\leq q-1 \\ h\sum_{j=0}^{i}\sum_{\nu=1}^{m}(W_{ij})_{\sigma\nu}G(t_{i\sigma},t_{j\nu})y_{j\nu}, & 1\leq\sigma\leq m,\ q\leq i\leq N, \end{cases}$$

where $\tilde{y}_{i\sigma}$, $1\leq\sigma\leq m$, $0\leq i\leq q-1$, are precomputed starting values and $y_{i\sigma}$ denotes an approximation to $y(t_{i\sigma})$, $t_{i\sigma} = (i+\eta_\sigma)h$, $1\leq\sigma\leq m$, $0\leq i\leq N$, where $\eta = (\eta_1,\eta_2,\ldots,\eta_m)\varepsilon\ \mathbb{R}^m$ is given. The W_{ij}, $0\leq j\leq i\leq N$, are m x m matrices of quadrature weights with entries $(W_{ij})_{\sigma\nu}$, $1\leq\sigma,\nu\leq m$, and W_{ii} is non-singular.

A method of the form (6.2) is said to be an (A^h,B^h) m-block quadrature method if there exist m x m matrices $\{A_j,B_j\}_{j=0}^{\tau}$, with A_0, B_0 non-singular, such that

$$W_{ij} = \bar{W}_{i-j} \text{ for } j\geq q,\ i-j\geq 0 \tag{6.3}$$

$$\text{where } \sum_{j=0}^{\tau} A_j \bar{W}_{i-j} = B_i,\ \sum_{j=0}^{\tau} A_j e = 0,\ e = (1,1,\ldots,1), \tag{6.4}$$

with the convention A_j, $B_j = 0$, $j \notin \{0,1,\ldots,\tau\}$ and $\bar{W}_{i-j} = 0$ for $i<j$.

The class of $(A^h B^h)$ m-block quadrature methods is extensive and includes linear multistep methods (MCKEE), block-by-block methods (DE HOOG AND WEISS), reducible quadrature

(WOLKENFELT) and multilag methods (WOLKENFELT).

Using the identity

$$G(t_{i\sigma},t_{j\nu}) = G(t_{j\nu},t_{j\nu}) + h((G(t_{i\sigma},t_{j\nu})-G(t_{j\nu},t_{j\nu}))/h)$$

ψ^h is decomposed into the sum $\psi^h = W^hG^h + h\overline{W}^{h(1)}$, where G^h is an $(N+1)m \times (N+1)m$ diagonal matrix with the qm x qm identity matrix in the top left hand corner and entries $G(t_{j\nu},t_{j\nu})$ for $1\le\nu\le m$, $q\le j\le N$, and W^h is the matrix of quadrature weights.

Using the decomposition of ψ^h in (6.2) yields

$$y^h = h(W^hG^h)^{-1} f^h + H^h(y^h) \tag{6.5}$$

where $H^h(y^h) = -h(W^hG^h)^{-1}\,\overline{W}^{h(1)}y^h$ satisfies

$$(|H^h(y^h) - H^h(z^h)|_m)_i \le h\,M\,C \sum_{j=0}^{i} (|y^h-z^h|_m)_j,\ 0\le i\le N,$$

where $M = \max_{0\le t\le T} |G(t,t)|^{-1} > 0,$

provided

$$\max_{i,j} |((W^h)^{-1}\,\overline{W}^{h(1)})_{ij}|_m \le C. \tag{6.6}$$

(Here $|((W^h)^{-1}\,\overline{W}^{h(1)})_{ij}|_m$ denotes the infinity norm of the m x m matrix $((W^h)^{-1}\,\overline{W}^{h(1)})_{ij}$.)

In general inverting W^h will be difficult and the relations (6.3), (6.4) are used to derive sufficient conditions for (6.6) to hold; details are given in DIXON AND MCKEE (1984b). If (6.6) is satisfied then (6.5) is the discrete fundamental form for (6.2) with $k_{ij} = MC$, $0\le j\le i\le N$, which satisfies DI - DIII with $\mu=1$. Invoking theorem 5.2 then yields

$$C_L'||\theta^h||_\infty \le ||r^hy - y^h||_\infty \le C_U'\,||\theta^h||_\infty \tag{6.7}$$

where θ^h is the r- consistency error. If r^h is the usual grid restriction operator then

$$\theta^h = (hW^hG^h)^{-1}\,T^h \tag{6.8}$$

where T^h is the quadrature error given by

$$h\psi^hr^hy = f^h + T^h.$$

Given an (A^h,B^h) m-block method satisfying (6.6) the bound (6.7) may be used to determine the exact order of r- convergence. For example, for a reducible quadrature method

(6.6) is satisfied provided the characteristic polynomials of the underlying linear multistep method are simple von Neumann polynomials with no common roots. Furthermore, if the linear multistep method is of order s and the starting values are of order s then using (6.8) the reducible quadrature can be shown to be optimally r- consistent of order s; (6.7) then implies the reducible quadrature is r- convergent of order exactly s.

Acknowledgements This work forms part of the author's D.Phil. thesis at Oxford University which was supervised by Dr S McKee and funded by the Science and Engineering Research Council.

Jennifer A Scott, Oxford University Computing Laboratory,
8-11 Keble Road, Oxford OX1 3QD, England.

References

Aubin, J.P.(1972) Approximation of Elliptic Boundary-Value Problems. Wiley - Interscience.

Céa, J.(1964) Approximation variationelle des problèmes aux limites. Ann. Inst. Fourier 14, 345-441.

Dixon, J. A. and McKee, S.(1984a) A unified approach to convergence analysis of discretization methods for Volterra type equations. IMA J. Numer. Anal., to appear.

Dixon, J. A. and McKee, S.(1984b) Two-sided error bounds for discretization methods, submitted for publication.

Dixon, J. A. and McKee, S.(1984c) Weakly singular discrete Gronwall inequalities, submitted for publication.

Hoog, F.de and Weiss, R.(1973) On the solution of Volterra integral equations of the first kind. Numer. Math. 21, 22-32.

McKee, S.(1979) Best convergence rates of linear multistep methods for Volterra first kind equations. Comput. 21, 343-358.

Noble, B. (1973) Error analysis of collocation methods for solving Fredholm integral equations. In : Topics in Numerical Analysis, ed. J.H.H. Miller, Academic Press.

Scott, J. A.(1984) A unified analysis of discretization methods. D.Phil thesis, University of Oxford.

Wolkenfelt, P. H.M.(1981) The numerical analysis of reducible quadrature methods for Volterra integral and integro-differential equations. Ph.d thesis, Amsterdam.

International Series of
Numerical Mathematics, Vol. 73

WIENER - HOPF INTEGRAL EQUATIONS: FINITE SECTION APPROXIMATION AND PROJECTION METHODS

I.H. Sloan* and A. Spence**

*University of New South Wales, Sydney, Australia.
**University of Bath, Bath, England.

We consider the numerical solution of integral equations on the half-line by their finite-section approximation and by projection methods. Convergence results for the finite-section approximation are discussed, and are shown to be important in the analysis of the convergence of the projection method. Piecewise-constant collocation is discussed in detail, and numerical results are given.

1. Introduction

In this paper we consider the approximate solution of Wiener-Hopf integral equations of the form

$$y(t) = f(t) + \frac{1}{\lambda}\int_0^\infty \kappa(t-s)y(s)ds, \qquad t \in \mathbb{R}^+, \tag{1.1}$$

and also generalizations of the form

$$y(t) = f(t) + \frac{1}{\lambda}\int_0^\infty k(t,s)y(s)ds, \qquad t \in \mathbb{R}^+, \tag{1.2}$$

where $\kappa \in L_1(\mathbb{R})$,

$$k(t,s) = \kappa(t-s) + \ell(t,s), \tag{1.3}$$

and $\ell(t,s)$ is appropriately restricted (see Section 2).

We shall be interested only in situations in which f and y are bounded, continuous functions on $\mathbb{R}^+$. Many practically important problems, including some that arise in astrophysics (see, for example, [3]), are of this character.

We shall consider here two kinds of approximation method. The first is the 'finite-section' approximation, in which (1.2) is approximated by

$$y_\beta(t) = f(t) + \frac{1}{\lambda}\int_0^\beta k(t,s)y_\beta(s)ds, \quad t \in \mathbb{R}^+, \tag{1.4}$$

where β, the 'cut-off' parameter, is a positive number. The second is a class of projection methods, with particular emphasis on collocation methods.

A natural setting for our study of (1.4) is X^+, the Banach space of bounded, continuous functions on $\mathbb{R}^+$ with the uniform norm. In this space the integral operator K, defined by

$$Kg(t) = \int_0^\infty k(t,s)g(s)ds, \quad t \in \mathbb{R}^+,$$

is a bounded operator, with norm

$$||K|| = \sup_t \int_0^\infty |k(t,s)|ds, \tag{1.5}$$

but is not in general a compact operator; whereas the finite-section operator

$$K_\beta g(t) = \int_0^\beta k(t,s)g(s)ds$$

is a compact operator (see [1,5]) under the conditions given in Section 2.

At first sight it may not be clear that there is any useful sense in which y_β approximates y, since simple examples (see [2]) made it clear that uniform convergence of y_β to y is generally not possible if y does not vanish at infinity. However, in a recent paper Anselone and Sloan [1], extending earlier results of Atkinson [2], have shown, under appropriate conditions, that as $\beta \to \infty, y_\beta(s)$ does converge pointwise to y(s), and even converges uniformly on arbitrary finite intervals. The result is stated as Theorem 1(ii) in the next section, the only assumption being that λ is not in $\sigma(K)$, the spectrum of K in the space X^+.

The main result proved in [1], from which the stated convergence result follows, is that for $\lambda \notin \sigma(K)$ the approximate inverse $(I - \lambda^{-1}K_\beta)^{-1}$ exists and is uniformly bounded as an operator in X^+ for all β sufficiently large. (Here I is the identity operator.) Thus in some sense the approximate spectrum is close to the exact spectrum for β sufficiently large. The result, which is stated as Theorem 1(i) in the next section, is trivial for $|\lambda| > \|K\|$, but much less so for $|\lambda| \leq \|K\|$.

The proof of Theorem 1 is sketched briefly in Section 2. An interesting aspect is that the proof is non-constructive, being based on repeated applications of the Arzelà-Ascoli theorem. Thus nothing is proved in [1] about the magnitude of the uniform bound on the approximate inverses, or on the rate of convergence of $y_\beta(s)$ to $y(s)$.

Many practical problems have an important simplifying feature, namely that the inhomogeneous term f in (1.2), and hence also the solution y, has a limit at infinity. The importance is firstly that, as shown in [6], the value of $y(\infty)$ can easily be obtained explicitly (see Section 3); and secondly that the existence of the limit at infinity can be exploited in numerical methods. In Section 4 we review briefly a recent study [6] of projection methods for (1.2), in which the approximating functions (e.g. piecewise-constant functions) have limits at ∞.

The connection between the two parts of this paper is that the existence and uniform boundedness of the finite-section inverses provide the theoretical foundation for the study of projection methods.

In Section 5 numerical results are given for a collocation method which is a particular example of the projection method introduced in Section 4.

Finally, in Section 6 we discuss some of the special features of numerical methods for (1.2), when compared with methods for integral equations of the second kind over finite intervals.

2. Finite-section Approximation

The kernel $\ell(t,s)$ in (1.3) is assumed to satisfy

$$\sup_t \int_0^\infty |\ell(t,s)|ds < \infty ,$$

$$\int_0^\infty |\ell(t',s) - \ell(t,s)|ds \to 0 \quad \text{as } t' \to t ,$$

$$\int_0^\infty |\ell(t',s) - \ell(t,s)|ds \to 0 \quad \text{as } t',t \to \infty ,$$

under which assumptions $\ell(t,s)$ is the kernel of a compact operator in X^+ (see [5]).

Then the following theorem holds.

Theorem 1 [1] Assume $\lambda \notin \sigma(K)$.
(i) For β sufficiently large $(I - \lambda^{-1}K_\beta)^{-1}$ exists and is uniformly bounded as an operator in X^+.
(ii) Assume also that $f \in X^+$, so that (1.2) has a unique solution $y \in X^+$. Then for β sufficiently large (1.4) has a unique solution $y_\beta \in X^+$, and

$$\lim_{\beta\to\infty} y_\beta(s) = y(s) ,$$

uniformly for s in any finite interval.

The full proof is given in [1]. The arguments there are inspired by, and make use of, an earlier result of Atkinson [2], who showed that part (ii) of the theorem follows if the existence and uniform boundedness of $(I - \lambda^{-1}K_\beta)^{-1}$ is assumed for large β. It may be instructive to sketch Atkinson's argument. Since $y_\beta = (I - \lambda^{-1}K_\beta)^{-1}f$, it follows from the uniform boundedness assumption that $\{y_\beta : \beta \geq \beta_0\}$ is bounded for some $\beta_0 > 0$, from which it follows (see [1,2]) that the set $\{K_\beta y_\beta : \beta \geq \beta_0\}$ is bounded and uniformly equicontinuous on finite intervals. In turn, since $y_\beta = f + \lambda^{-1}K_\beta y_\beta$ it follows that $\{y_\beta : \beta \geq \beta_0\}$ is bounded and uniformly equicontinuous on finite intervals. Then a simple extension (see [1,2]) of the Arzelà-Ascoli theorem implies that there exists a sequence $\{\beta_i\}$ and a $y^* \in X^+$ such that $y_{\beta_i}(s) \to y^*(s)$, uniformly on finite intervals. It follows in turn (see [1]) that $K_{\beta_i} y_{\beta_i}(s) \to Ky^*(s)$ uniformly on finite intervals, so that by taking pointwise limits in the finite-section equation we obtain $y^* = f + \lambda^{-1}Ky^*$. Thus y^* is y, the unique solution of (1.2), and $y_{\beta_i}(s) \to y(s)$ uniformly on finite intervals. It only remains to show that the limit holds as $\beta \to \infty$ through all real numbers, not just through a particular subsequence $\{\beta_i\}$. This follows easily (see [1]) from the fact that, by the same argument as above, every subsequence of $\{y_\beta\}$ has a subsequence that converges to y uniformly on finite intervals.

Similar arguments are used in [1] to prove part (i) of Theorem 1, with the additional feature that a 'sliding' variant of the Arzelà-Ascoli argument is employed - i.e. the Arzelà-Ascoli theorem is applied after a suitable translation of individual members of a family of functions. The argument proceeds by making the contrary assumption, namely that the inverses $(I - \lambda^{-1}K_\beta)^{-1}$ either do not exist or are not uniformly bounded, and proves that under this assumption λ is an eigenvalue of at least one of the following equations, in the spaces X^+, X^- and X of bounded continuous functions on $\mathbb{R}^+$, $\mathbb{R}^-$ and $\mathbb{R}$ respectively:

$$\int_0^\infty k(t,s)z(s)ds = \lambda z(t), \qquad t \in \mathbb{R}^+,$$

$$\int_{-\infty}^0 \kappa(t-s)z(s)ds = \lambda z(t), \qquad t \in \mathbb{R}^-,$$

$$\int_{-\infty}^\infty \kappa(t-s)z(s)ds = \lambda z(t), \qquad t \in \mathbb{R}.$$

Since it is known from the classical Wiener-Hopf theory (see [1,4]) that $\lambda \in \sigma(K)$ if and only if λ is an eigenvalue of at least one of those equations, a contradiction is obtained, and the argument is complete.

An interesting byproduct of the arguments in [1] is a non-standard proof of part of the classical result on the spectrum mentioned above: it is shown in [1], by arguments similar to those indicated above, that $\sigma(K)$ is contained in the union of 0 and the eigenvalues of the three equations in the preceding paragraph.

3. The Value at Infinity

If f, the inhomogeneous term in (1.2), has a limit at ∞ then a more appropriate space within which to set the analysis may be C_ℓ^+, the space of bounded continuous functions with a limit at ∞. Equipped with the uniform norm, it is again a Banach space.

From now on it will be convenient to replace the third condition on $\ell(t,s)$ in Section 2 by the more stringent condition

$$\int_0^\infty |\ell(t,s)|ds \to 0 \qquad \text{as } t \to \infty .$$

The condition seems to be satisfied in most practical problems.

Under this condition the spectrum of K in the space C_ℓ^+ is known (see [6]) to be $\sigma(K)$, i.e. to be the same as the spectrum in the space X^+. Thus for each $\lambda \notin \sigma(K)$ the equation (1.2) has, for each $f \in C_\ell^+$, a unique solution $y \in C_\ell^+$. It is then an easy matter to show, as observed in [6], that the value of y at infinity is

$$y(\infty) = \frac{1}{1 - \lambda^{-1}\chi} f(\infty), \tag{3.1}$$

where

$$\chi = \int_{-\infty}^{\infty} \kappa(u)du .$$

The denominator in (3.1) cannot vanish for $\lambda \notin \sigma(K)$, thus an explicit expression for $y(\infty)$ is always available. For a formal proof of (3.1) see [6].

4. The Projection Method

In this section we briefly describe a general theory of a projection method for equations of the form (1.2), as given in [6]. In Section 5 we illustrate this theory by the method of collocation with piecewise-constant basis elements.

In the convergence analysis described below it proves to be convenient to introduce the iterated projection solution, which enables us to set the analysis in the space C_ℓ^+ and to apply the theory described in Section 2. For convenience we set $\lambda = 1$.

For each positive integer n, let U_n be a finite dimensional space of functions within which an approximate solution, y_n, say, is to be sought. To allow the possibility of piecewise-constant approximating functions, we do not require that $U_n \subset C_\ell^+$. However, we shall assume that each function in U_n has only a finite number of discontinuities, and has a limit at infinity. For each n, let $P_n: C_\ell^+ \to U_n$ be a bounded linear operator onto U_n. Also, we shall now consider K as an operator from $C_\ell^+ + U_n$ to C_ℓ^+. This causes no difficulty, since the norm of K with this domain and range is again given by (1.5), and has the advantage of allowing us to consider KP_n as an operator on C_ℓ^+.

The projection method for (1.2) is given, in operator form, by

$$y_n = P_n f + P_n K y_n \ , \tag{4.1}$$

and the iterated projection solution, $y_n^{(1)}$ say, is defined by

$$y_n^{(1)} = f + K y_n \ . \tag{4.2}$$

It follows from (4.1) and (4.2) that

$$y_n = P_n y_n^{(1)} \ , \tag{4.3}$$

and, hence, that $y_n^{(1)}$ satisfies

$$y_n^{(1)} = f + KP_n y_n^{(1)} \ . \tag{4.4}$$

It is well known that the solutions of (4.1) and (4.4) are in one-to-one correspondence via the connecting equations (4.2) and (4.3). However, equation (4.4) has several advantages over (4.1). First, since KP_n can be regarded as an operator on C_ℓ^+, the equation (4.4) can be analysed in C_ℓ^+, and hence the results in Section 2, which are firmly rooted in a continuous function setting, are applicable. Second, as in the finite-interval case, there is the possibility that $y_n^{(1)}$ may converge faster than y_n for large n. Finally, the theoretical results are simpler and more powerful than any that have so far been obtained by a direct study of (4.1).

Now, provided $(I - KP_n)^{-1}$ exists, $y_n^{(1)}$ exists and is unique in C_ℓ^+, and the following error analysis is then standard:

$$\begin{aligned} y - y_n^{(1)} &= (I - K)^{-1}f - (I - KP_n)^{-1}f \\ &= (I - KP_n)^{-1}(K - KP_n)y , \end{aligned}$$

and so

$$\|y - y_n^{(1)}\| \leqslant \|(I - KP_n)^{-1}\| \; \|K(I - P_n)y\|. \tag{4.5}$$

Since $y_n^{(1)}$ exists and is unique, equation (4.1) has a unique solution $y_n = P_n y_n^{(1)} \in U_n$. Now

$$y - y_n = y - P_n y + P_n y - P_n y_n^{(1)} ,$$

and so

$$\begin{aligned} \|y - y_n\| &\leqslant \|y - P_n y\| + \|P_n\| \; \|y - y_n^{(1)}\| \\ &\leqslant (1 + \|P_n\| \; \|K\| \; \|(I - KP_n)^{-1}\|) \; \|y - P_n y\|. \end{aligned} \tag{4.6}$$

The above analysis raises the following questions:

(a) Does $(I - KP_n)^{-1}$ exist in C_ℓ^+ and is it bounded independently of n?

(b) Can we ensure that $\|y - P_n y\|$ will converge to zero reasonably rapidly?

(c) Is it possible to exploit the form of the error bound (4.5) by choosing P_n in such a way that $y_n^{(1)}$ converges faster than y_n?

We shall consider (a) in the remainder of this section and shall return to (b) and (c) in Section 5.

Clearly, if $\|K\| < 1$ and $\|P_n\| = 1$ then $\|(I - KP_n)^{-1}\| \leqslant (1 - \|K\|)^{-1}$, and question (a) is answered immediately. The mathematically interesting case is $\|K\| \geqslant 1$, and this is where we require the results of Section 2, applied to the finite-section operator $K_n = K_{t_n}$ defined by

$$K_n g(t) = \int_0^{t_n} k(t,s)g(s)ds, \qquad g \in C_\ell^+ + U_n . \tag{4.7}$$

We shall also assume that

$$\lim_{n\to\infty} t_n = \infty . \tag{4.8}$$

It is now necessary to restrict P_n so that it has the property of yielding the correct value at infinity i.e.,

$$\lim_{t\to\infty} P_n g(t) = g(\infty) , \qquad g \in C_\ell^+ . \tag{4.9}$$

It then follows, by the argument used to prove (3.1), that y_n and $y_n^{(1)}$ have the correct limits at ∞. Also, it is convenient to introduce a linear operator $\Pi: C_\ell^+ + U_n \to C_\ell^+$ defined by

$$\Pi g(t) = g(\infty) , \qquad t \in \mathbb{R}^+, \quad g \in C_\ell^+ + U_n . \tag{4.10}$$

Clearly, (4.9) is equivalent to

$$\Pi P_n g = \Pi g , \qquad g \in C_\ell^+ .$$

We can now state a theorem which answers question (a) above.

Theorem 2 [6] (i) Assume that $1 \notin \sigma(K)$ and that (4.8) and (4.9) hold. Assume also that the operators $K_n P_n$ are uniformly bounded in C_ℓ^+, and that

$$\lim_{n\to\infty} \| K_n(I - P_n)K_n P_n \| = 0 . \tag{4.11}$$

Then for n sufficiently large $(I - K_n P_n)^{-1}$ exists as an operator on C_ℓ^+ and is bounded uniformly in n.

(ii) Assume also that

$$\lim_{n\to\infty} \| (K - K_n)(P_n - \Pi) \| = 0 , \tag{4.12}$$

where the operator norm is understood to be taken in the space C_ℓ^+.

Then for n sufficiently large $(I - KP_n)^{-1}$ exists as an operator on C_ℓ^+ and is bounded uniformly in n.

Proof We merely outline the steps in the proof. The details are given in [6].

(i) The first step is to show that Theorem 1(i) on the uniform boundedness of $(I - K_n)^{-1}$ holds in C_ℓ^+ as well as in X^+. Next, the inverse of $(I - K_nP_n)$ in C_ℓ^+ is calculated as

$$(I - K_nP_n)^{-1} = [I + (I - K_n)^{-1}K_n(I - P_n)K_nP_n]^{-1}[I + (I - K_n)^{-1}K_nP_n],$$

which, for large enough n exists and is uniformly bounded under the assumptions on K_nP_n and (4.11).

(ii) If n is large enough that $(I - K_nP_n)^{-1}$ exists and

$$\|(K - K_n)(P_n - \Pi)\| < \|(I - K_nP_n)^{-1}\|^{-1}$$

then

$$B_n := [I - (I - K_nP_n)^{-1}(K - K_n)(P_n - \Pi)]^{-1} \tag{4.13}$$

exists as a bounded operator on C_ℓ^+. It may then be verified that

$$(I - KP_n)^{-1} = \frac{1}{1 - \chi}\Pi + B_n(I - K_nP_n)^{-1}(I - \Pi)(I + \frac{1}{1 - \chi} KP_n\Pi), \tag{4.14}$$

where the operator on the right hand side of this expression is uniformly bounded. The motivation behind the representation (4.14) is given in [6].

5. Piecewise-constant Collocation

The aim of this section is to apply the convergence theory given in Section 4 to a piecewise-constant collocation method, similar to one used by Finn and Jefferies [3]. In particular, we consider an example and give theoretical and numerical results.

First we define the method. Let U_n be the space of piecewise-constant functions over $[0,\infty)$, with possible discontinuities at the breakpoints $t_2^{(n)}, \ldots, t_n^{(n)}$, where

$$0 = t_1^{(n)} < t_2^{(n)} < \ldots < t_n^{(n)} < t_{n+1}^{(n)} = \infty . \qquad (5.1)$$

For convenience we shall omit the superscript n from now on. To avoid ambiguity at the breakpoints we assume that the elements of U_n are right-continuous at t_i. In each subinterval $[t_i, t_{i+1})$, $i = 1,\ldots,n-1$, we choose a collocation point τ_i, and in $[t_n, \infty)$ we take $\tau_n = \infty$. Thus if

$$u_i(t) = \begin{cases} 1, & t_i \leqslant t < t_{i+1} , \\ 0, & \text{otherwise}, \end{cases}$$

then for $g \in C_\ell^+$

$$P_n g(t) = \sum_{i=1}^{n-1} g(\tau_i) u_i(t) + g(\infty) u_n(t). \qquad (5.2)$$

It is easy to see that $\|P_n\| = 1$ and that (4.9) holds. It follows, as mentioned in Section 4, that the projection solution y_n has the correct value at infinity, namely $y_n(\infty) = (1-\chi)^{-1} f(\infty)$. In practice we may represent y_n as

$$y_n(t) = \sum_{i=1}^{n-1} y_n(\tau_i) u_i(t) + y_n(\infty) u_n(t),$$

with the unknown coefficients being found from the system

$$\sum_{i=1}^{n-1} [\delta_{ji} - Ku_i(\tau_j)] y_n(\tau_i) = f(\tau_j) + y_n(\infty) Ku_n(\tau_j), \qquad j = 1,\ldots,n-1.$$

We note that if $\|K\| < 1$ then there is no need to choose τ_n at infinity, since the uniform boundedness of $(I - KP_n)^{-1}$ is immediate, and other choices for τ_n are possible [3,6]. However, in this paper we consider only the choice which leads to (5.1).

We turn now to the questions (b) and (c) which were suggested by the error analysis in Section 4. In any practical application we have to choose the breakpoints t_i, $i = 1,\dots,n$ and the collocation points τ_i, $i = 1,\dots,n-1$. The error bound (4.6) suggests that we might try to minimise $\|y - P_n y\|$. An alternative strategy suggested by the bound on $\|y - y_n^{(1)}\|$ given by (4.5) is to minimise $\|K(I - P_n)y\|$. This might be a better choice, since in the finite-interval case $y_n^{(1)}$ would be the product-integration solution, which in some circumstances is known to show a superior convergence rate when compared to the collocation solution.

For the semi-infinite interval case considered here one needs some prior knowledge of the exact solution y, which may not be easily obtainable in practice. To illustrate the possibilities if the form of the solution is known, we consider an equation for which the exact solution is known analytically: the equation is

$$y(t) = (1 - \tfrac{1}{\lambda}) + \frac{1}{2\lambda}\int_0^\infty e^{-|t-s|}y(s)ds, \tag{5.3a}$$

and the exact solution, for $\lambda \notin [0,1]$, is (cf.[2])

$$y(t) = 1 - (1 - \mu)\, e^{-\mu t}, \qquad \mu = \left(\frac{\lambda-1}{\lambda}\right)^{\frac{1}{2}} > 0\,. \tag{5.3b}$$

The value at infinity, from (3.1), is $y(\infty) = 1$, and the norm of the operator in (5.2) is $\|K\| = |\lambda|^{-1}$.

If we assume that we know only that the solution is a smooth function of $e^{-\mu t}$, then it is natural to choose the t_i to be equally spaced with respect to $T = e^{-\mu t}$, i.e.

$$t_i = \frac{1}{\mu}\log\left(\frac{n}{n - i + 1}\right), \quad i = 1,\dots,n, \tag{5.4}$$

and the τ_i to be the midpoints with respect to T, i.e.

$$\tau_i = \frac{1}{\mu}\log\left(\frac{n}{n - i + \frac{1}{2}}\right), \quad i = 1,\dots,n-1. \tag{5.5}$$

Table I Numerical results for equation (5.3) with $\lambda = \frac{4}{3}$ and with t_i and τ_i given by (5.4) and (5.5) respectively.

n	$\|y - y_n\|$	$\|y - y_n^{(1)}\|$	$\max_i \|y(\tau_i) - y_n(\tau_i)\|$
2	.250	.826 E - 1	.389 E - 1
4	.125	.415 E - 1	.193 E - 1
8	.622 E - 1	.207 E - 1	.963 E - 2
16	.310 E - 1	.104 E - 1	.481 E - 2
32	.155 E - 1	.518 E - 2	.241 E - 2

Numerical results for this choice for example (5.3) with $\lambda = \frac{4}{3}$ are given in Table I. The expected $O(n^{-1})$ convergence rate for $\|y - y_n\|$ is observed. The same rate is also observed for $\|y - y_n^{(1)}\|$ and for $\max|y(\tau_i) - y_n(\tau_i)|$. Clearly, for this choice of the t_i, $y_n^{(1)}$ exhibits little improvement in accuracy over y_n. The reasons for this, discussed in detail in [6], are roughly speaking as follows: the smoothing effect of K in the $\|K(I - P_n)y\|$ factor in (4.5) is most effective near 0, where $t_{i+1} - t_i$ is smallest, and becomes less effective as the width of the intervals $[t_i, t_{i+1})$ increases. In order to balance these effects one must push the breakpoints t_i further out towards infinity. A good choice turns out to be

$$t_i = \frac{2}{\mu} \log\left(\frac{n}{n - i + 1}\right), \quad i = 1,\ldots,n, \tag{5.6}$$

with the collocation points chosen as

$$\tau_i = \frac{2}{\mu} \log\left(\frac{n}{n - i + \frac{1}{2}}\right), \quad i = 1,\ldots,n-1. \tag{5.7}$$

Table II Numerical results for equation (5.3) with $\lambda = \frac{4}{3}$ and with t_i and τ_i given by (5.6) and (5.7) respectively.

n	$\|y - y_n\|$	$\|y - y_n^{(1)}\|$	$\max_i \|y(\tau_i) - y_n(\tau_i)\|$
2	.232	.345 E - 1	.132 E - 1
4	.122	.816 E - 2	.446 E - 2
8	.620 E - 1	.200 E - 2	.149 E - 2
16	.312 E - 1	.528 E - 3	.428 E - 3
32	.156 E - 1	.136 E - 3	.114 E - 3

Numerical results for this choice are given in Table II. The rate of convergence of $\|y - y_n^{(1)}\|$, and of $\max|y(\tau_i) - y_n(\tau_i)|$, is now observed to be $O(n^{-2})$. This improvement is predicted by the following lemma, which is proved in [6].

<u>Lemma 1</u> Consider the example (5.3). Define Y by $Y(T) = y(t)$, $t \geq 0$, with $T = e^{-\mu t}$, and assume $Y \in C^2[0,1]$. With the choice of t_i and τ_i given by (5.6) and (5.7) we have

$$\|K(I - P_n)y\| \leq A\, n^{-2},$$

where A depends only on μ and the (uniform) norms $\|Y'\|$ and $\|Y''\|$.

We now seek to apply Theorem 2 in Section 4 to this method, with t_n in (4.7) chosen to be the last breakpoint $t_n^{(n)}$. The first task is to check the conditions (4.11) and (4.12). With P_n given by (5.2), we have immediately

$$(P_n - \Pi)g(t) = 0 \quad \text{for} \quad t \geq t_n ,$$

and hence (4.12) holds trivially. The condition (4.11) can be shown to hold (see [6]) if

$$\max_{1 \leq i \leq n-1} |t_{i+1} - t_i| \to 0 \qquad \text{as } n \to \infty . \tag{5.8}$$

Now for the choice (5.6) condition (5.8) does not hold. However, the choice (5.6) is a good one for minimising $\|K(I - P_n)y\|$, where K is the integral operator corresponding to example (5.3), even when $\|K\| > 1$. This is seen from the numerical results given in Table III, which correspond to the case $\lambda = -\frac{1}{3}$, and hence $\|K\| = 3$, and which show the same good convergence rates as observed in Table II for the case of $\|K\| < 1$. In [6] it is shown that (5.8) is a sufficient condition for the uniform boundedness of $(I - KP_n)^{-1}$, but this may not be a necessary condition, and, indeed, no numerical instability is evident for this choice of t_i for the $\|K\| > 1$ example. This highlights a possible conflict between choosing the t_i to ensure the stability of $(I - KP_n)^{-1}$, which is independent of y, and choosing the t_i to minimise $\|K(I - P_n)y\|$, which depends crucially on the behaviour of y as $t \to \infty$. This conflict is in contrast to the finite-interval case, where a condition like (5.8) appears naturally in both stability and convergence results. However, we remark that a choice for t_i which does satisfy (5.8), and which produces satisfactory, if not optimal, convergence results, is given in [6].

Table III Numerical results for equation (5.3) with $\lambda = -\frac{1}{3}$ and with t_i and τ_i given by (5.6) and (5.7) respectively.

n	$\|y - y_n\|$	$\|y - y_n^{(1)}\|$	$\max_i \|y(\tau_i) - y_n(\tau_i)\|$
2	.400	.900 E - 1	.375 E - 1
4	.228	.208 E - 1	.634 E - 2
8	.119	.510 E - 2	.167 E - 2
16	.611 E - 1	.127 E - 2	.448 E - 3
32	.309 E - 1	.317 E - 3	.117 E - 3

6. Discussion

It seems appropriate to mention briefly some of the special features of numerical methods for (1.2) which distinguish the half-line integral equation with kernel given by (1.3) from the finite-interval type.

First, the noncompactness of the integral operator in (1.2) means that standard finite-interval error analysis, say involving a degenerate-kernel approximation, is not applicable. Thus, when $\|K\| \geq 1$, the proof of the uniform boundedness of the approximate inverses, necessary for ensuring stability of the numerical approximations, is much more complicated.

Second, to achieve a satisfactory rate of convergence we must have some information as to the behaviour of the solution $y(t)$ as $t \to \infty$. If this information is available then it may be possible to choose P_n such that $\|(I - P_n)y\|$ converges reasonably quickly, and hence so does $\|y - y_n\|$. The third difference is that, for reasons indicated in Section 5, this choice for P_n may not be the best for minimising $\|K(I - P_n)y\|$, and so possibly obtaining superconvergence of the iterated approximation $y_n^{(1)}$. The fourth difference is that it appears to be more difficult to determine the important information about the behaviour of $y(t)$ than it is in the finite-interval case.

Finally, we see in the example in Section 5 a conflict arising between the stability and convergence criteria in the case of piecewise-constant collocation: the sufficient condition for stability is that the maximum length of a sub-interval $[t_i, t_{i+1}]$, for $i = 1,..,n-1$, should converge to zero, and this may seem little enough to ask; and yet we have seen that the best partition for ensuring fast convergence of either y_n or $y_n^{(1)}$ may not have this property. Clearly, further work is needed.

7. Acknowledgement

I.H. Sloan acknowledges the support of the U.K. Science and Engineering Research Council.

8. References

[1] Anselone, P.M. and Sloan, I.H. (1983) Integral equations on the half-line, J. Integral Equations (to appear).

[2] Atkinson, K.E. (1969) The numerical solution of integral equations on the half-line, SIAM J. Numer. Anal. 6, 375-397.

[3] Finn, G.D. and Jefferies, J.T. (1968) Studies in spectral line formation. I. Formulation and simple applications, J. Quant. Spectrosc. Radiat. Transfer, 8, 1675-1703.

[4] Krein, M.G. (1963) Integral equations on a half-line with kernel depending on the difference of the arguments, Amer. Math. Soc. Transl. (2), 22 163-288.

[5] Sloan, I.H. (1981) Quadrature methods for integral equations of the second kind over infinite intervals, Maths. Comput., 36, 511-523.

[6] Sloan, I.H. and Spence, A. (1984) Projection methods for integral equations on the half-line (submitted).

Dr I.H. Sloan,
Department of Applied Mathematics,
University of New South Wales,
Sydney,
NSW 2033,
AUSTRALIA

Dr A. Spence,
School of Mathematics,
University of Bath,
Claverton Down,
Bath, BA2 7AY.
U.K.

International Series of
Numerical Mathematics, Vol. 73
© 1985 Birkhäuser Verlag Basel

STABILITY RESULTS FOR ABEL EQUATION

Sergio Vessella

1.   We study some stability question for the Abel equation

(1.1) $$\frac{1}{\Gamma(\alpha)} \int_0^x \frac{K(x,t)u(t)}{(x-t)^{1-\alpha}} \, dt = f(x) \qquad (0 \le x \le 1)$$

Here $0 < \alpha < 1$, f and K are given, u is the unkown.
We assume trought

(1.2) $K, \dfrac{\partial K}{\partial t} \in C^\circ(T)$, where $T = \{(x,t) \in R^2 : 0 \le t \le x \le 1\}$,

(1.3) $K(x,x) = 1$ for $x \in [0,1]$.

2.   For the equation (1.1) there is not a continuous dependence of the
solution u from the data f in L^p- spaces. The reasons of this instability
phenomenon are in the regularizing properties of the operator A_α defined
by :

(2.1) $$(A_\alpha u)(x) = \frac{1}{\Gamma(\alpha)} \int_0^x \frac{K(x,t)u(t)}{(x-t)^{1-\alpha}} \, dt \qquad (0 \le x \le 1) .$$

For example it can be shown that the operator (3.1) is a compact operator from $L^p(0,1)$ for $1 \leq p \leq +\infty$ (see [12]). Other regularizing properties of A_α can be derived from [8] .

Before giving an example that illustrates the instability we recall that if $K=1$ on T the equation (1.1) becomes

$$J^\alpha u(x) = \frac{1}{\Gamma(\alpha)} \int_0^x \frac{u(t)dt}{(x-t)^{1-\alpha}} = f(x) \qquad (0 \leq x \leq 1) \tag{2.2}$$

and the solution u is given by the formula

$$u(x) = f^\alpha(x) = \frac{1}{\Gamma(1-\alpha)} \frac{d}{dx} \int_0^x \frac{f(t)dt}{(x-t)^\alpha} .$$

See for instance [13] .

Let $K \equiv 1$ and

$$f_n(x) = \frac{\sin \pi n x}{(\pi n)^\alpha} . \tag{2.3}$$

We obtain

$$u_n(x) = \frac{1}{\Gamma(1-\alpha)} \int_0^{\pi n x} \frac{\cos(\pi n x-\xi)}{\xi^\alpha} d\xi$$

and

$$\| f_n \|_{L^\infty(0,1)} \to 0 \quad \text{for} \quad n \to \infty ,$$

$$\| u_n \|_{L^1(0,1)} \geq \frac{2}{\pi} \quad \text{for every } n.$$

It follows that the operator A_α^{-1} is not a continuous operator from $L^p(0,1)$ to $L^q(0,1)$ for $1 \leq p \leq +\infty$ and $1 \leq q \leq +\infty$.

In the next theorem we prove some estimates which show the stability of solutions to equation (1.1) . We use Sobolev spaces of fractional order $H^{\theta,p}(0,1)$, defined by (see [2, ch.VII])

$$H^{\theta,p}(0,1) = \{u \in L^p(0,1) : \int_0^1 \int_0^1 \frac{|u(x)-u(t)|^p}{|x-t|^{1+p\theta}} dxdt < +\infty \} ,$$

for $0 < \theta < 1$, $1 \leq p < +\infty$. $H^{\theta,p}(0,1)$ is a Banach space under the norm :

$$\| u \|_{\theta,p} = \| u \|_p + | u |_{\theta,p} ,$$

where

$$| u |_{\theta,p} = \left(\int_0^1 \int_0^1 \frac{|u(x)-u(t)|^p}{|x-t|^{1+p\theta}} \, dxdt \right)^{1/p}$$

<u>Theorem 2.1</u> *Suppose* K *satisfies* (1.2) , (1.3) *and* $p \in [1,+\infty]$. *Let* u *the* $L^p(0,1)$ *- solution of* (1.1). *If* u *is known to be absolutely continuous with a p-integrable derivative, we have the following estimate :*

$$\| u \|_p \le C_1(\alpha,p,M) \; \{ \; \| u' \|_p^{\frac{\alpha}{1+\alpha}} + \| A_\alpha u \|_p^{\frac{\alpha}{1+\alpha}} \} \; \| A_\alpha u \|_p^{\frac{1}{1+\alpha}} \quad , \tag{2.4}$$

where $C_1(\alpha,p,M)$ *is a computable constant that depends on* α,p *and* $M = \sup_T |\frac{\partial K}{\partial t}|$ *only.*

If u *is known to lie in* $H^{\theta,p}(0,1)$ *for* $0 < \theta < 1, 1 \le p < +\infty$ *we have :*

$$\| u \|_p \le C_2(\alpha,p,\theta,M) \; \{ \; | u |_{\theta,p}^{\frac{\alpha}{\theta+\alpha}} + \| A_\alpha u \|_p^{\frac{\alpha}{\theta+\alpha}} \} \; \| A_\alpha u \|_p^{\frac{\theta}{\theta+\alpha}} \quad , \tag{2.5}$$

where $C_2(\alpha,p,\theta,M)$ *is a computable constant that depends on* α,p,θ *and* M *only.*

<u>Proof</u>. Before we observe that

$$A_\alpha = (I + B_\alpha) J^\alpha \quad \text{in} \quad L^p(0,1) \tag{2.6}$$

where I is the identity operator in $L^p(0,1)$; J^α is defined by (2.2) and B_α is defined by

$$B_\alpha v(x) = - \frac{\sin \pi\alpha}{\pi} \int_0^x \{ v(\xi) \int_\xi^x \frac{\partial}{\partial t} \left(\frac{H(x,t)}{(x-t)^{1-\alpha}} \right) \frac{dt}{(t-\xi)^\alpha} \} \, d\xi$$

where $H(x,t) = K(x,t) - K(x,x)$

For every $v \in L^p(0,1)$ we have

$$(2.7) \qquad \| v \|_{L^p(0,1)} \leq C(M,p) \, \| (I + B_\alpha) v \|_{L^p(0,1)}$$

where

$$(2.7a) \qquad C(M,p) = \sum_{n=0}^{\infty} (2M)^n \, \frac{\Gamma(p)}{\Gamma(p+n)}{}^{1/p}$$

By (2.6) and (2.7) we obtain

$$(2.8) \qquad \left\| J^\alpha u \right\|_{L^p(0,1)} \leq C(M,p) \left\| A_\alpha u \right\|_{L^p(0,1)}$$

Therefore if we prove the theorem for $K \equiv 1$, we can easily prove the theorem in the general case using (2.8).

If $K \equiv 1$ on T the equation (1.1) becomes

$$(2.9) \qquad \frac{1}{\Gamma(\alpha)} \int_0^x \frac{u(t)dt}{(x-t)^{1-\alpha}} = f(x) \qquad (0 \leq x \leq 1)$$

Equation (2.9) is equivalent to the following

$$(2.10) \qquad \int_0^x u(t)dt = f_{1-\alpha}(x) \qquad (0 \leq x \leq 1) \, ,$$

where $$f_{1-\alpha}(x) = \frac{1}{\Gamma(1-\alpha)} \int_0^x (x-t)^{-\alpha} f(t)dt \, ,$$

Let $0 < h \leq \frac{1}{2}$ and

$$(2.11) \qquad u_h(x) = \frac{1}{h} \int_0^{x+h} u(t)dt \qquad (0 \leq x \leq 1 - h)$$

we have

$$(2.12) \qquad u_h(x) = \frac{f_{1-\alpha}(x+h) - f_{1-\alpha}(x)}{h}$$

At this point we observe that

$$\frac{f_{1-\alpha}(x-h) - f_{1-\alpha}(x)}{h} = \frac{1}{h\Gamma(1-\alpha)} \int_x^{x+h} (x+h-t)^{-\alpha} f(t)dt - \int_0^x [(x+h-t)^{-\alpha} - (x-t)^{-\alpha}] f(t)dt$$

Young's inequality for convolutions (see [9]) gives :

$$(2.13)\qquad \left\| \frac{f_{1-\alpha}(x+h)-f_{1-\alpha}(x)}{h} \right\|_{L^p(0,1-h)} \le \frac{2h^{-\alpha}}{\Gamma(2-\alpha)} \| f \|_{L^p(0,1)}$$

From lemma 1.A (see appendix) we have

$$(2.14i)\qquad \| u - u_h \|_{L^p(0,1-h)} \le \frac{h}{2} \| u' \|_{L^p(0,1)} ,$$

$$(2.14ii)\qquad \| u \|_{L^p(1-h,1)} \le 2h \| u' \|_{L^p(0,1)} + \| u \|_{L^p(0,1-h)}$$

Furthermore by (2.12) and (2.13) we have

$$(2.15)\qquad \| u_h \|_{L^p(0,1-h)} \le \frac{2h^{-\alpha}}{\Gamma(2-\alpha)} \| f \|_{L^p(0,1)}$$

and by using (2.14i-ii) and (2.15) we have :

$$(2.16)\qquad \| u \|_{L^p(0,1)} \le h \| u' \|_{L^p(0,1)} + \frac{h^{-\alpha}}{\Gamma(2-\alpha)} \| f \|_{L^p(0,1)} .$$

Minimizing the function

$$h \to h \| u' \|_{L^p(0,1)} + \frac{h^{-\alpha}}{\Gamma(2-\alpha)} \| f \|_{L^p(0,1)}$$

in $(0,{}^1/_2]$ and using the inequality (2.8) we have the estimate (2.4).

The estimate (2.5) can be found in an analogous way by using the lemma (2.A).

Remark 2.1. *If replacing the hypothesis* (1.2) *by assuming the following one :*

$$(2.17)\qquad K, \frac{\partial K}{\partial x} \in C^\circ(T)$$

the estimates (2.4) *and* (2.5) *are still valid with different constant* C_1 *and* C_2 *that depend on* α,θ,p *and* $\sup_T |\frac{\partial K}{\partial x}|$ *only.*

Appendix

Lemma A.1 . *Let* $0 < h \le \frac{1}{2}$ *and*

(A.1) $$u_h(x) = \frac{1}{h}\int_x^{x+h} u(t)dt \qquad (0 \le x \le 1-h) \quad .$$

We have the following estimates.

(A.2) $$\| u - u_h \|_{L^p(0,1-h)} \le \frac{h}{2} \| u' \|_{L^p(0,1)} \quad ,$$

(A.3) $$\| u \|_{L^p(1-h,1)} \le 2h \| u' \|_{L^p(0,1)} + \| u \|_{L^p(0,1-h)} \quad ,$$

Lemma A.2. *Let* u_h *defined by (A.1). For* $0 < \theta < 1$, $1 \le p << +\infty$ *we have the following estimates :*

(A.4) $$\| u-u_h \|_{L^p(0,1-h)} \le h^\theta |u|_{\theta,p} \; \textit{for} \; 0 < h \le \frac{1}{2} \quad ,$$

(A.5) $$\| u \|_{L^p(1-h,1)} \le 2|u|_{\theta,p} h^\theta + \| u \|_{L^p(0,1-h)} \; \textit{for} \; 0 < h \le \frac{1}{2} \quad ,$$

The proofs of Lemma A.1 and Lemma A.2 can be found by using Hölder inequality and Young inequality for convolutions.

References

[1] N.H. Abel, "Resolution d'un problème de mecanique". *Oeuvres, vol. 1 Christiania (1881), 97 - 101.*

[2] R.A. Adams, *Sobolev spaces.* (Academic Press, New York, 1975).

[3] N.Yu.Bakaev - R.P. Tarasov, "Semigroups and a method for stability solving the Abel equation". *Siberian Math.J. 19 (1978)n.1, 1-5.*

[4] A.L.Bugheim, *Volterra equations and inverse problems.* (in russian).(Nauka Publishing Company, Siberian Branch, Novosibirsk 1983).

[5] J. Dieudonné, *Calcul infinitesimal.* (Hermann, Paris, 1968).

[6] J. Garmany, "On the inversion of travel times". *Geophys. Res. Lett. 6, (4), (1979), 277-279.*

[7] J. Garmany-J.A. Orcutt-R.L. Parker, "Travel time inversion: a geometrical approach". *J. Geophys.Res. 84, (B7), (1979), 3615-3622.*

[8] G.H. Hardy-J.E. Littlewood, "Some properties of fractional integrals". *Math. Zeit., 27 (1928), 565-606*

[9] G.H.Hardy-J.E.Littlewood-G.Pòlya, *Inequalities*. (Cambridge University Press, Cambridge, 1978).

[10] G.Kowalewskii, *Integralgleichungen*. (Waltes de Graytes & Co., Berlin, 1930).

[11] M.M.Lavrent'ev-V.G. Romanov-S.P. Šišatskij, *Problemi non ben posti in Fisica Matematica e Analisi*. (Quaderno I.A.G.A.; Serie "problemi non ben posti ed inversi"; n.12, 1983).

[12] S.G.Mikhlin, *Mathematical Physiscs, an advanced course*. (North-Holland Publishing Co., Amsterdam-London, 1970).

[13] F.G. Tricomi, *Integral equations*. (Interscience Publisher, New York, 1957).

Dr. Sergio Vessella c/o I.A.G.A. (CNR)- Via S. Marta 13/A-

50139 - Firenze (Italia)

International Series of
Numerical Mathematics, Vol. 73

Problems

One evening during the conference was devoted to a joint discussion, in which several open problems were presented. Three of these problems have been formulated by the authors in written form and are given here.

Problem 1 (proposed by R. Gorenflo, Berlin):

HOW TO COMPUTE VERY ROUGH SOLUTIONS OF ABEL INTEGRAL EQUATIONS?

There is no lack of good methods for computing (very) smooth solutions of Abel integral equations. However, there are applications where the solution is a physical intensity or density or a probability density and in these instances the (numerical) analyst should be able to handle also intensities and densities with very sharp peaks or even such ones which behave like (a linear combination of) delta functions. The appropriate general model thus requires that we look for a measure instead of a function as solution.

For any real function u of bounded variation in $[0,b]$, where $b \in \mathbb{R}^+$, and $0 < \alpha < 1$, the function

$$x \to v(x) := \int_0^x (x-t)^{\alpha-1}\, du(t) \quad , \quad 0 < x \leq b \; ,$$

being in $L^1\,[0,b]$, we pose the following desideratum.

There should be worked out a theory of approximating a measure du as solution of the Abel integral equation

$$(1) \qquad \int_0^x (x-t)^{\alpha-1}\, du(t) = v(x) \;, \quad 0 < x \leq b \;,$$

for given values of a finite set of linear functionals of v. Because $v \in L^1$ these functionals cannot be point evaluations, but should be of the form $\int_0^b p(x)\, v(x)\, dx$ with suitable weight-functions p. A theory of refinement of discretization and of convergence should be worked out. Of interest is also the rapidity of convergence. Analogous theories should be worked out for the Abel equations of spectroscopy (see [1]) and of stereology (see [2]), these equations having exponent $\alpha = 1/2$ and being transformable into the classical Abel integral equation.

References:

[1] H. Hörmann: Temperaturverteilung und Elektronendichte in frei brennenden Lichtbögen. Zeitschrift für Physik 97 (1935), 539-560.

[2] S.D. Wicksell: The corpuscle problem. A mathematical study of a biometric problem. Biometrika 17 (1925), 84-99.

Problem 2 (proposed by J.T. Marti, Zürich):

Find an efficient algorithm for the numerical solution of strongly ill-posed problems in form of a Fredholm integral equation of the first kind $Kf = g$, $K : L_2(0,1) \rightarrow L_2(0,1)$,

$$Kf(s) := \int_0^1 k(s,t)f(t)dt, \quad f \in L_2(0,1), \quad 0 < s < 1 .$$

An example of such a problem is given by

$$k(s,t) = \begin{cases} s(1-t), & 0 < s \leq t < 1 , \\ t(1-s), & 0 < t < s < 1 , \end{cases}$$

$$g(s) = s - s^3 , \quad 0 < s < 1 .$$

This problem shows an extremely slow convergence when it is solved by Tikhonov's regularization method based on the functional $\| Kf - g\|^2 + \lambda \| f \|^2$ and appropriate choice of the regularization parameter λ, where $\| \ \|$ is the norm of $L_2(0,1)$.

Remark concerning the open problem presented by J.T. Marti:

The exact solution is $x_0(t) = 6t$. Since for any $z \in L^2[0,1]$, $(K^*z)(1) = 0$, $x_0 \notin R(K^*)$. Hence, one cannot expect reasonably fast convergence of Tikhonov regularization of order 0 (cf. our paper in this volume and the references [6], [8] quoted there). If one uses Tikhonov regularization of order 2 based on $\| Kf - g\|^2 + \alpha \| f'' \|^2$, then one can expect faster convergence, since the smoothness condition quoted as (3.8) in our paper is fulfilled. This assertion is supported by our Example 1 and much more by Example 1b of [19] .

Heinz W. Engl and Andreas Neubauer, Linz

Problem 3 (proposed by H.J.J. te Riele, Amsterdam)

Consider the weakly singular second kind Volterra integral equation

$$(1) \qquad y(t) = g(t) + \int_0^t K(t,s)(t-s)^{-1/2} y(s)ds, \; t \in [0,T] ,$$

and suppose that it has a unique solution $y(t)$. Moreover, consider the perturbed equation

$$(1_\varepsilon) \qquad y_\varepsilon(t) = g(t) + \int_0^t K(t,s)(t-s+\varepsilon)^{-1/2} y_\varepsilon(s)ds, \; t \in [0,T] ,$$

where ε is a fixed, positive, small number. Suppose that (1_ε) has a unique solution $y_\varepsilon(t)$. This equation is no longer weakly singular so that solving this equation might be easier than solving (1). For $t = s$ the derivative to y of the integrand in (1_ε) may assume very large values, so that (1_ε) may be considered as a stiff Volterra integral equation.

Do there exist efficient numerical methods for solving (1_ε), producing $\hat{y}_\varepsilon$, say, such that $\hat{y}_\varepsilon$ is also a good numerical approximation to y, i.e., for which $\| y - \hat{y}_\varepsilon \| \to 0$ as $\varepsilon \to 0$?